The CEO, Strategy, and Shareholder Value

The CEO, Strategy, and Shareholder Value

Making the Choices That Maximize Company Performance

PETER KONTES

WILEY

John Wiley & Sons, Inc.

Published by John Wiley & Sons, Inc., Hoboken, New Jersey.
Published simultaneously in Canada.

No part of this publication may be reproduced, stored in a retrieval system, or transmitted in any form or by any means, electronic, mechanical, photocopying, recording, scanning, or otherwise, except as permitted under Section 107 or 108 of the 1976 United States Copyright Act, without either the prior written permission of the Publisher, or authorization through payment of the appropriate per-copy fee to the Copyright Clearance Center, Inc., 222 Rosewood Drive, Danvers, MA 01923, (978) 750-8400, fax (978) 646-8600, or on the Web at www.copyright.com. Requests to the Publisher for permission should be addressed to the Permissions Department, John Wiley & Sons, Inc., 111 River Street, Hoboken, NJ 07030, (201) 748-6011, fax (201) 748-6008, or online at www.wiley.com/go/permissions.

Limit of Liability/Disclaimer of Warranty: While the publisher and author have used their best efforts in preparing this book, they make no representations or warranties with respect to the accuracy or completeness of the contents of this book and specifically disclaim any implied warranties of merchantability or fitness for a particular purpose. No warranty may be created or extended by sales representatives or written sales materials. The advice and strategies contained herein may not be suitable for your situation. You should consult with a professional where appropriate. Neither the publisher nor author shall be liable for any loss of profit or any other commercial damages, including but not limited to special, incidental, consequential, or other damages.

For general information on our other products and services or for technical support, please contact our Customer Care Department within the United States at (800) 762-2974, outside the United States at (317) 572-3993 or fax (317) 572-4002.

Wiley also publishes its books in a variety of electronic formats. Some content that appears in print may not be available in electronic books. For more information about Wiley products, visit our web site at www.wiley.com.

Library of Congress Cataloging-in-Publication Data:

Kontes, Peter W.
  The CEO, strategy, and shareholder value: making the choices that maximize company performance/Peter W. Kontes.
    p. cm.
  Includes bibliographical references and index.
  ISBN 978-0-470-59630-2 (cloth); ISBN 978-0-470-87590-2 (ebk);
  ISBN 978-0-470-87591-9 (ebk); ISBN 978-0-470-87592-6 (ebk)
  1. Strategic planning. 2. Organizational effectiveness. 3. Corporations—Valuation. I. Title.
  HD30.28.K6654 2010
  658.4'012–dc22   2010009569

Printed in the United States of America

10 9 8 7 6 5 4 3 2 1

To my sons, Chris and Alex, who tolerate with reasonable grace the distracted curiosity and tedious work habits of their father, and without whom there could never be enough joy to offset the more mundane demands of life.

Contents

Preface

THE DECISION TO WRITE this book was stimulated by a conversation with the CEO of one of the world's most admired companies in which he expressed his concern that "we are not very good at strategic planning." This statement struck me as remarkable because his company is the largest and, by nearly any measure, the most successful in its industry. The company has a history of formulating and executing very profitable strategies, with a record of tremendous innovation and bold competitive initiatives, and the company's shareholders have enjoyed spectacular increases in the value of their investment. Thus, even if it were true in a formal sense that the company was "not very good at strategic planning," that did not seem to have been much of a handicap.

The CEO understood this. What he was saying, I think, was that after delivering exceptional results for several decades, the company's embedded beliefs and practices were beginning to show signs of diminishing effectiveness. It was time to begin challenging some of the old precepts, to consider new ways of doing business, and to bring fresh thinking into the organization—all without destroying what was still good and effective from the old paradigm. This would be a tremendous task for any company, and his sense of urgency was no doubt justified. But this was not a task that could be addressed through the strategic planning process, which is at best a useful analytical exercise. The real task was to determine whether and how the company needed to change its approach to *strategic management*—to reexamine how the biggest choices affecting the company's future performance would need to be made.

This book presents a strategic management framework that has been developed through my consulting experience and my teaching at the Yale School of Management. It contains concepts and ideas that are new and some that are well known. My goal is to show how these ideas fit together into a pragmatic framework that can help CEOs lead their companies to significantly higher levels of performance.

A few words on the scope and timing of the book follow.

SCOPE

As with any book on management, there is a balance to be struck between the breadth and depth with which subjects are treated. The framework I wanted to present here is necessarily broad, focusing much more on the "what" than on the "how" of strategic management. It is about the responsibilities of the CEO and business unit leaders, defining the most important choices they are responsible for making, elaborating on those choices, and laying out general recommendations for addressing them. Some specifics pertaining to measurement and analytical techniques are included in the endnotes and appendices, but I have deliberately kept these to a minimum to avoid digressing into long and, for most readers, mind-numbing explications of various finance, accounting, and strategic methodologies.

The book is written from the perspective of a large, public, multibusiness company, with almost all examples and cases drawn from U.S. and European companies many readers will recognize. This perspective simply reflects my own experience in management consulting, as nearly all of my clients have been companies fitting this profile. However, I believe the principles and practices put forward here are equally valid for smaller companies and private companies, though their implementation might have to be modified to suit a more entrepreneurial environment.

TIMING

The book was written during 2009 and 2010, tumultuous times for the U.S. and world economies. Many companies have, of necessity, been focusing on their immediate survival and shorter-term liquidity issues. Reducing head counts, rationalizing product portfolios, consolidating production facilities, selling assets, deferring investments, and finding financing have been top priorities. Also during this time, at least in the United States, there has been massive government intervention in many of our most important industries including housing, banking, insurance, health care, automobiles, and energy, resulting in what may be permanent but as yet not fully predictable changes to the economics of these and related sectors.

So this was perhaps not the best time to be writing about long-term strategic management.

One very practical problem in writing a book during this time has been the rapidly changing situation at many companies I had intended to use as case examples. Some, like the Saturn division of General Motors, and as a practical matter General Motors itself, either ceased to exist or were so completely changed as to no longer serve my original purpose. Others, like the NBC/Universal unit of General Electric, became involved in ownership changes. There were many of these moving targets to contend with, and some no doubt will have changed yet again by the time the book is published and read. I have tried to select cases that will still resonate with readers in the coming years, but recognize that some may fade from relevancy sooner than I hoped.

In early 2010, the question remains as to whether CEOs are ready to turn their energies back to the longer-term strategic choices about which this book has been written, and on that score I am optimistic. As bad as the Great Recession has been, there are already signs that businesses are beginning to stabilize and start growing again. So long as the smothering and wasteful influences of state control can be minimized, the world's economies will resume their upward path of increasing wealth for all people. With that happy future in mind, I hope this book can play a role in improving the strategic management practices at many companies.

Acknowledgments

OVER A CAREER OF advising several dozen chief executives, I find each has added to my own knowledge of the special demands of that role and the ways in which CEOs can, for better or worse, affect the performance of their companies. Two giants who deserve special mention are Roberto Goizueta (The Coca-Cola Company, 1981–1997) and Sir Brian Pitman (Lloyds TSB, 1983–1997), each of whom led his company to perform at levels seldom matched among large public corporations. Roberto was an early adopter of some of the basic tenets described in this book, and he showed as much as any CEO how powerful these ideas can be in revitalizing an organization, raising it from modest to exemplary performance. Brian Pitman was also an early adopter in the UK and Europe, showing the way for many other companies through the spectacular rise of Lloyds TSB from a second-tier UK bank to one of the most valuable financial institutions in the world. Sadly, neither of these great leaders is still with us, but perhaps a small part of their legacies can be found in these pages.

Among the many colleagues who have influenced my thinking over the years, the late Dr. William Alberts stands apart for the enormous intellectual contributions he made to his two beloved institutions, the University of Washington and Marakon Associates. Bill, more than anyone, started me on the journey that led to writing this book. I also wish to acknowledge Deans Sharon Oster and Stan Garstka of the Yale School of Management for allowing me the time off to write, and professors Rick Antle, Jake Thomas, and Nick Barberis, who graciously responded to some of my decidedly unscholarly questions.

Special thanks are due to my three "readers," Andy Bryant, David Coulter, and Peter Mulford, who did me the great favor of providing their reactions and suggestions to the late stage drafts. They were encouraging, as I hoped they would be, and challenging, as I knew they would be. My gratitude goes also to

David Pugh of John Wiley & Sons, who was most helpful in improving the clarity and flow of ideas throughout the book.

Other friends and colleagues who made important contributions and deserve recognition are Alan Hamilton, Michael Mankins, James Mossman, and Greg Rotz.

I was fortunate to be joined in this effort by three associates without whom it would have been impossible to complete the job. Sarah Gross and Noel Bottjer were my resourceful researchers, overcoming fickle databases and a sometimes fickle author to carry out the necessary searches and analyses. My longtime assistant Mary Jo Amato made sure I had the uninterrupted time I needed to write, produced many of the graphics, and generally would not let me off the hook until the book was done. To all three, my deepest thanks.

Finally, the responsibility for any errors or omissions rests with the author.

Introduction

MANAGEMENT HAS A DUTY to produce goods and services with real and growing value for both customers *and* shareholders. Companies that provide customer value without earning adequate returns for shareholders do not last long. Or, like General Motors, they simply bump along in corporate intensive care awaiting an ignominious takeover by a competitor or a government. Even shorter life expectancies await companies that try to fool investors into thinking they are providing customer value when they really are not, becoming the failures we know as Enron or the hundreds of now defunct "dot-coms" from the late 1990s.

All great companies focus intently on their customers' needs and work constantly to add more customer value to their offer, as well as more customers who value their offer. Customer feedback, in the form of changing market share, changing prices, or requirements for new or different product attributes, is constant, challenging all competitors to adjust their strategies in ways that, at a minimum, can sustain good revenue growth year in and year out.

But there are myriad ways that companies can drive revenue growth, and not all are equal: Some create a great deal of shareholder value, some result in adequate but not exceptional increases in shareholder value, and some, unfortunately, actually destroy shareholder value. If increasing customer satisfaction and revenue growth were the sole objectives of business, formulating at least adequate strategies would be relatively easy. It is the duty to increase value for both customers and shareholders that makes formulating great strategies interesting, and hard.

Much has been written about accounting and financial market metrics that management should employ when evaluating investments and strategic options. Most of this literature is technical, tedious, and extremely difficult to relate to high-level strategic decision making. This book is about management, not measurement, but a solid economic underpinning is essential to successful strategic thinking and action. When it comes to financial metrics, choices are

EXHIBIT I.1 Economic Profit Illustrated

The General Electric Company (2007)	
Earnings	$22.5 billion
Equity	$112.3 billion
Cost of equity	× 10%
Capital charge	−$11.2 billion
ECONOMIC PROFIT	$11.3 billion
Source: Datastream.	

not without controversy, including the three that will be mentioned most frequently: economic profit, equity value, and total shareholder returns.

The concept of economic profit is so central to the framework proposed here that it deserves special mention at the outset. Most executives have had some experience with economic profit, which is simply a measure of earnings minus a charge for the equity capital employed to generate that income. A simple calculation of economic profit is illustrated in Exhibit I.1.

The significance of economic profit, its measurement, applications, and its advantages will be developed more fully in Chapter 2. Here, it is not being argued that economic profit is a new idea, or that it is the holy grail of business management, or that it is the best measure of economic benefit in every circumstance, or that its measurement and application cannot be manipulated by executives who are intent on doing so.

The principle argument is that economic profit, both as a single- and a multiperiod measure, offers executives substantial pragmatic advantages for the purposes of generating insights, formulating options, and making strategic decisions. In particular, three recurring themes of this book—the role of the CEO, the choices that shape strategy, and the creation of shareholder value—can each be described in economic profit terms, allowing them to be integrated into the overall strategic management framework, which is described in Chapter 1.

For readers skeptical of the validity or usefulness of economic profit and the other financial measures to which it will be related, try not to put the book down quite yet. As the broader framework unfolds, perhaps their conceptual and practical utility will prove greater than you might imagine, and greater too than any of the alternatives.

CHAPTER ONE

Foundations

HIS BOOK IS ABOUT strategic management, the process by which the chief executive shapes a company's strategies and drives its financial performance over time. Strategic management is not strategic planning, or strategy formulation, or setting the strategic direction of the company, though these activities may be part of it. It is a broader concept, encompassing all of the CEO's major decisions and their ultimate impact on the quality of a company's strategies and the height of its economic success.

Strategic management comprises five high-level choices every CEO must make:

1. *Performance objective choices*—deciding what the company will define as success
2. *Participation choices*—deciding where the company will compete to achieve its performance objectives
3. *Positioning choices*—deciding how the company will compete to achieve its performance objectives
4. *Organizational choices*—deciding how to build an institution that can sustain high performance over time
5. *Risk management choices*—deciding how the company will protect its performance from catastrophic setbacks

Companies vary enormously in how, and how well, they make these choices. Many factors can influence these choices, including a company's history, industry practices, its understanding of customers, its competitive situation, its embedded resource allocation processes, the quality of information available to its executives, and the effects of its reward systems. These and others factors combine in unique ways that predispose one company to make certain strategic management choices one way, while other companies facing similar choices tend to make them in entirely different ways.

The fundamental question for the CEO, and for all executives, is: How do we make the right choices?

The ability to make the "right" strategic management choices is based on two governing principles, one relating to the purpose of strategy itself and the second relating to the role of the CEO. These governing principles and their impact on how companies should address each of the five choices are the foundations of superior strategic management.

 ## THE PURPOSE OF STRATEGY

As a first principle, the purpose of business strategy is to maximize the growth of economic profit over time. It is not to do anything else. If a new strategy will increase economic profit over time, it is better than the old strategy. If a new strategy would reduce economic profit over time, it is inferior to the old strategy regardless of other benefits it might bring. Specifically, it is not the purpose of strategy to achieve competitive advantage as measured by indicators such as having the largest market share, having the most satisfied customers, or being the low-cost producer. For some businesses, achieving these goals will increase economic profit growth, but in other cases, achieving some or all of these goals will reduce economic profit growth. As the following chapters will show, pursuing these and other commonly accepted strategic objectives is simply not a reliable path to improving, let alone maximizing, the economic performance of a business.

There will be a chorus of objections to this principle. One curious objection is that the principle is "obvious," as though that somehow diminishes its validity. As obvious as it may be, few companies or CEOs have actually embedded this principle at the core of their strategic management processes, nor is it even mentioned in most of the strategy literature. Another objection is that strategy is about much more than mere financial results and cannot be reduced to a simple financial metric. Well, certainly formulating and executing great strategies requires capabilities far beyond measuring financial outcomes, but the greatness of a strategy is not determined by the skill or cleverness with which it is constructed but by the concrete economic results that it produces. Yet another objection to the principle is that maximizing shareholder value, not economic profit growth per se, is the purpose of business strategy. This is a fair objection, but not a particularly useful one in the conduct of everyday strategic management. As will be shown, maximizing economic profit growth is an excellent proxy for maximizing value under most circumstances, not only theoretically but in the observed results of top performing companies, and it is much easier to employ in everyday decision making.

The idea behind this principle appears simple, but appearances can be misleading. The task of formulating and executing the strategies that maximize economic profit growth over time is extremely demanding, much more demanding than conventional goals like gaining market share or increasing operating income, earnings, or even return on investment (perhaps this is why the principle is admired more in the breach than in the observance). A first step toward understanding, and then accepting and utilizing the principle is to examine the explicit linkages between strategic decisions and financial outcomes. A framework describing these key linkages is the subject of Chapter 2.

Principles are fine, but is there good evidence that maximizing economic profit growth over time has real consequences? Do companies that achieve higher economic profit growth also achieve higher valuations and returns for their shareholders over time? The answer, with appropriate qualifications, is yes, they do. Exhibit 1.1 shows the results of an analysis of S&P 500 companies comparing their 10-year economic profit growth and total shareholder return performance.

The results here show the EP-dominant group (companies that grew economic profits per share faster than they grew earnings per share) generated far higher total shareholder returns than the earnings-dominant group (companies that grew earnings per share faster than they grew economic profit per share). The nearly 7 percent annual compound difference in total shareholder returns between these two groups is enormous, and the nearly four percentage point difference between the EP-dominant and middle groups is also significant. These results, which are explained more fully in Appendix I, offer compelling evidence of a strong link between companies' longer-term economic profit growth and their total shareholder returns, reinforcing the proposition that maximizing economic profit growth is both the purpose and the result of good strategic management.

EXHIBIT 1.1 Economic Profit (EP) Growth and Total Shareholder Returns (TSR)

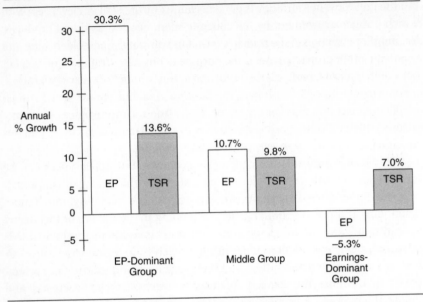

Notes:
EP-Dominant: Companies where 10-year annualized EP growth rate exceeds earnings growth rate by five percentage points or more.
Middle: Companies where 10-year annualized EP and earnings growth rates are within five percentage points of each other.
Earnings-Dominant: Companies where 10-year annualized earnings growth rate exceeds EP growth rate by 5 percentage points or more.
Analysis covers S&P 500 companies during the time period of 1998 to 2007. A more complete discussion of methodology and results is in Appendix I.

 THE ROLE OF THE CEO

The primary job of the CEO is to determine the proper level and disposition of a company's resources. Whether adding a new product line, making an acquisition, entering a new market, increasing research and development, promoting a key executive, or divesting a business, the CEO is constantly reshaping the configuration of the company's human and capital resources. For major resource commitments, the CEO may make the decisions directly, or with other executives, with support or authority from the board. For the many other decisions made by management at all levels, the CEO's influence on the level and disposition of resources will be indirect, though powerful, through the people, performance standards, and approval processes he or she has put into place.

The majority of a company's resources are committed through strategic decisions about how, and how fast, to grow (or shrink) lines of business or business units. Some investments may be evaluated on a stand-alone project basis, but a company's chosen business strategies will ultimately determine the nature and magnitude of its total resource commitments. These strategies will also determine the rate of economic profit growth the company is able to sustain over time.

Therefore, the second principle of strategic management can be stated more precisely:

The paramount role of the CEO is to ensure that all resources of the company are committed to strategies that maximize the growth of economic profits over time.

The role defined here is "paramount" because although there certainly are other tasks a CEO must perform, none is more important to the long-term strategic and financial health of the company. Enforcing the company's values, meeting with employees and key customers and suppliers, maintaining good community relations, or responding to a sudden crisis might all be legitimate demands on a CEO's time, but consistently directing resources to achieve superior economic profit growth is the *sine qua non* of the CEO's leadership role. The benefits from doing other tasks well would pale in comparison to the costs to all of the company's stakeholders if the CEO performs this supreme task poorly.

Looking at the definition in more detail, "all resources" means all of the human, technological, and financial resources the company can bring to bear on the strategies that will increase economic profit. The company's inventory of resources is not assumed to be fixed; if more resources can be invested to meet the objective, they should be added; if fewer resources are needed, they should be reduced. In addition, and of critical importance, is the implied corollary to this principle, which is that the CEO has a responsibility to ensure that *none* of the company's resources are committed to strategies that diminish economic profit growth.

The term "strategies" refers to both business unit and corporate center strategies. The CEO of a multibusiness company obviously cannot formulate individual business unit strategies personally; that is the job of the business unit leaders. But at the end of the day, the CEO must approve each of the business unit strategies, together with the commitment of resources needed to support those strategies. This approval should be subject to a number of tests designed to determine whether the proposed strategies are likely to maximize economic profit growth. As will be elaborated in later chapters, rigorous strategy reviews are one of the most effective tools a CEO has available to execute his or her role successfully.

"Maximizing" any economic benefit is a somewhat slippery concept. Two of the most difficult complications involve trade-offs and time frames. For example, what does the CEO do if maximizing economic profits means reducing revenues or earnings for a period of time? Or, over what time frame is "maximizing" economic profits supposed occur: one year, five years, the "long term," infinity? These are eminently fair questions of any economic objective, and they will be addressed in subsequent sections of the book.

Finally, it should be emphasized that nothing about the role of the CEO defined here is meant to imply the acceptance of illegal or unethical behavior to achieve the objective. Maximizing economic profits is itself an entirely ethical pursuit, an honest attempt by the CEO and top management team to create the wealth that results in new products and services, new technologies, growing employment, growing taxes, and growing returns on savings and investment. It is never a good commercial decision, let alone a proper legal or ethical decision, to put that growing stream of wealth at risk by evading or ignoring the requirements of good citizenship and good conscience.

FIVE CHOICES THAT SHAPE STRATEGY

Transforming the two governing principles into the real work of a CEO requires understanding strategic management choices in terms of concrete economic goals. In Exhibit 1.2, each of the five big choices is characterized in terms of the role it plays in driving the company's economic profit growth over time.

Each of these choices will be described briefly here and then developed more fully in the chapters that follow:

1. *Choosing the right performance objectives.* The choice of performance objectives has an enormous impact on the shaping of strategy. For instance, a company that gives precedence to increasing return on investment will pursue markedly different strategies than a competitor that gives precedence to earnings growth. An error in choosing the right performance objectives can be, and usually is, magnified many times over by the resultant errors in choosing the best strategies. To assure alignment of strategic choices with the governing principles, performance objectives

EXHIBIT 1.2 Five Choices that Shape Strategy

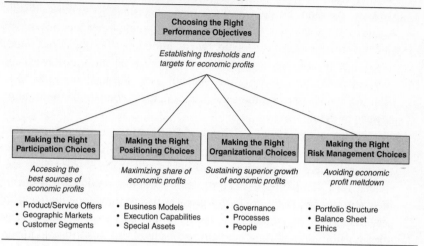

should be based on maximizing the growth of economic profits over time. Pragmatically, these objectives must also be translated into something more concrete and measurable than the fairly abstract notion of "maximizing" economic profit growth. Specific recommendations for setting these objectives will be the subject of Chapter 3.

2. *Making the right participation choices.* Participation choices should be directed at committing the company's resources to product markets that are likely to be good sources of economic profit growth and avoiding those product markets that are unlikely to be so. Specifically, participation choices consist of which products and services to offer, in which geographic markets, and to which customer segments. Most important, these are also choices of which products and services *not* to offer and which geographic markets and customer segments *not* to serve. Of all of the strategic choices a business unit head or the CEO makes, participation choices frequently have the biggest overall impact on the magnitude and potential growth rate of economic profit. A framework for assessing participation options is the subject of Chapter 4.

3. *Making the right positioning choices.* Within the product markets in which the company chooses to participate, its competitive objective should be to maximize its share of the total economic profit pie over time. The biggest single factor that will determine economic profit share is the choice of the business model, or set of core convictions, based on which the business unit

head or CEO will commit the resources for growth. Among all aspects of strategy, creating the right business model is probably the most difficult, requiring tremendous creativity and often entailing a fair amount of risk. Once a business model is adopted, two additional positioning choices need to be made: the execution capabilities in which the business must excel and the best means of exploiting any special assets the business may have. Chapter 5 addresses business models and their companion positioning choices in detail.

4. *Making the right organizational choices.* Sustaining superior economic profit growth over long periods of time is the hallmark of a well-managed company. There are many examples of excellent CEOs who were able to lead their companies to achieve great economic profit growth during their tenures, but there are far fewer cases where that same high level of performance is sustained through the terms of successive CEOs. This phenomenon hints at the underlying problem of the "institutional imperative," a relentless propensity of large organizations to revert to mediocrity. To overcome this powerful force, CEOs usually need to make substantive changes in many areas of the organization, including governance, executive processes, and executive capabilities. Governance choices include clarifying the roles and responsibilities of the business units, the corporate center, and the board of directors. Executive process choices include the design and functioning of information management, strategy formulation, capital management, control, and compensation processes. And executive capability choices cover the selection of executives for specific roles, as well as the development of key executive skills that support economic profit growth. These topics are covered in Chapter 6.

5. *Making the right risk management choices.* Ultimately, risk management must be about protecting a company's economic profit from imploding, either suddenly or over longer time periods. The main choices that influence economic profit resiliency are a company's portfolio choices, its balance sheet choices, and its ethical choices. Of the three, portfolio choices—the boundaries the CEO sets for business units' participation and competitive positioning performance—is the most important driver of both the level and variability of the company's economic profits over time. Making the right balance sheet choices, in turn, depends importantly on the company's overall participation and competitive positioning. And the ethical choices that impact the resiliency of economic profit are mainly about information quality and transparency, inside and outside the company. These choices are discussed in Chapter 7.

These are the five big strategic management choices. The quality with which these choices are made throughout the company must be the responsibility of the CEO. They form the inescapable agenda of the CEO, the essential activities that define the job. The issue for the CEO is not whether these choices will be made, because they will be. They are made every day in every company. At issue is whether they will be made well or badly, ahead of or behind the competition, coherently or incoherently across the company. This does not mean the CEO needs to make all of the key decisions personally, which in a large company would be impractical. But it does mean the CEO has to establish and enforce the ground rules within which all of the most important corporate and business unit decisions will be made.

A STRATEGIC MANAGEMENT FRAMEWORK

Bringing the principles and choices together creates the basic structure of a pragmatic strategic management framework, as shown in Exhibit 1.3.

This framework gives us a clear picture of the CEO's vital leadership domain, of the fundamental responsibilities, tasks, and outcomes that should

EXHIBIT 1.3   A Strategic Management Framework

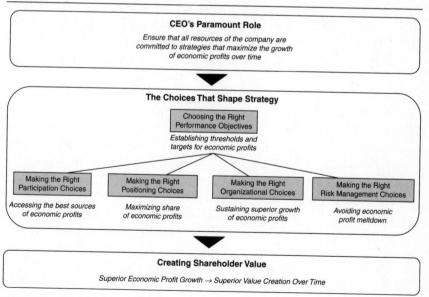

constitute the highest priorities and ultimate responsibilities of the chief executive. But this clarity should not be read as implying rigidity or inflexibility with respect to the pathways to success. Every business unit and every company will face different strategic and organizational challenges in pursuit of economic profit growth. There is no one-size-fits-all strategic nostrum, there is no esoteric financial engineering solution, and there is no one style of leadership or organization structure that will assure success. What the framework provides is a coherent set of metrics, standards, guidelines, and practices that, if employed in a thoughtful and disciplined fashion, will greatly increase the odds that a company's chosen strategies will generate superior economic profit growth and value creation over time.

CHAPTER TWO

The Economics of Strategic Management

B USINESS STRATEGY MUST BE about achieving concrete, measurable, and important economic objectives. Yet most of the theory and practice of business strategy lacks a sound economic foundation. The strategy literature contains strong presumptions, stated and unstated, that by pursuing certain seemingly desirable goals, such as increasing customer satisfaction or achieving economies of scale, good or improved economic results for the business will naturally follow. Unfortunately, many of these widely accepted presumptions are myths: unproven, unreliable, and often incorrect guides to good strategic decision making.

The purpose of this chapter is to demonstrate the link between economic profit and strategy, to highlight some of the most common strategic myths, and to lay an economic foundation for making the best strategic management choices.

 ## ECONOMIC PROFIT

As noted in the Introduction, economic profit, or EP, is a simple concept, defined as earnings minus a charge for the equity capital employed to generate those

EXHIBIT 2.1 Economic Profit (EP) Calculation

Big Dog Business Unit

Key Data

Earnings	$ 1.2 billion
Equity employed	$10.0 billion
Cost of equity capital	10%

Calculations

Earnings	$ 1.2 billion
Capital charge	− $ 1.0 billion [Capital charge: $10.0 billion ×.10]
ECONOMIC PROFIT	$ 200 million

earnings. Exhibit 2.1 shows a general example of how economic profit would be calculated for a single business unit.

This economic profit calculation is the dollar amount by which the business unit's annual earnings exceed the return on capital required by investors who assume the risk of supplying the equity used in the business. Here, investors require a minimum 10 percent return on the $10 billion of equity they have supplied, meaning there is an implicit capital charge of $1 billion the business must earn in order to truly "break even." In this case, the business unit has earnings of $1.2 billion, or $200 million more than the minimum capital charge; therefore it is considered economically profitable.

As a managerial metric, economic profit has important advantages over earnings, return on investment, or even cash flow. Uniquely, it contains an income statement measure, a related balance sheet measure, and an external capital market measure all in one number. This combination gives EP a signaling attribute that is superior to other financial metrics. In a single-year example like that shown in Exhibit 2.1, it is a measure of how much equity value a business strategy has *created* (or, if this were a forecast, is *expected to create*) during the period. Further, as we will see, EP represents a much closer linkage than any other metric between a company's strategic, or product-market, performance and its financial, or capital-market, performance. It is not too strong a statement to say that without EP measures, a proper managerial understanding of the strategic position of a business and the strategic options it faces would be nearly impossible.

The economic profit metric has many manifestations. Some versions, like the well-known economic value-added (EVA®), can become quite complicated.[1] For economic profit to be a really useful managerial metric, however, it is best

EXHIBIT 2.2 Company EP Identity Rule

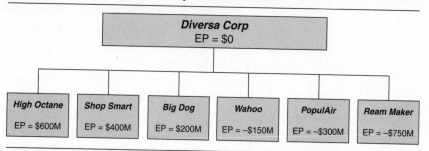

Notes:
Business unit strategies and financial results are assumed to be independent.
All company revenues, expenses, assets, liabilities, and equity have been imputed to the business units.

to err on the side of simplicity. The CEO does not want to have strategic management degenerate into a debate on how the company's "true" EP measurement is impacted by factors such as mark-to-market accounting, depreciation methodologies, capitalized leases, or deferred taxes. These refinements, while appropriate for making some company-to-company EP comparisons, are generally not necessary for strategic decision-making purposes. In particular, when evaluating strategic choices at the product and customer level, measurement complexity can quickly lead to a loss of focus on the more important commercial and organizational factors that actually determine the potential for EP growth.

One attribute of economic profit that is obvious but often overlooked or ignored is that essentially all of a company's EP comes from customers buying products sold by the business units. It follows, therefore, that the total EP of the company is ultimately determined by the product-market strategies of individual business units. We might think of this as the company EP identity rule as illustrated by Exhibit 2.2, where Diversa Corp's total EP of zero is the summation of the economic profits of its six individual business units.

The significance of this rule will become apparent in the following section on company valuation.

 ECONOMIC PROFIT AND STRATEGY VALUATION

Defining the objective of strategic management as maximizing economic profit growth represents an apparent departure from a strictly orthodox tenant of finance. The generally accepted, and often stated, financial objective of a public company is to "maximize shareholder value," meaning, usually, to maximize the market value of the company's equity or common stock. And there is no doubt that growing the per-share value of the company at some "maximum" rate is the proper theoretical objective. This objective is sometimes restated as maximizing total shareholder returns (TSR) over time.

There are three main justifications for the CEO and other executives to focus their energies on "maximizing economic profit growth" rather than "maximizing shareholder value." First, they are essentially the same thing: Continuously choosing strategies that maximize economic profit growth over time will, in virtually all cases, also maximize the value of the company. Second, EP is simply easier to understand and apply than a present value calculation, whether measuring the profitability of a product line or assessing the profitability of a competitor. Third, CEOs cannot manage the company's share price or TSRs anyway, but they can and should have a big influence on the size and growth of economic profit. (For a more complete discussion of the relationship between EP and equity value, please refer to Appendix II.)

For strategic management purposes, the most important application of valuation at the business unit level would be to compare two or more strategic options, where the presumption is that the option with the highest equity value will be chosen. Exhibit 2.3 provides an example of this application.

In this example, the business should choose to compete on quality because that is the strategy that maximizes its equity value. But it is also the strategy that maximizes its expected intermediate term economic profit growth of 6 percent, so using the EP growth projection would lead to the same decision.

It should be stressed here that both EP growth and equity value are being used to determine the best strategy among the options available within a single business unit, *not for comparing strategic options across business units.* The key question for each business unit is "What strategy will produce the highest EP

EXHIBIT 2.3 Comparing the Strategic Options for a Single Business Unit

Strategic Option	EP Growth	Equity Value
Compete on price	4%	$200 million
Compete on service	5%	$220 million
Compete on quality	6%	$250 million

Notes:
Assumes initial book value of $100 million and a base year EP of $6 million in all cases.
Assumes cost of equity of 10 percent in all cases.
Assumes constant growth into perpetuity (for illustration only; not normally a realistic assumption); see Appendix II for valuation methodology.

EXHIBIT 2.4 Company Equity Value (EV) Identity Rule

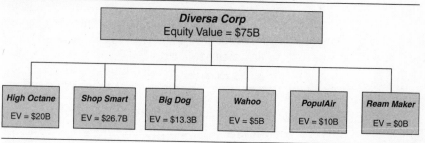

Notes:
Business unit strategies are assumed to be independent.
All company revenues, expenses, assets, liabilities, and equity have been imputed to the business units.
See Appendix III for full details of EP calculations and equity valuations.

growth rate and equity value?" The answer to this question should not normally be dependent on what happens in any other business unit in the company's portfolio. This is a vitally important distinction that will be developed further in later chapters.[2]

As with the economic profit identity rule, there is an equity value identity rule for multibusiness corporations. Just as EP can be generated only in the product markets, so equity value can come only from the product markets, meaning that all of the equity value of a corporation must come from the equity values of its business units, as illustrated in Exhibit 2.4.

This rule has important strategic management implications. The most important is that the business units are the building blocks of the company's total equity value. It is only the strategies of the business units that generate EP and equity value for the company, *therefore the company's total EP growth and equity value can only be maximized when every business unit is pursuing its own highest EP growth strategy.* This suggests another way to state the primary responsibility of the CEO, which is to ensure that every business unit in the portfolio is pursuing the strategy that maximizes its EP growth over time.

THE FINANCIAL DRIVERS OF ECONOMIC PROFIT AND EQUITY VALUE

As noted, one of the great advantages of economic profit over the other most commonly used managerial metrics is that it alone includes earnings, investment, and the cost of capital. In their simplest form, these three factors can be related as shown in Exhibit 2.5.

EXHIBIT 2.5 Financial Drivers of EP

Big Dog Business Unit Illustration

$$EP = BE\,(ROE - COE)$$
$$EP = \$10B\,(12\% - 10\%)$$
$$EP = \$\,200M$$

Notes:

BE: "Book" equity (imputed) = $10B

ROE: Return on equity = $1.2B/$10B = 12%

COE: Cost of equity = 10%

From this example it is easy to see that when a business strategy generates a return on equity (ROE) greater than the cost of equity (COE), economic profit will be positive. To the extent that the business can sustain this positive "spread" between ROE and COE over time, it will be creating value and making a positive contribution to the company's value. And to the extent the business can continue to invest new equity at a positive (ROE − COE) spread, that new investment will increase both future EP and current equity value.

Conversely, if a business strategy produces an ROE that is less than the cost of equity, EP will be negative and the business will be economically unprofitable. If this negative (ROE − COE) spread is persistent, the business unit will produce a capital loss and actually destroy equity value for itself and the company. Importantly, attempting to grow a persistently negative EP business by increasing the equity capital investment can accelerate value destruction and reduce the equity value of the company.

The examples in Exhibit 2.6 illustrate these points more precisely for a company with three geographically defined business units.

Exhibit 2.6 reveals a number of important relationships. First, the company's total EP and equity values are determined by the EPs and equity values of the three business units. Second, the company overall just earns its cost of capital with a zero EP, neither creating nor destroying value; therefore, its equity value is equal to its book equity. Third, only one business unit, the United States, has a positive EP and is creating equity value, whereas France, with an EP of zero, is simply conserving value, and Russia, with an (ROE − COE) spread of minus 5 percent, is destroying value. This means two-thirds of the company's equity capital is invested in strategies that do not generate positive EP or create value. In addition, every business unit is being funded to grow at the same

EXHIBIT 2.6 Economic Profit and Equity Value Comparisons

Business Unit	Book Equity	ROE	COE	ROE – COE Spread	EP	Growth	Equity Value
United States	$50M	15%	10%	5%	+$2.5	5%	$100M
France	$50M	10%	10%	0%	$ 0	5%	$ 50M
Russia	$50M	5%	10%	−5%	−$2.5	5%	$ 0
Company	$150M	10%	10%	0%	0	5%	$150M

Notes:

To make comparisons easier, only ROE is varied, whereas imputed book equity, the cost of equity, and growth (both book equity and earnings growth) are assumed to be the same for all three geographic units.

EP: First-year economic profit.

Equity Value: See Appendix II for valuation methodology.

5 percent rate, a kind of communitarian philosophy of capital allocation. Yet simply stopping further investment in the Russia unit would actually increase the company's equity value by $25 million. No CEO should accept this funding pattern as the best possible investment of the company's resources.

The financial drivers of economic profit, their implications, and the options for changing them for the better will be examined in much more detail throughout the book. But one critical organizational implication must be highlighted at this point, which is that, at more than 95 percent of all companies, the financial drivers of EP and equity value shown here are not even measured or reported. Yet without this information, it is impossible for a CEO, or any executive, to know how to do his or her job nearly as well as it can be done. Consistently creating, reporting, and acting on this kind of financial information at quite fine levels of granularity within the company is one of the critical elements of superior strategic management. This will be a topic for more detailed examination in Chapter 6.

THE STRATEGIC DRIVERS OF ECONOMIC PROFIT AND EQUITY VALUE

The financial drivers of economic profit and equity value provide the CEO with excellent insight into company performance and they are essential for analyzing strategic choices. They tell us a lot about the condition of a business, and what alternative strategies could be worth, but they do not tell us much about *why* a business performs the way that it does. For instance, in Exhibit 2.6, once we see the differences in the financial drivers of economic profit for the United States, France, and Russia business units, we naturally want to know why they are so different and, more important, what those differences imply for changing their strategies to achieve higher EP growth in the future. To understand the "why" of business unit and company performance, we must look beyond the financial drivers to the strategic drivers of EP and equity value.

There are two high-level strategic drivers of economic profit for a business:

- *Market economics:* the average investment returns and growth rates achieved by competitors in the product markets in which the business competes
- *Competitive position:* the economic performance advantage or disadvantage the business enjoys relative to its competitors within those product markets

The combined effects of market economics and competitive position, together with the amount of equity employed in the business, determine its level and growth rate of EP at any point in time.

A key measure of market economics is the average (ROE – COE) spread generated by all competitors in a product market. In a given year, this market EP spread is the combined net incomes divided by the combined book equities attributable to the participation of all competitors in the product market, minus the average cost of equity capital of those players. This is illustrated in Exhibit 2.7.

When the financial performance of all competitors combined generates a positive EP spread, as in the Global Lunch Food illustration, we can label that an economically profitable product market. The petroleum exploration and production industry would be another example where positive economic profits have

EXHIBIT 2.7 Market Economics Calculation: Global Lunch Food Product Market

Competitor	Net Income	Book Equity	ROE	COE	Spread	EP
Old Dog	$ 500	$ 5,000	10.0%	10%	0.0%	$ 0
Hot Dog	$ 2,000	$ 8,000	25.0%	10%	15.0%	$1,200
Big Dog	$ 1,200	$10,000	12.0%	10%	2.0%	$ 200
Mad Dog	$ 500	$ 7,000	7.1%	10%	−2.9%	−$ 200
Total Market	$4,200	$30,000	14.0%	10%	4.0%	$1,200

EXHIBIT 2.8 U.S. Product Market Profitability (1998–2007)

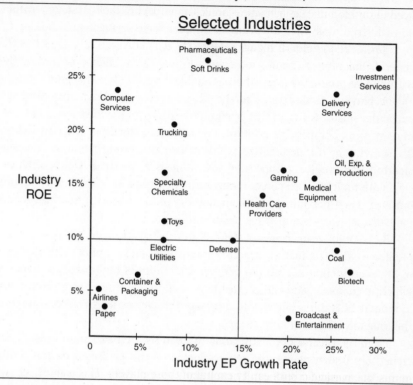

Selected Industries

Source: Datastream.

Note: Average COE for all companies estimated at 10%. Average EP growth for total sample was 14.7% during this period.

persisted for many years. Conversely, if the collective performance of all players generates a negative (ROE – COE) spread, that defines an economically unprofitable product market. One example of a chronically unprofitable product market would be the airline industry in the United States, where there are few, if any, years during which industry EP exceeds zero. Exhibit 2.8 illustrates the 10-year average EP spreads of some selected U.S. product markets.

These data display the wide variations in product-market economics over this time period. Broadcast & Entertainment might be a glamorous high-growth business, but the companies in this group collectively generated enormous negative EP and destroyed shareholder value. Trucking may be boring and slow growing, but its return was a lot better than that for the music and movie industries and actually created equity value for investors. It should be emphasized that these examples are not forecasts, although businesses do need to develop market economics forecasts as part of their strategy formulation efforts, a topic that will recur in Chapter 4 on participation choices.

Market economics as measured by ROE only is a high-level signal of the general difficulty of earning a positive EP for an average competitor. But within most product markets there is a wide range of EP performance among all the players, as illustrated in the Global Lunch Food example. Where a particular business sits on this profitability spectrum provides a first approximation of its competitive position. For instance, Hot Dog, with an ROE of 25 percent, or 11 percentage points above the product-market average, clearly has a tangible competitive advantage over its rivals. Conversely, Old Dog, with an ROE of 10 percent, may be just earning its cost of equity capital, but it is also 4 percentage points below the product-market average, which indicates it is at a competitive disadvantage.

By combining measures of these high-level strategic drivers of economic profit, we can begin to draw a picture of why a business earns a particular level of EP as a function of both the general economics of the product markets in which it competes and the competitive position it occupies at a given point in time. Exhibit 2.9 is one way to represent this picture for an entire company, the imaginary Diversa Corp.

From the Diversa Corp illustration, we can see that important insights can come from understanding the relative impact of the EP drivers on the performance of a particular business. The company overall earns an economic profit of zero, with its ROE of 10 percent just equal to its cost of equity. But the underlying performance of its six business units presents a much more complex, interesting, and useful picture of what is behind Diversa Corp's aggregate profitability.

High Octane, an oil and gas exploration and production business, earns an ROE of 16 percent, well above its 10 percent cost of equity. What the exhibit shows are the sources of that ROE. The first 13 percent of High Octane's ROE comes from its participation strategy, competing in a product market where the average of all its competitors' ROEs is 13 percent. The rest of High Octane's ROE, an additional 3 percent, comes from having a competitive advantage of some kind. This is the strategic sweet spot, where the conditions for sustaining and growing EP are usually most favorable. Ideally, a company's portfolio would include many High Octane–type business units.

Shop Smart, a big box retailer, is in a very different position. It actually has an even bigger competitive advantage than High Octane, earning an ROE 4 percent above its product market average. But, unlike the economically profitable oil and gas business, Shop Smart's retailing competitors do not,

EXHIBIT 2.9 Market Economics/Competitive Position Profitability Matrix

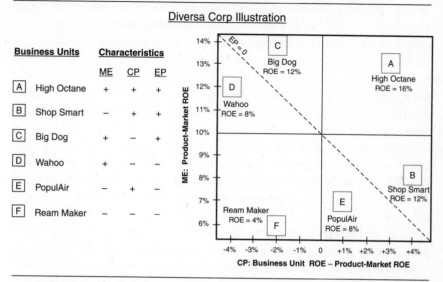

Diversa Corp Illustration

Source: The Market Economics–Competitive Position Profitability Matrix (and a number of variants) was developed by Marakon Associates and first published as "The Marakon Profitability Matrix" in its *Commentary* (April 1981).

Note: Cost of equity: 10% in all cases

on average, earn their cost of equity, having a product-market average ROE of just 8 percent. Thus, while Shop Smart's 12 percent ROE may appear somewhat modest, the business unit is clearly very well managed with a terrific strategy that generates positive EP under difficult circumstances. A business unit with these characteristics would also be value creating and a welcome part of any company's portfolio.

Big Dog is a branded food business. It earns an ROE of 12 percent, the same as Shop Smart, but its market economics and competitive positions are entirely different. Big Dog is in a very profitable product market where the overall average ROE of 14 percent is 4 percent above the cost of equity, so if Big Dog were just an average player it too would earn a 14 percent ROE (see Exhibit 2.7). But in this example, Big Dog is actually at a competitive disadvantage as reflected in 12 percent ROE, which is 2 percent below the product market average. The business unit is earning a positive EP based solely on the strength of its product-market economics. This type of business unit, economically profitable but strategically disadvantaged, is value creating for now but faces some important challenges for protecting and growing EP in the future.

The Wahoo business unit is an Internet retailing business, which on average generates an ROE of 12 percent for all players combined. However, Wahoo finds itself at such a competitive disadvantage that it earns an ROE of only 8 percent, 4 percent below the product-market average, producing a negative EP and destroying value for Diversa Corp's shareholders. For Wahoo, simply becoming an average competitor would create good EP growth and equity value. The strategic challenge for Wahoo's management is to determine whether an entirely different business model could raise the unit's performance to at least that level.

PopulAir is a commuter airline that is competitively advantaged but still not EP positive or value creating for shareholders. Like Wahoo, it earns an ROE of just 8 percent, but the PopulAir management is clearly doing a much better job of making the best of a bad situation. PopulAir's product-market economics are very poor, with an average ROE of just 7 percent, so to earn a positive EP requires not just any competitive advantage but a huge competitive advantage similar to the position Shop Smart is in. Unfortunately, even with a relatively good strategy and good management, PopulAir has not so far been able to overcome the adverse economics of the product market in which it competes.

Finally, Ream Maker is a paper manufacturing business that operates at a competitive disadvantage in a very unprofitable product market, resulting in an ROE of only 4 percent and massive value destruction on an ongoing basis. For a business like Ream Maker to find and execute a strategy that moves it all the way to becoming a value-creating business like Shop Smart is very rare. Nor can it count on a big improvement in product-market economics, which is also a rare occurrence. So its choices are limited, with a restructuring of some kind likely to be necessary.

The Market Economics/Competitive Position (ME/CP) Profitability Matrix does not capture all aspects of competitive advantage or economic profit growth, but it is a useful diagnostic tool. At the portfolio level shown here, the CEO can quickly see the drivers of economic profit for each business unit and of the total company in the context of its strategic positioning. With this perspective, it is clear that participation choices weigh heavily on the level and growth prospects of economic profit. It is also clear that competitive advantage alone, though certainly important, is not a good proxy for value creation: A competitively advantaged business like PopulAir can still be value consuming, whereas a competitively disadvantaged business like Big Dog can nevertheless be value creating.

These high-level measures are by no means all we want to know about the market economics and competitive position of a business, but they form an essential foundation for a CEO to understand the underlying sources of EP growth and value for each of the company's business units and the company as a whole. Unfortunately, even this very basic financial and strategic information exceeds what most CEOs have to work with when evaluating business strategies, so capturing and reporting this kind of information on a regular basis should be a top priority.

DEALING WITH MYTHOLOGY

The basic framework linking economic profit, equity value, and strategy may seem straightforward and even powerful, but in practice its influence on decision making is often overwhelmed by the deeply ingrained doctrines of other frameworks that are based on quite different principles. Collectively, these doctrines constitute the mythology of strategic management. It is not possible to address every aspect of the mythology here, but elaborating on a few of the more prominent doctrines will demonstrate why CEOs would be wise to expunge them from serious strategic discussions within the company.

Earnings Growth

Perhaps the most deeply embedded practice impacting the quality of strategic management at most public companies is the almost single-minded drive to increase annual (or quarterly) earnings or earnings per share. Despite overwhelming evidence that earnings growth alone is not a reliable indicator of either superior strategic decision making or of creating shareholder value, many CEOs continue to pursue it as their overriding objective.

The central problem with earnings growth is that it can be purchased at any price. If a sustainable $1 increase in earnings per share can be purchased by investing $5 per share, that is probably a good thing. But if that same $1 of earnings per share is purchased by investing $20 per share, that is almost certainly a bad thing. In Exhibit 2.10, three companies with identical earnings growth performance are compared to drive home this point.

In this example, each of the companies achieved its goal of growing earnings at 15 percent per year for five years. Consequently, all three doubled their earnings per share from $1 to $2.01. But their paths to make those earnings gains were entirely different:

- Company A was able to grow its earnings at 15 percent while increasing its book equity by only 10 percent per year, meaning that its incremental ROE was well above the cost of equity and EP was increasing.

EXHIBIT 2.10　Earnings Growth versus EP Growth

Three Companies with 15% Annual Earnings-per-Share Growth

	Base Year			Year 5		
	Earnings	Book Equity	EP	Earnings	Book Equity	EP
Company A						
(Grows equity @ 10%)	$1.00	$10.00	0	$2.01	$16.11	$ 0.40
Company B						
(Grows equity @ 15%)	$1.00	$10.00	0	$2.01	$20.11	$ 0
Company C						
(Grows equity @ 20%)	$1.00	$10.00	0	$2.01	$24.88	−$ 0.48

Notes:

All figures are per share.

All companies grow earnings at 15% compounded annually.

Cost of equity for all three companies = 10%.

- Company B grew both earnings and book equity at the exact same rate, 15 percent, meaning that its incremental ROE held constant at just equal to the cost of equity and EP remained constant at zero.
- Company C was buying earnings at an uneconomic rate, with book equity over the period increasing nearly $15 per share in order to increase earnings by only $1.01 per share, meaning its incremental ROE was less than the cost of equity and its EP was declining. By the end of the period, its EP was a *negative* $0.48 per share versus a positive $0.40 per share for Company A.

Over the five-year period, Company A would have seen its equity value increase by as much as 240 percent, while Company C would have achieved only a 50 percent increase in its equity value.[3]

The message in this hypothetical example is echoed in the real world. Taking another look at the EP-dominant versus earnings-dominant company data in Exhibit 2.11, the empirical evidence shows the consequences of putting too much emphasis on earnings growth, especially if it is not accompanied by a similar or higher level of economic profit growth.

The EP-dominant group had the highest earnings per share growth rate of the three groups, not surprising because earnings growth is a large component of EP growth. The bigger insight is in the differences in per share book equity

EXHIBIT 2.11 Differential Growth and Total Shareholder Returns

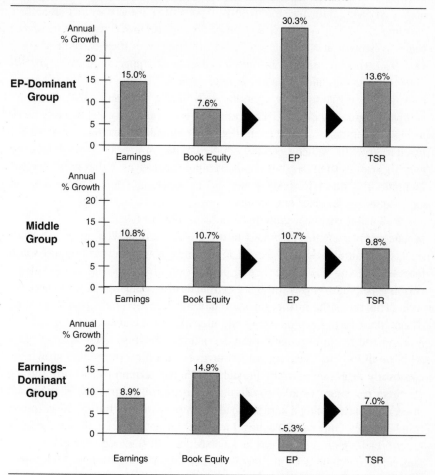

Notes:

EP-Dominant: Companies where 10-year annualized EP-per-share growth rate exceeds earnings-per-share growth rate by 5 percentage points or more.

Middle: Companies where 10-year annualized EP and earnings-per-share growth rates are within 5 percentage points of each other.

Earnings-Dominant: Companies where 10-year annualized earnings-per-share growth rate exceeds EP-per-share growth rate by 5 percentage points or more.

Analysis covers S&P 500 companies during the time period of 1998 to 2007.

For a more complete discussion of methodology and results, see Appendix I.

growth between the top and bottom groups. The EP-dominant companies increased their equity investment only 50 percent as fast as they increased their earnings (7.6% vs. 15%), whereas the earnings-dominant companies increased their investment at a rate *almost 70 percent faster* than their earnings (14.9% vs. 8.9%). This investment differential had as much impact on their EP growth differential as did differences in earnings growth. Although it cannot be said that there is a one-to-one correlation, it is hardly surprising that a group of companies growing EP at 30.3 percent per year would have TSRs nearly twice as high as companies that were trying hard to increase earnings per share but failed to grow EP. When CEOs are tempted to pay or invest too much to grow earnings rather than EP, they should remind themselves of that great Beatles' admonition: "Can't Buy Me Love." (See Appendix I for a more detailed explanation of the data and results.)

If chasing earnings growth alone is so obviously an error, why is this practice so persistent? A key part of the answer is that Wall Street securities analysts are unquestionably fixated on earnings growth and earnings per share forecasts, giving CEOs the strong impression that meeting Wall Street's earnings per share expectations is essential for the company's stock to perform well. (This raises the further question of why so many bright people on Wall Street continue to focus on the wrong metrics, but the answer to that may be more in the realm of religion than economics.) Because CEOs interact often with analysts, the seeming importance of earnings per share growth is constantly being reinforced. Further, a "miss" on projected earnings or earnings per share usually results in a short-term pummeling of the stock price, again reinforcing a false sense of the importance of "hitting the earnings number." Yet if one considers how incomplete a performance picture earnings growth alone paints, and if one looks objectively at the long-term evidence as illustrated in Exhibit 2.11, the fact is inescapable: Making strategic investment decisions based exclusively on increasing earnings or earnings per share is a fool's errand. Perhaps CEOs should consider Wall Street analysts to be similar to theater critics: If you perform only to satisfy the critics/analysts, your commercial success is far from assured; but if your performance consistently makes audiences/investors happy, you can ignore the critics.

Other Myths

Besides the fixation with earnings growth, there are other troublesome "strategic" goals that are deeply engrained in management thinking. These include such well-known aspirations as having the highest market share, or having the highest customer satisfaction, or building on core competencies. The utility of pursuing these goals must be tested against the CEO's objective of maximizing the company's EP growth: Does pursuing them help achieve that objective? The general answer is no. As is the case with earnings growth, the substantive linkage between these goals and the financial performance of the company is weak and unreliable.

Seeking to be number one, or having the highest share of revenue or volume in served markets, has almost sacred status in the business world. Possibly no phrase pertaining to strategy has appeared more often in CEOs' analyst presentations, company planning documents, and annual reports to shareholders. Belief in the primacy of being number one presumes that achieving it will result in superior financial performance, but the evidence on this point is decidedly mixed. There are companies with high revenue market share, such as International Paper, Alcoa, and Delta Airlines, that struggle to reach positive EP even in their best years. And there are companies, such as Apple in personal computers and Honda in the U.S. automobile market, that earn higher economic profits than many of their larger, higher market share competitors.

A similar observation can be made with the goal of increasing or maximizing customer satisfaction. It is certainly true that all great companies place a high value on customer satisfaction, but that is also true of many poorly performing companies. In reality, the most satisfied customers are not necessarily the most economically profitable customers—indeed, in some industries keeping high-volume customers happy simply drives EP downward. Commercial and investment banks have many satisfied corporate customers from whom they are unable to earn economic profits. And the European aircraft giant Airbus could not exist unless it was able to satisfy extremely demanding airline customers, yet the company seems unable to wean itself of EU taxpayer subsidies, let alone consistently earn economic profits.[4]

What about building on core competencies—surely that must be a sound approach to strategy? Not necessarily. It is often better (though not ideal) to compete having only mediocre competencies in a profitable product market than to compete even with above-average competencies in an unprofitable product market. Put another way, the one core competency issue the CEO should worry about above all others is this: "Are we exceptionally good at generating economic profit growth?" If the answer is yes, chances are good that many of the competencies required to do well are already in place. If the answer is no, taking an inventory of the company's existing skill set is unlikely to get at the heart of the problem.

Every company wants to have higher share, lower costs, more satisfied customers, and better skills than the competition. But there is nothing distinctive in pursuing these ends, *nor is there necessarily even any economic advantage in achieving them.* There are many companies with large share, happy customers, and good cost controls—like some basic chemical manufacturers and oil refiners—that create little or no long-term value for their shareholders. And there are many small and midsize companies that grow economic profits faster than their larger and presumptively advantaged competitors.

Why are these and similar platitudes so widespread and ingrained in management thinking? One reason is confusing cause and effect: A relentless pursuit of economic profit growth is likely to lead a company into building meaningful competitive advantages over time, but a relentless pursuit of "competitive advantages" will in no way guarantee high economic profit growth. This critical point will be developed further in Chapter 5.

Another reason for the appeal of these platitudes is that they seem to make easy something that is normally hard—the formulation of great strategies. Every year, thousands of business unit strategic plans are approved and funded based on a collection of promises that sound almost identical, regardless of the business unit or the company in which they occur—for example, "to deliver the company's earnings growth targets through increasing market share and customer satisfaction while becoming a low-cost producer" (and perhaps while building on core competencies and achieving "sustainability" as well). These shopworn phrases constitute a kind of strategic planning checklist, and business units dutifully tick the boxes *du jour.* The incontrovertible fact that so few of these "strategies" ever prove to be exceptional in terms of growing EP and equity value seems to have little effect on their appeal, or at least on their packaging.

All of these conventional doctrines of strategic management present the CEO with a major problem because they usually impede rather than accelerate the achievement of great performance. Despite their simplicity, their intuitive appeal, their validation (and often origination) by "experts," and their entrenched position in the language of strategy and strategic planning, they must be excised from a CEO's thinking and decision making. Strategy must be about economic results, specifically EP and equity value growth, not about mythology. A CEO must make it clear that he or she absolutely does not care whether a business unit increases earnings 10 percent, is number one in its markets, is the lowest cost producer, has the most delighted (or delightful) customers, or positively exudes competencies. If a strategy having all or some these characteristics cannot consistently produce growing economic profits, it is not a good strategy. And if a strategy having none of these characteristics does produce consistently superior EP growth, then it is at least a good, maybe even a great, strategy.

 ## CHAPTER SUMMARY

The concepts in this chapter establish a basic analytical framework for making the right strategic management choices. Having an understanding of both the financial and strategic drivers of economic profit and equity value can be of immense help to executives in evaluating the strengths and weakness of their current strategies and in formulating new strategic options. Knowing how each business unit creates economic profit is essential if the CEO and board of directors are to understand the sources of the company's overall economic profit performance and its total equity value.

One critical insight of this framework is that the near universal belief of CEOs, that their top financial priority should be to grow earnings or earnings per share, is simply wrong. Growing earnings and growing economic profit are certainly related, but they are not the same thing. Moving away from an earnings growth obsession to an economic profit growth obsession is a liberating and necessary step to making the best strategic management choices.

Another insight is the danger of strategic myths. Starting in the 1960s, when business strategy first emerged as a distinct discipline, a number of powerful ideas have come into general favor, including for example the importance of having the most market share, of being the low-cost producer, and of maximizing customer satisfaction. CEOs should be wary of allowing these concepts to influence their strategic thinking because pursuing them does not necessarily lead to higher economic profit growth and may well result in lower economic profit growth. Too often, accepting these strategic myths is simply a substitute for the hard thinking and hard work of finding and executing strategies that produce exemplary EP growth and value creation.

3

Choosing the Right Performance Objectives

THE STARTING POINT OF good strategic management is choosing the right performance objectives for each business unit and for the company overall. The entire future of the enterprise will be affected by how well or badly these objectives are chosen. If, for example, a company chooses to give priority to increasing earnings growth, then its strategies will evolve very differently than they would if it chooses instead to emphasize increasing return on investment. Over time, this divergence of strategies could result in two completely different companies, with different business unit portfolios, different competitive positioning, different share price performance, and different risk-taking behaviors.

Recognizing this problem, but not having a good solution, many companies try to finesse the choices by seeking a "balance" between growth and returns, or between the short term and the long term, or between cash generating and cash consuming business units. But "balancing" tends to produce a profusion of competing objectives which, more often than not, means having no meaningful objectives at all. For example, almost all strategic decisions involve trade-offs: raise prices (but reduce growth), add product features (but raise costs), start a new marketing campaign (but, again, raise costs), expand into a new market (but increase investment and reduce return on investment). The fundamental question of how to strike the proper "balance" among these commonly encountered trade-offs is usually left unanswered.

The choice of performance objectives is so fundamental to the success of the company that it falls naturally to the CEO. In making that choice, the CEO should establish business unit and company performance objectives that are consistent with, and supportive of, committing the company's resources to the strategies that maximize the growth of economic profits over time. Unfortunately, the most widespread practices for choosing performance objectives do not even begin to meet this requirement. The most common choices of performance goals, like earnings or operating income growth, are simply not appropriate. And the typical "top-down" processes for setting business unit and company performance targets also have serious shortcomings. Following these conventional practices for setting performance objectives will usually make it less, not more, likely that managers will be able to determine and pursue their best strategies.

This chapter addresses these issues and suggests how the CEO can choose performance objectives that are fully aligned with the highest value business unit and company strategies.

 ## ASPIRATIONS

The proposition that maximizing shareholder value is the ultimate objective of a publicly owned company is the subject of constant debate, even among CEOs. In Europe, "maximizing shareholder value" is often seen as a synonym for the "Anglo-Saxon" model of supposedly cutthroat capitalism, wherein the social costs of private wealth creation are alleged to exceed the benefits. In the United States, some CEOs recoil from expressing goals that imply a primacy of their shareholders' interests over those of the company's other stakeholders, preferring to assert a more "balanced" approach. For perhaps a majority of CEOs, maximizing shareholder value is an abstract academic idea, fine in principle but somewhat divorced from the complexities of making everyday business decisions and undermined by the vagaries of stock market pricing fluctuations.

Despite these and other reservations, however, no CEO wants to preside over a company that actually destroys shareholder value or that earns poor returns for shareholders during his or her tenure. Nor would a responsible board of directors tolerate such performance were it to continue for very long. So maximizing shareholder value or total shareholder returns over time remains, as it should, a preeminent if sometimes unspoken aspiration of most CEOs and boards.

Although maximizing shareholder value or total shareholder returns may be accepted in principle as legitimate aspirations, there are significant practical problems that limit their suitability for making everyday management decisions. Three problems in particular are common in most companies: measurement, motivation, and markets.

Measurement

Most resource allocation decisions take place at the business unit level and below, within product lines, customer groups, and geographic markets. But making good estimates of equity values at these levels is not always easy. The calculations themselves can be complex, and valuation efforts can quickly degenerate into resolving methodological rather than commercial issues. Essentially, conducting full-blown present value calculations in order to determine the best options for, say, increasing penetration into a customer segment is often impractical. And, with some exceptions, it is also overkill, unlikely to lead to better decisions than choosing the options with the highest expected economic profit (EP) growth over the forecast horizon.

Motivation

There is no doubt that the words "maximize shareholder value" lack motivational power for most people, including many CEOs. Even if the left brain recognizes maximizing value or shareholder returns as legitimate expressions of the company's aspirations, the right brain finds them decidedly abstract and uninspiring. These are not the sort of energizing concepts that get the blood coursing through the veins or the team spirit up to a fever pitch. Indeed, much of the appeal of some of the strategic myths, like being number one or having the most satisfied customers, is that they are more inspirational than being asked to win for the shareholders. As this perception is unlikely to change, some CEOs will hesitate to trumpet maximizing shareholder value or shareholder returns as their primary preoccupation, particularly in lower levels in the company.

Markets

When trying to link the company's financial performance to its actual stock market performance, CEOs and boards encounter serious linkage problems. In the short term, the main problems are the volatility and seeming arbitrariness of stock price movements. Observing these, CEOs and directors understandably question whether shareholder value as reflected in the price of their stock can be relied on as a fair and accurate indicator of the company's performance at any point in time. In markets where quarterly earnings falling one penny short of analysts' estimates can cause a company's stock to drop 5 percent in one day, who can blame them for being skeptical?

Over the longer term, as measured in years, there does appear to be better linkage between companies' actual EP growth rates and total shareholder return performance (see Exhibit 2.11), but still great care must be taken before drawing conclusions about any one company over any particular time frame. Total shareholder return is driven by investors' expectations about a company's future, not past, performance, and it is also sensitive to the exact time periods over which it is measured. One example of the difficulties that can arise as a result is in measuring CEO performance. The median CEO tenure in the United States in 2008 was only about four and a half years,[1] and it is possible that a company's total shareholder return measured over such a relatively short period could be at odds with its EP growth performance. For instance, if investors happened to be overly optimistic about the company's prospects at the beginning of a CEO's tenure, total shareholder returns over the next four or five years might appear to be mediocre, even if the company's EP growth versus competitors was exceptional.

Some of the problems with using the total shareholder return measure can be mitigated by looking at it relative to an index of competitor or peer group returns, but even then anomalies can occur. As is the case with "maximizing shareholder value," "maximizing total shareholder return" is best seen as an aspirational goal rather than as an entirely reliable measure of management or company performance over specific time periods.

 ## BUSINESS UNIT OBJECTIVES

Because the business units are the building blocks of company value, setting the right performance objectives needs to start at that level. Of course, the primary objective of a business unit is to maximize economic profit growth over time, but the maximum potential EP growth rate of a business is not a concrete or observable number. As a practical matter, a business unit needs to adopt concrete measures that will correctly influence its choice of strategies and also serve as the standards, or targets, against which its progress is to be measured. For most businesses, there are three concrete performance objectives, each based on economic profit, that are most helpful in guiding decisions and controlling performance. Two of these objectives represent threshold, or minimum, performance standards, and the third represents the business unit's targets, or promised EP performance levels.

The Financial Performance Threshold

Every business unit must create at least some equity value to justify its place in the company's portfolio. This means every business unit must consistently earn a positive economic profit; that is, its return on equity (ROE) must be consistently greater than its cost of equity. CEOs, most of whom would never accept a capital project proposal or approve an acquisition that does not show an adequate return on investment, are too often tolerant of business units that go year after year without generating an economic profit. Recalling the Diversa Corp portfolio (Exhibit 2.9), three of the business units, each for different reasons, were not earning positive EP. In the cases of PopulAir and Wahoo, it is possible that changes in their strategies could improve their sustainable ROEs and move them into positive EP territory. The CEO certainly should not approve of any strategies that do not promise a solid prospect of quickly achieving that objective. The Ream Maker business unit is in too deep a negative EP hole for anything other than a complete strategic makeover to bring it back to the ranks of the value creators. If that is not achievable, then some form of restructuring must occur. Management has an affirmative duty to withdraw capital from any businesses that clearly consume value.

Many readers will recognize this financial performance threshold as what is sometimes called the "hurdle rate" of a business. For too many executives, however, the term "hurdle rate" carries with it the implication of sufficiency; that is, once the business unit has cleared the hurdle rate and is earning its cost of capital, it is deemed to be performing adequately. This is a serious misconception. Earning the cost of capital, and therefore a positive EP, is just the beginning of the journey, not the destination. It is the *minimum* required performance, not the highest or even the average expected performance of a well-managed business.

The positive economic profit threshold standard also applies to activities *within* the business units. Ideally, each of the business unit's product or service lines, geographic markets, and customer segments will achieve a consistently positive EP as the minimum requirement for inclusion in future strategies. The same capital discipline that the CEO applies to the business units overall should be applied to each element of a business unit's strategy as well.

Are there any exceptions to the requirement that every business unit must consistently earn a positive economic profit over time? There could be some short-term exceptions, particularly for businesses in highly cyclical industries and in the case of certain acquisitions. For cyclical businesses, like some basic metals, commodities, and chemicals companies, generating a positive economic profit each year may prove impossible. However, strategies should be constructed to allow these businesses to earn a substantial positive economic profit through the cycle.

In the case of a newly acquired business for which a substantial premium is paid, it is theoretically possible that a strategy that maximizes economic profit over time might still produce negative economic profits for, at most, a year or two after the transaction is completed. This can be a slippery slope, however, and CEOs should be careful about tolerating the argument that "we would have positive economic profits if only we could ignore the accounting goodwill from the acquisition." The accounting goodwill should not be ignored. It represents real money paid for real assets and should be included in setting performance objectives and assessing strategic options for the business.

The Strategic Performance Threshold

Assuming the financial threshold is being met, the next threshold is the minimum standard for strategic performance, which is that every business unit should strive to grow its economic profit faster than the competition; that is, it should challenge itself to gain share of available EP in all of its product markets. This threshold might be considered the dividing line between strategies that are adequate, in that they are value accretive, and strategies that are excellent, in that they grow the equity value of the business unit faster than the competition.

For example, if Diversa Corp's High Octane business unit (Exhibit 2.9) was competing in a product market where the total economic profit was growing at about 4 percent per year, the CEO should be looking for that business to propose a strategy that would grow its economic profit by more than 4 percent per year. On the other hand, Shop Smart might be competing in markets where the average EP growth is only 2 percent per year, so it would be doing very well to grow its own EP by 3 percent per year—or 50 percent faster than the competition.

Unlike the threshold requirement to earn positive economic profits, which should be absolute, the strategic threshold of growing economic profits faster than the competition is presumptive but not inviolable. For most businesses participating in profitable product markets, it is an appropriate threshold standard, or test, to be applied when formulating and evaluating strategic options. However, there could be circumstances where it should be modified. For instance, in a rare product market like PC microprocessors where only one company, Intel, historically has earned 100 percent or more of the total economic profit, its strategic objective would be to help grow the total demand for microprocessors as fast as possible, rather than to gain EP share at the expense of a competitor. Or in the case of other highly profitable and dominant players in mature or slow-growing markets, experiencing some EP share erosion from smaller, more agile competitors may be inevitable. For these giants, finding ways to sustain overall market EP growth, while minimizing their own EP share losses, will be the top strategic priorities.

Meeting the financial and strategic threshold standards assures that a business is creating value and pursuing at least an adequate strategy. Indeed, most publicly traded companies would experience an enormous increase in their market capitalizations, at least as much as 50 percent, if every product market strategy in each of their business units at least met these two tests.[2]

Gold Strategies

Even if a business unit is meeting the two performance thresholds, it may well have more EP growth potential. To determine that, the business unit must evaluate all of its high-potential strategic options, consisting of both participation and positioning choices, to identify the combination most likely to yield the highest EP growth over the forecast period. This combination, which we will call the Gold strategy, is illustrated in Exhibit 3.1.

In this simplified example, the business unit is comparing three strategic options, all of which meet the minimum financial threshold of generating positive economic profits and creating equity value. However, the Red strategy, with its focus on providing a lower price than competitors, does not meet the strategic threshold of growing EP faster than the competition. The Blue strategy of competing primarily on service does meet the strategic threshold and is value accretive. It is certainly a good, though not the best, strategy. The Gold strategy, with its focus on offering superior quality, exceeds the strategic threshold and is also the option with the highest expected EP growth rate of 6 percent per year. Therefore, this is the strategic option the CEO will want to approve, along with the resources required to execute it successfully.

So what are the right performance targets for this business unit? First, the business unit management must commit to delivering the rate of future EP growth promised in the Gold strategy that was approved by the CEO: In the

EXHIBIT 3.1 The Gold Strategy

Business Unit Options in a Product Market Where EP Growth Is 5%

	Red Strategy	Blue Strategy	Gold Strategy
	Focus: Price	Focus: Service	Focus: Quality
	$EP_0 = \$6M$	$EP_0 = \$6M$	$EP_0 = \$6M$
	EP Growth: 4%	EP Growth: 5%	EP Growth: 6%
	Equity Value: $200M	Equity Value: $220M	Equity Value: $250M
Performance Objectives Met			
Financial Threshold (EP > 0)	Yes	Yes	Yes
Strategic Threshold (business unit EP growth equal to or greater than product market EP growth)	No	Yes	Yes
Maximize EP Growth	No	No	Yes

preceding example, this is 6 percent per year over the next five years. What if, for some reason, the business unit and CEO had chosen to pursue the Blue strategy? In that case, the primary financial target for the business would have been to grow EP at 5 percent, not 6 percent. It would not be appropriate to ask the business unit to pursue the Blue strategy but to deliver Gold strategy performance. This would make no sense and yield only unproductive tension between the business unit and the CEO. Strategy and targets must be aligned, and choosing the right performance targets is dependent on first choosing the right strategy.

A secondary performance target that can be useful is annual revenue or volume growth. It is secondary in the sense that it should always be subordinate to achieving the promised EP growth. But meeting the revenue/volume growth targets promised in the Gold strategy can provide some reassurance that the business unit is not meeting its short-term EP growth targets at the expense of sustaining superior longer-term EP growth. If a business unit consistently meets both the EP and revenue/volume growth targets as projected in the Gold strategy, it is more likely than not delivering on most other elements of the strategy as well.

In setting business unit performance objectives in this way, two implications should be noted. First, a business unit neither needs nor benefits from any "stretch" goals emanating from the corporate center; indeed, dispensing top-down targets, such as revenue or earnings growth goals, can be a dangerous distraction, as will be discussed in a later section. Second, the choice of the right performance objectives for one business unit should be independent of the choices made for other business units. All businesses share the need to meet the financial minimum of consistently generating positive EP, but the strategic minimums and the Gold strategy targets are unique to each business. In the preceding example, the 6 percent EP growth target is grounded in the market economics and strategic options available to that particular business; the target could not have come from the corporate center, nor could it be inferred in any way by referencing the performance possibilities of other business units in the portfolio.

COMPANY OBJECTIVES

What does this bottom-up, business-unit-focused approach imply for company-level financial objectives? Clearly, the company itself must adhere to the financial threshold of consistently earning a positive economic profit and creating value for shareholders. Of course, if all of the business units are held to that minimum standard, then the company will easily surpass it. The strategic threshold is suitable primarily as a business unit or product-market objective. It cannot easily be measured or applied to the consolidated results of a multibusiness company, although comparisons of relative economic profit growth among similar companies can be instructive.

The company's overall financial targets should be no more and no less than the consolidated economic profit and revenue growth targets of the business unit Gold strategies.[3] On a consolidated basis, these business unit targets already represent the best overall performance the company believes it can deliver. There is no additional stretch to be had from setting even higher targets at the company level, but neither should the CEO and board hold themselves accountable for achieving anything less. Of course, in any one year, some business units will perform better than promised and some not as well, but on average the CEO should expect the collective Gold strategies to produce as promised, so that the company should normally achieve its target objectives.

THE TYRANNY OF TOP-DOWN TARGETS

The bottom-up strategy based approach to setting objectives is fundamentally different from the top-down command and control approach followed in most companies. The differences are not superficial but deep, going in some cases to the core of institutional beliefs and processes.

The most widespread approach for setting performance objectives begins with the CEO first establishing earnings and revenue growth objectives, sometimes augmented with an ROI or ROE objective, for the company overall. This seems like an eminently sensible thing for the leader of the enterprise to do, signaling to the organization ahead of the annual planning and budgeting cycle what his or her performance expectations are for the coming year and beyond. But what exactly do these objectives mean and what behavior do they drive?

The general problems caused by using earnings growth or even rate of return measures as proxies for value creation have already been discussed, but it needs to be stressed again that by choosing such inappropriate performance metrics the CEO's ultimate purpose of maximizing economic profit growth is already starting to derail. Even assuming, however, that the CEO avoids the earnings and ROE target pitfalls and wants to establish an overall company EP growth objective, what should that overall company target be? And what, exactly, are individual business units supposed to do with that number?

As has already been shown, the answer to the first question is that, unless the CEO knows what all of the business unit Gold strategies are, there is no way of knowing what the right economic profit growth target for the company overall should be. The CEO may have aspirational EP growth objectives in mind, but setting overall company EP targets will not usually inspire the business unit strategies that can achieve those aspirational objectives over the long run.

In the example shown in Exhibit 3.2, a toy company with just two business units illustrates some of the problems with the conventional approach.

In Scenario 1, the main behavioral problem is that the top-down target of 10 percent EP growth makes it unlikely that either business unit would even try to determine its Gold strategy, let alone execute it. Because there is no linkage at all between the CEO's top-down company target and the product market realities the businesses are facing, the effort to formulate a Gold strategy would be largely wasted—in effect, that strategy has already been ruled out by the top-down mandate.

Even if each business unit somehow knew what its Gold strategy should be, it would have to largely ignore that knowledge and "stretch" to produce one-year operating plans to reach the mandated 10 percent EP growth. It could probably do this only by under-investing in capital, marketing, research and development, or other "discretionary" areas, thereby endangering its longer-term EP growth and equity value. This means that even if there were a way for

Gold Strategy Potential

Conventional Toys Business Unit

Maximum EP Growth 3%

+

Electronic Toys Business Unit

Maximum EP Growth 7%

▶

Total Toy Company Consolidated Business Units

Maximum EP Growth 5%

Scenario 1
CEO Sets EP Growth Target = 10%

- Probably not possible to achieve 10% for even one year
- Trying for 10% would distort expense and investment choices away from Gold strategy
- Probably would never even discover Gold strategy—it would be irrelevant
- Result: LT EP growth < 3%

+

- Possible business might attain 10% for a year or two
- Trying for 10% would distort expense and investment choices away from Gold strategy
- Probably would never even discover Gold strategy—it would be irrelevant
- Result: LT EP growth < 7%

▶

- Company would not achieve 10% EP growth
- Neither business unit would discover or pursue its Gold strategy
- Company LT EP growth < 5%
- Company fails to maximize equity value and shareholder returns

---

Scenario 2
CEO Sets EP Growth Target = 5%

- Might be able to stretch to EP growth of 5% for a year or two
- Trying for 5% would distort expense and investment choices away from Gold strategy
- Probably would not discover Gold strategy—it would be irrelevant
- Result: LT EP growth < 3%

+

- Might formulate and pursue Gold strategy
- Or, might opt for lower EP growth strategy, still ≥ 5% but easier to achieve than Gold strategy and bonuses might be larger
- LT EP growth = between 5% and 7%

▶

- Company might achieve 5% EP growth for several years, but
- At best, only one business unit is pursuing its Gold strategy, more likely that neither business unit is maximizing EP growth
- Company LT EP growth < 5%
- Company fails to maximize equity value and shareholder returns

---

EXHIBIT 3.2 Problems with Setting Top-Down Performance Targets—Toy Company Illustration

each business unit and the company overall to achieve 10 percent EP growth for next year, it would not be maximizing equity value. Continuing to use top-down "stretch" targets in this way year in and year out, as many companies do, would actually cause the company to underperform over the longer term—precisely the opposite of what the CEO intended.

Scenario 2 illustrates other subtle effects of top-down targets on business unit behavior, even when the company's economic profit growth target is notionally correct. Here, the CEO has set the top-down economic growth target at 5 percent, which, by coincidence, would be the correct target for the company if the business units actually knew what their respective Gold strategies were. Even though the 5 percent number may be coincidentally correct for the company overall, however, it can still cause both business units to depart from their highest value strategies. For instance, the Conventional Toys unit may choose to cut back on investment and marketing to get to the one-year 5 percent EP growth level, deviating from what would have been its Gold strategy. What is the Electronic Toys unit likely to do? Perhaps nothing, because its Gold strategy is projected to produce EP growth higher than 5 percent anyway. But what if the business unit leadership team's annual bonuses are based on meeting the company's target? Then there may be an incentive to low-ball the business unit forecast, to move away from a Gold strategy that is challenging to implement to a less difficult strategy with lower EP growth. Both of these natural behaviors undermine maximizing EP growth and equity value. Again, over time the overall results for the business units and the company would likely fall short of what the CEO intended.

The GE Story

One example of the unintended consequences arising from a top-down target setting approach would appear to be the experience of the General Electric Company (GE) during the period 2001–2007.[4] The company's annual reports in these years are a veritable anthology of every strategic and financial cliché known to mankind, so that both investors and GE's own managers could be excused for having no idea at times what the CEO's actual intentions were. But buried in all the public relations jargon, several top-down targets are consistently asserted.

The one target that is highlighted and repeated more often than any other is the old chestnut, 10 percent annual earnings growth. This target is intended to apply not just to GE's consolidated performance but to each of the business units as well.[5] Other objectives prominently asserted included industry leadership in served markets, revenue growth of two to three times gross domestic product (GDP), return on capital employed (ROCE) of 20 percent, various references to growing cash flow, and achieving above-average returns for shareholders. Of course, these objectives are interdependent and some even conflict with one another, but no mention is made of these difficulties or how the company would cope with them. A fair inference is that the ubiquitous 10 percent earnings growth target dominated the others for internal decision-making purposes, much as it did for external communications.

With so many stated targets, the company might have been expected to achieve at least some of them. In this case, however, GE was unsuccessful in meeting any of its high-priority commitments. Shareholders were especially disappointed. Over this time period, the Standard & Poor's 500 index delivered a total return to shareholders of 6.1 percent, while GE managed to deliver only 1.4 percent, or less than its dividend yield alone.[6] A key reason for this underperformance can be seen in the data shown in Exhibit 3.3.

Although annual revenue growth fell far short of the company's unrealistic target of two to three times GDP growth, this would not necessarily have an adverse effect on economic profit or shareholder returns. Earnings growth of 8.1 percent was also short of the targeted 10 percent, but for a company the size of GE to achieve over 8 percent annual earnings growth over a six-year period is not unimpressive, depending on the underlying investment needed to fund that growth. In GE's case, however, this seems to have been

EXHIBIT 3.3 GE's Financial Performance 2002–2007

	2001	2007	Annual Growth Rate	Top-Down Target
Revenue	$126.1	$169.7	5.1%	10–15%[a]
Earnings	$14.1	$22.5	8.1%	10%
LT Debt[b]	$82.1	$260.8	21.2%	AAA Rating
Equity	$50.5	$112.3	14.2%	Unknown
Economic Profit[c]	$9.1	$11.3	3.7%	None

Source: Datastream, Value Line.

Notes:

[a]Global GDP ~ 5% during this period (*Economist*).

[b]Not needed to calculate EP, but reinforces the scale of new investment.

[c]Assumes cost of equity = 10% for entire period; total EP and EP-per-share growth were nearly identical.

precisely the problem. Overall capital growth exploded during this period, with long-term debt and equity combined increasing at over 18 percent per year. Equity alone grew at an annual rate of over 14 percent, far faster than earnings. As a result, economic profit growth was an anemic 3.7 percent during a period of fairly robust economic growth throughout the world. As was shown in earlier chapters, when a company's economic profit growth lags earnings growth by a significant amount, the consequences for total shareholder returns are usually not good, and GE proved no exception.

Can any of this performance shortfall be attributed to GE's approach to setting top-down targets? After all, if all of the targets, including earning an ROCE of 20 percent, had actually been achieved, economic profits might have grown faster than 10 percent per year and it is likely that shareholder returns would have been at least average for the period. But that is a big "if." To find answers to this question, we have to look into the mind-set that produced the targets and the probable business unit behaviors encouraged by the targets.

We cannot know for certain what was in the mind of the CEO when setting GE's top-down targets. But from what is contained in the annual reports and from the company's actual performance, two important inferences can be drawn. First, the CEO may have had an incorrect model of the linkage between earnings growth and shareholder returns, apparently pursuing the simplistic notion that meeting 10 percent earnings guidance would propel the share price forward. Following this incorrect model then led him to make fateful strategic investment errors. Nearly all investment decisions involve trade-offs, frequently between earnings growth and capital or equity growth. It appears from GE's numbers that when these trade-offs arose (which happens with great frequency in a company the size of GE, usually involving large amounts of capital), they were overwhelmingly made in favor of trying to meet the 10 percent earnings growth target, even when the capital required to support the new earnings was excessive. Subordinating disciplined equity growth to a fixation with earnings growth almost guarantees that economic profit growth will suffer over time, as it did in GE's case.

A second inference to be drawn is that the CEO seems not to have appreciated that this combination of top-down financial targets actually set the company up to overpromise and underdeliver. For a company the size of GE to sustain a 20 percent ROCE *and* grow earnings at 10 percent or more per year is, in the absence of high inflation, a near impossibility. The number of new investment opportunities with a sustainable 20 percent average return on capital employed that can be identified and implemented in any one year is obviously limited for any company, especially one the size of GE. For instance, to achieve these dual objectives in 2008 alone, GE would have had to create the equivalent of one entirely new business unit with an equity capital investment of $11 billion and first-year net income of $2.2 billion, and then grow that business at 10 percent per year while sustaining a 20 percent ROCE over the long term. In 2009, this same feat would have had to be repeated on an even larger scale, as it would every year thereafter. That a single enterprise, even one as impressive as GE has been over the years, could accomplish this year in and year out is most unlikely.

Thus, it appears that GE's top-down targets contained the seeds of their own failure. They seem inherently unrealistic and, because of the primacy given to earnings growth over capital growth, they were unlikely to succeed in their intended purpose of generating great financial or stock market performance.

As if these problems were not bad enough, the top-down targets may well have created even more unintended consequences within the business units. GE's large number of diverse businesses, participating in markets with very different economics and positioning choices, could not possibly have similar Gold strategies or the same performance objectives. It is inconceivable that the Gold strategies for business units that make jet engines, commercial loans, TV programs, wind turbines, and medical imaging machines would all produce performance that meets or exceeds the company's top-down mandated targets. Even *trying* to meet those targets could undermine long-term performance of many business units. As noted, the 10 percent earnings growth target, in particular, was clearly intended to set the standard for each GE business unit. But for any one business unit, that objective may be completely at odds with achieving its true Gold strategy, which might promise earnings growth of only 6 percent but EP growth of 8 percent in a product market that is not economically profitable. This would be a spectacular strategy that would never even be uncovered in search of the requisite corporate 10 percent earnings growth number. The business units are being told, in effect, that their value maximizing strategies are irrelevant unless they happen to produce 10 percent earnings growth. Even then, if the notional Gold strategy were to produce more than 10 percent earnings growth, it might possibly be ignored in favor of a less challenging strategy that still meets that target. In either case, there will be a tremendous temptation throughout the company to overinvest in earnings growth, both organically and through acquisitions, further fueling the downward pressure on business unit and company economic profit.

A final distortion that top-down targets can cause results from imposing the responsibility on some business units to make up for earnings shortfalls in other business units. This can have calamitous effects. In GE's case, there are some who argue that this is precisely the responsibility that was placed on some of the finance units during 2002–2007, resulting ultimately in the collapse of GE's earnings in 2008 and 2009 and the need for federal government support to protect the entire company from a potential bankruptcy. There is indirect evidence to support this argument. While the nonfinance units struggled collectively to meet the company's 10 percent earnings growth target, the finance units could purchase earnings quickly and in large amounts, simply by making more loans (or buying securities) and by doing more deals, both of which GE's units did during this time. The rapid growth in the finance units was the biggest driver on the enormous capital increases, particularly the debt increases, shown in Exhibit 3.3. It was also a big contributor to GE's earnings growth, but ultimately not to its economic profit growth or shareholder value.

Many other large financial institutions were caught up in the same problems that plagued GE, so it is possible that the company would have encountered some reverses even with properly set objectives. But the combination of GE's errors—the primacy given to earnings growth, the combination of unrealistic financial targets, the disconnect between company targets and business strategies, the lack of capital discipline, and the risks assumed in the finance business units (in part perhaps to make up for the earnings shortfalls in other business units) were a recipe for disappointing performance no matter what the economic environment.

 ## CHAPTER SUMMARY

The CEO's choice of performance objectives exerts a profound influence on a company's strategies and financial results over time. The most widespread choices—top-down, earnings-based mandates—provide misleading guidance to most business units and will not usually lead to maximizing economic profit or equity value for business units or the company. As well intentioned as the CEO is in setting these objectives, the consequences may well be far less than what was possible or than what he or she was hoping for.

Business units should have three levels of performance objectives: a financial threshold to earn at least the cost of capital, a strategic threshold to grow EP faster than the competition, and a Gold strategy target to maximize EP growth over time. Meeting the financial threshold will ensure that the business is not destroying value. Meeting the strategic threshold will stretch the business to maximize its share of available EP. And meeting the Gold strategy threshold will ensure that the business is delivering on its promises, justifying the investment of resources necessary to support the strategy.

For the company overall, performance objectives should be determined from the bottom up, with the consolidated business unit Gold strategy EP and revenue growth targets becoming the total company's EP and revenue growth targets. Achieving the EP growth generated by collective performance of the business unit Gold strategies will ensure the best possible results for shareholders and other stakeholders over time.

4

Making the Right Participation Choices

PARTICIPATION CHOICES ARE ABOUT answering the "what," "where," and "for whom" questions of business strategy: What products and services will the business offer, in which geographic markets will it provide the offer, and to which customer segments will it target the offer? Although these questions will be addressed somewhat separately here, they are in fact interdependent and usually need to be answered together for each product market. Collectively, they constitute the overall participation strategy of the business.

The objective of participation strategy is to concentrate the company's resources in those product markets with the highest potential of generating positive economic profit for the business over time, primarily in the "northern hemisphere" of the ME/CP Profitability Matrix in Exhibit 2.9. Generally these product markets have a history of allowing even average competitors to earn positive economic profit, though the fact that a product market has favorable structural characteristics does not mean that the market would necessarily be profitable for new entrants or even for all incumbents. Still, with the objective of maximizing EP growth in mind, a business needs to seek out and participate in those product markets where earning a positive EP is reasonably likely, and to exercise the discipline to exit, or stay out of, those product markets where it is not likely.

GENERAL CONSIDERATIONS

The first consideration is that participation choices, both at the business-unit and corporate-portfolio levels, are critically important determinants of a company's current and future levels of economic profit. Although it is difficult to generalize, for a typical company, at least half—and perhaps as much as three-quarters—of its economic profit and equity value are determined by the structural characteristics of its chosen product markets, with the rest determined by its competitive positioning choices within those product markets. If a company consistently makes good participation choices, odds are high that it will at least earn its cost of capital and perform reasonably well for investors. If, on the other hand, it makes consistently poor participation choices, the odds that it can achieve positive EP or grow EP very much over time are greatly reduced.

A second important consideration is that participation choices should be made based on judgments about *future* economic profitability. In general, economic profitability declines over time as product markets reach maturity. But some product markets remain highly profitable for long periods of time: Photographic film, as an example, generated enormous economic profits for more than 100 years before digital photography finally ended that impressive run. Other product markets generate positive economic profits for short periods of time and then quickly implode; one example would be subprime mortgages in the United States, which appeared hugely profitable for nearly a decade before collapsing in 2007. In some cyclical industries such as basic chemicals, economic profit rises and falls with the demand cycle, perhaps averaging slightly positive or slightly negative over an entire cycle. Occasionally, a product market that has been unprofitable for incumbents turns out to be a gold mine for one or two new entrants who are able to change the structure of the market in fundamental ways: This is what Nucor was able to do in the U.S. steel market. Thus, regardless of past history or current product-market economics, management must always be alert to impending changes in those economics that would also require a decisive change in participation strategy.

A third consideration is that participation choices are almost entirely within management's control. At the business unit level, the choices of which products to sell, in which markets, and to which customer segments should constantly be reviewed and refined. As the economic profit outlook for a product market changes so should the participation strategy. Although sudden changes in product-market profitability cannot always be foreseen, most changes occur over a number of years, allowing management ample time to adjust its strategy and level of investment accordingly. As a general rule, except in special situations where the business unit has an enormous competitive advantage, all of the equity capital employed in the business should be invested in economically profitable product markets. For the CEO to maximize the company's overall EP growth, he or she has to be sure that each business unit pursues participation strategies that attain that level of capital efficiency.

ASSESSING PARTICIPATION OPPORTUNITIES

There are many, mostly qualitative, criteria commonly used to characterize a product market as attractive. These criteria include high growth, high entry barriers, few competitors, few substitutes, and low customer power. When managers use these criteria to describe a product market, they are making a big assumption that certain combinations of these criteria are highly corre-lated with product-market profitability. In other words, they presume that "attractive," as defined by these criteria, equals "profitable." But to make the right participation choices, it is critical to reverse this way of thinking: If, and only if, a product market is or can be economically profitable is it inherently attractive. Managers need to understand whether markets are, and in the future are likely to be, good sources of economic profits for the average competitor. This understanding should not be based on a list of qualitative characteristics but—whenever possible—on the actual measurement of economic profits.

As an example of the pitfalls from starting an analysis of market attract-iveness with qualitative rather than quantitative criteria, what would be the presumed attractiveness of a mature product market that is highly regulated, relatively slow growing, has low entry barriers, has hundreds of competitors and vast production capacity, offers customers an almost unlimited choice of me-too products, and where there is a constant threat of substitution from other product providers? The conventional wisdom would almost certainly peg this as an unattractive product market. But this product market consistently generates among the highest absolute levels of EP of any product market in the United States—it is the basic retail deposit gathering and lending business of commercial banks.[1]

Or what about a product market that provides high-tech goods with very high customer benefit, has had high growth historically, has high rates of innovation, has moderate entry barriers, and has no real substitutes. Again, conventional wisdom would probably peg this as a fairly attractive product market, but it would be wrong. These were the characteristics of the U.S. personal computer market from the 1980s to the early 2000s. Only one player, Dell, managed to earn consistent economic profits throughout that period. Others either broke even or—like IBM, Gateway, Compaq, and many others—earned negative economic profits. (More recently, Apple, following an entirely different business model, has experienced a resurgence that has brought it dominance not in total personal computer market share but in the high-priced segment where it appears to earn excellent EP.[2])

To the extent that generalizations about market attractiveness are possible, there are certain factors that do tend to limit the total EP generated in a product market, among them poor government regulation (airlines), weak property laws (Venezuela), and endemic corruption (Russia). However, other conditions often associated with unattractive product markets—excess capacity, too many competitors, and too many similar or substitute offerings—should not be accepted at face value. For example, "excess" production capacity can be just as much a consequence of poor profitability as it is a cause. Is a U.S. auto factory idle because its output cannot be sold profitably, or is the U.S. auto industry unprofitable (in part) because it has too many underutilized factories? The somewhat complicated answer is "both," but it is a lack of industry profitability that usually creates the excess capacity that then acts as a damper on any subsequent recovery. And there are examples of product markets with lots of "extra" productive capacity, including banks and mutual funds, which have generated significant economic profits over long periods of time.

Another frequently cited driver of market attractiveness is the number of competitors, but again, as a proxy for economic profitability, this has little predictive power. There are only a half dozen major aluminum producers in the entire world, yet collectively they earn negative economic profits.[3] There are hundreds of oil exploration companies (including business units that are part of larger oil companies) that, though volatile, on average earn very good economic profits;[4] there are far fewer oil refining companies (including business units of the larger integrated companies), but they, on average, earn negative economic profits.[5]

As one final example of the limitations of using qualitative criteria to assess product market profitability, we can look at "customer choice." Normally, the more choices customers have to buy the same or similar products and services, the less attractive a product market is thought to be. But look at the U.S. mutual fund industry. It comprises approximately 8,000 funds offering customers a vast choice of investment strategies in stocks, bonds, and other securities.[6] And, overall, this industry does not even provide an exceptional service to its customers. The industry is so large and diversified and manages so much money ($12 trillion in the United States in 2007) that it can do no better than earn average market returns (minus fees) for its customers.[7] By definition, this means that the expected investment returns for most customers are less than they would be if the customers just selected their own investments by throwing darts at a list of stocks and bonds. Yet despite the huge number of participants and the relatively low customer benefits they provide, the mutual fund business itself appears to been a gold mine for most participants. In part, this is because the funds have succeeded in decoupling their own compensation (fees) from their performance: The funds are paid a percentage of assets under management whether they make money for their customers or not. Why investors accept this arrangement is a mystery, but historically they have, and as long as they continue to, operating a mutual fund will likely remain an economically profitable activity for the average player.[8]

The point of these examples is not to prove that the qualitative and quantitative criteria for estimating economic profit are never aligned. They are usually at least partly aligned, but not in any consistent or predictable ways. Because of this, the qualitative criteria are not good proxies for, or reliable predictors of, product market economic profits. For existing product markets, knowledge of EP must be factual and therefore empirically grounded, either by observing incumbents or through direct participation. Actually knowing product-market EP, not making qualitative guesstimates, is the first step to understanding the true drivers of profitability in any existing product market.

Even with good data, however, managers want to have some general guidelines to narrow the number of choices they can reasonably be expected to consider in formulating strategies. Six common scenarios capture many of the possible situations a business may be evaluating. They can provide managers with a first approximation of what the economic profit potential for their business might be in a given product market. The first four scenarios may be described as standard cases and the last two as special cases for evaluating EP growth potential.

Four Standard Product Market Scenarios

As illustrated in Exhibit 4.1, these four scenarios are described in terms of actual or estimated product-market EP potential and the barriers to entry or exit. They are intended to frame understanding and suggest possible options but are not entirely prescriptive—there can always be exceptions.

EXHIBIT 4.1 Standard Product Market Scenarios

Scenario	Product-Market Characteristics	Example (2001–2007)
I	Positive EP, high entry barriers	Money transmission
II	Positive EP, low entry barriers	Educational services
III	Negative EP, low exit barriers	Entertainment
IV	Negative EP, high exit barriers	Paper and forest products

When making participation choices within any of these scenarios, either as an incumbent or as a potential new entrant, there are four basic questions to be answered first:

1. How much EP is currently being generated by each major competitor and for the total product market?
2. What are the current structural drivers of EP?
3. What factors seem likely to impact the drivers of overall product-market EP in the future?
4. What EP growth rate is likely to occur over the next several years? (The number of years that are relevant depends on the nature of the business.)

Looking at each scenario with some examples will help illustrate this approach.

Scenario I: Product Markets with Positive EP and High Entry Barriers

These are product markets with structural characteristics that allow incumbents to earn high ROEs and economic profits, even if they posses no outright competitive advantage. The specific structural characteristics that allow for this performance will vary by product market—there is no list of positive EP factors that applies generally to all product markets.

One example fitting this product-market scenario is global money transmission. This is the service large banks like Citigroup, Bank of America, and JPMorgan Chase provide to commercial and government clients for managing their cash and near-cash transactions on a nearly real-time worldwide basis: Taking deposits in almost any location, providing local and global balances, exchanging currencies, investing short-term funds, and administering payrolls and pension payments are some examples of the many critical services these companies provide. For most competitors, it is a very profitable business. Over the years, the resiliency of positive EP in this product market has been impressive. Indeed, this seemingly staid service may well have earned more EP for banks over the years than their more glamorous investment banking businesses.

To illustrate answers to the four basic product-market questions, here (briefly) is how they might look for global money transmission:

▪ *Estimated global market EP (2007).* In excess of $4.0 billion.[9]
▪ *Current EP drivers.* (1) Adequate fee levels because of the high value customers place on having absolute confidence in the security, access, record keeping accuracy, currency and investment flexibility, speed, and privacy offered by incumbents; (2) generally high customer deposit balances in the system, earning the prevailing interest rate spread; (3) scale effects, especially from leverage of IT assets, and scope to serve clients anywhere in the world limit competitive entry.
▪ *Future EP drivers.* Likely to be the same as current drivers. New entrants would need substantial time to build required reputations and global infrastructure. There could be a threat from technological changes allowing customers to do more of these activities themselves, but scale and scope advantages of the big banks would be difficult to overcome.
▪ *Future EP growth.* Probably in line with average global economic growth rates of 4.5 percent to 5.5 percent, with much higher growth in emerging markets and somewhat slower growth in mature economies. Increasing government outsourcing of payrolls and welfare payments could add to this growth rate. Pricing pressure on fees will be constant but should be largely offset by continued cost reductions from scale effects. Profit margins from deposits should remain stable or decline slightly with new regulations in the financial services industry.

What does this information and analysis imply for participation choices? For well-established players, future EP growth rates from money transmission are likely to be at GDP rates or perhaps slightly higher. Even at 5 percent growth, the total EP "pool" would be increasing by more than $200 million per year, an absolute dollar amount of annual EP growth matched in few other product markets.

For potential new entrants into global money transmission, making significant inroads into this big EP pool could be a challenge. Investment in the required technology is huge, and reputation for absolute reliability and safety is also of extreme importance to customers, as is the capacity to serve nearly anywhere in the world. Few new entrants could achieve these require-ments in less than a decade. One would expect new entrants to come in at the margins (e.g., pension administrators with their own systems) rather than on a wholesale basis. Incumbents must always be vigilant, but the threat of a rapid demise in the economic profitability of this product market seems modest in the near term.

Scenario II: Product Markets with Positive EP and Low Entry Barriers

Low entry barriers invite competition and normally suppress rather than enhance profitability, but there are striking examples of highly profitable product markets with low entry barriers. One previously cited is the retail banking deposit gathering and lending business in the United States, where entry barriers (as demonstrated by the large number of competitors) are not particularly high yet economic profits have historically been enormous. The mutual fund industry would be another example of a Scenario II product market.

Another interesting example in the United States is the secondary educa-tional services market, where there are literally thousands of public and not-for-profit schools and also a small number of for-profit, publicly traded suppliers. With entry barriers so low and with so many competitors, many of whom are completely subsidized and need show no earnings, it is remark-able that there is room for for-profit companies to enter and earn positive EP, but on a modest scale they do. A group of seven public educational services companies covered by Value Line have averaged ROEs well above 30 percent from 2000 to 2007 and are projected to remain above that level, at least through 2014, while growing at more than twice projected gross domestic product.[10]

The significant difference between participating in Scenario I and Scenario II type product markets is the greater threat posed by new entrants in Scenario II. The implosion of the U.S. home mortgage market serves as a powerful object lesson for how quickly these threats can alter product-market economics. For the decade prior to 2007, large incumbents along with many new entrants, abetted by low interest rates and government-imposed social engineering policies, expanded the availability of mortgages to virtually anyone claiming to be of the species *homo sapiens*. Profitability for the myriad of middle persons—originators, lenders, securitizers, processors, rating agencies, and the deeply corrupt Fannie Mae and Freddy Mac—was tremendous. The rapid expansion of new competitors alone did not cause the collapse but did contribute to the lowering of lending standards, the poor credit review practices, and the utter lack of due diligence all along the chain. Thus, except for the high-quality prime loan segment, the reasonably good but not spectacular market economics of the mid-1990s were transformed into a high-risk and low-reward product market within 10 years.

With only low entry barriers protecting their profitability, Scenario II incumbents can be especially sensitive to the threat of new rivals. One example of blocking a potential threat to industry profitability occurred when the U.S. community banking lobby, fearful of more effective competition in members' local markets, convinced the U.S. Congress in 2006–2007 to pass legislation preventing Wal-Mart from obtaining a banking charter. Despite such setbacks, Scenario II product markets continue to have attractive opportunities for potential entrants, particularly if the contemplated entry is related to their existing profitable business activities. This is why expanding into consumer finance makes economic sense for a company like Wal-Mart and why it will no doubt continue in its efforts to find legitimate ways to participate where it can.

Scenario III: Product Markets with Negative EP and Low Exit Barriers

Unless a business unit has a large and sustainable competitive advantage over virtually all other rivals, it will be unable to consistently earn its cost of capital in this type of product market. Among the examples of Scenario III product markets in the United States are various news and entertainment segments, automotive parts suppliers, furniture and clothing manufacturers, and many retailing segments.

Take the entertainment business as one example. For U.S. businesses engaged in radio and TV broadcasting, newspaper and magazine publishing, motion picture production, and theme parks, ROEs are well below the cost of equity in most years. Such luminous names as CBS Corp., News Corp., Time Warner, and NBC/Universal are perpetually unable to earn economic profits (Viacom has been a notable exception).[11] One reason for this generally poor profitability is that, similar to investment banking and professional sports teams, the "talent" and the executives in these businesses tend to take any economic excess as compensation before it reaches the shareholders. This presents a classic agency problem, where the business may be hugely attractive to employees but not so much so to public shareholders. None of these businesses face high exit barriers. But as long as there is no incentive for management or highly paid professionals to want to exit them, and as long as equity returns do not fall too low and the companies can still be financed (most carry substantial debt), many will struggle on.

Most multibusiness companies have a significant amount of capital tied up in Scenario III product markets where they have no offsetting competitive advantage large enough to earn a positive EP. Continuously identifying and dealing with these unpromising situations can be a major source of EP growth over time. Because of the low exit barriers, an economically unprofitable business unit can almost always increase its longer-term EP by exiting the Scenario III product market and redeploying the funds to other positive EP parts of its business or returning the capital to investors.

The question is why so many companies and CEOs fail to do this, or at least why they wait until performance becomes so poor they are forced to act. This question, one of the most important in strategic management, has a complicated set of answers. Elements of these answers are addressed more fully in other chapters, but the key explanations are as follows:

- *Management focus on earnings growth, not EP growth.* Many Scenario III product markets allow businesses to simultaneously generate positive accounting earnings and negative EP. Thus, to exit the product market would mean (even without a write-off) the business would have to reduce reported earnings, which would run counter to most companies' goal of increasing earnings or earnings per share. Unfortunately, this conflict occurs often, and many value-creating capital redeployment opportunities are deferred indefinitely.

- *Management rewards based on scale.* The absolute levels of a CEO's or business unit head's pay and prestige are normally correlated to the size of the company or business unit the individual leads. When reducing the size of a business by exiting a certain unprofitable product market would increase EP but decrease revenues, assets, and headcount, this presents a classic agency problem. The shareholders might be indisputably better off if the exit decisions are made, but management may fear its own pay and perks will be reduced or even eliminated at the same time. It is not surprising that few business unit heads come forward with exit strategies that would potentially threaten their own interests and those of their team.

- *Shaky synergies.* An example of this phenomenon might occur when selling a particular product in Country A is economically profitable but selling it in Country B is not. This would suggest exit as one option for Country B. It is often argued, however, that continued participation in Country B gives the total business unit much more manufacturing scale and therefore lower unit costs than if it participated only in Country A; that is, the alleged synergy translates into larger operating profits in Country A and therefore justifies continued participation in Country B. This argument should always be tested because it is frequently mistaken. Given the choice of either having to absorb somewhat higher manufacturing costs (if the volume in Country B was lost) or having to absorb all of the negative EP of Country B (because it is the beneficiary of the alleged scale effects), Country A might conclude that it would maximize EP without the "synergies" from Country B. Once all costs are properly taken into account, many alleged synergies between product markets can quickly evaporate.

■ *Poor capital allocation processes.* This topic will be covered more fully in Chapter 6. However, it needs to be noted here that there is a strong bias in the way most companies manage capital to look primarily at the prospective returns of investing incremental capital in new projects rather than looking at the prospective returns on the much larger amounts of capital already invested in all of the company's product markets. This bias causes capital myopia, where executives may argue for days or weeks over whether to fund a $50 million project, while ignoring for years the $1 billion invested in a product market that has not generated positive EP within living memory.

For all of these reasons, liberating capital from unprofitable product markets, even when external exit barriers are low, can prove to be difficult. This is one area where the CEO must take the lead and insist that, unless the business unit has a competitive advantage large enough to offset the unattractive characteristics of these markets, capital must be withdrawn and put to more productive uses. These businesses can often be sold at attractive prices to other competitors looking to increase their scale or scope.

In the case of a potential new entrant, a Scenario III product market offers little or no opportunity to earn positive EP. Only the conditions described in Scenario V would cause the CEO to justify participation in this type of product market.

Scenario IV: Product Markets with Negative EP and High Exit Barriers

Scenario IV businesses are a CEO's nightmare, terrible to be in, and perhaps worse to get out of. Among examples of Scenario IV product markets in the United States are the pulp and paper business, the oil refining business, and the airline industry.

Looking briefly at the U.S. pulp and paper product market, there is a strong alignment between qualitative and quantitative indicators of market attractiveness. In addition to dealing with increasing foreign competition, the companies in this market control few of their input costs (fiber, chemicals, power, and equipment) and have almost no influence on what their price-sensitive customers will be willing to pay. Thus, the industry is not well positioned to generate high EP under normal supply-demand conditions.[12] In addition, production costs have been driven relentlessly higher by the need to meet ever-more-stringent pollution rules because of the high toxicity of emissions from the paper-making processes. It now costs half-a-billion dollars or more to build a major new paper plant in the United States, and the environmental cleanup costs of shutting an older paper plant down are sometimes prohibitive, making exit an extremely unattractive choice.

In these situations, an analysis of choices may produce a perverse indication. The EP stream from continuing participation is usually very negative, but on a strictly analytical basis might still have a less negative equity value than absorbing the cost of a plant closing or a complete shutdown of part of the business. In that case, continuing to operate would appear to be the preferred strategy. Often, however, it is better for the CEO to override the present value calculation and find the least painful way to exit. One reason for this is that the structural factors driving negative EP from continuing operations almost never improve and usually only get worse with time. Another reason is that continued participation risks sending the wrong message to the rest of the organization, making it more difficult for the CEO to enforce good capital discipline generally; that is, if one clearly negative value participation choice is allowed to continue, why not others? A third, more subtle, reason to exit is the pressure that continued participation in Scenario IV (or Scenario III) product markets puts on the rest of the business. In an effort to compensate for the effects of a poorly performing part of the business, the leaders of other product markets may be encouraged to overpromise on performance or otherwise depart from what might be their Gold strategies to help make the (short-term) numbers for the company. This type of distortion, especially when repeated over many years, assures that the company will not be maximizing EP growth.

Two Special Product-Market Scenarios

The special cases comprise scenarios where product-market EP data either suggests a counterintuitive strategy (Scenario V) or is nonexistent (Scenario VI).

Scenario V: Product-Market Transformation Opportunity

This is an important variant to Scenario III and Scenario IV situations in which a company should ordinarily be withdrawing, not adding, capital in economically unprofitable product markets. However, the competitive conditions in these unattractive product markets can sometimes be transformed by the entry of a new player with a radically different business model. Business models as a source of competitive advantage will be discussed more extensively in Chapter 5, but for now we can generalize to say the new entrant has a very different way of delivering customer value or a very different way of organizing and managing the supply chain, such that it can succeed in generating a positive and growing stream of EP, whereas most incumbents cannot. In fact, the existing product-market structure becomes an absolute advantage to the new entrant because current competitors have such large and sticky investments in unprofitable business models that they cannot respond to the challenge of the new model easily or quickly.

It is worth stressing the potential in this scenario because some extremely successful companies have been built by participating in what were previously unprofitable product markets. Among the exemplars of this participation strategy (combined with their unique positioning strategies) are companies like Dell in personal computers, IKEA in furniture, Nucor in steel production, Danaher in basic industrial products, Valero in oil refining, and Amazon in bookselling. All of these companies saw opportunity in product markets that others understandably viewed as having limited, if any, economic profit growth opportunities.

Nucor Corp. illustrates how dramatically a new entrant can alter product-market economics. Although its roots go back to the early 1900s, Nucor took its modern form in the 1970s when it began to focus on the steel business. Though periodically earning economic profits during the peaks of economic cycles, companies in the U.S. steel industry at that time were facing, at best, marginal and declining industry economics. The least profitable segment of the steel business was the "nonflat" commodity segment, with basic products like rebar and rods. It was this seemingly unpromising segment that Nucor decided to enter, utilizing its new minimill technology that used steel scrap rather than iron ore as its feedstock.

Within a few short years, Nucor had succeeded in pushing the larger integrated steel companies out of the nonflat segment. At the same time, the company was earning ROEs nearly twice as high as what other companies were earning from remaining in the supposedly more attractive flat steel segment. Eventually, Nucor was also able to utilize its minimill technology to make flat steel, and it has continued to both grow faster and earn much higher returns than its older, more established competitors. There are other elements to Nucor's business model, besides its manufacturing technology, that differ markedly from the older competitors, including a relentless focus on profitability, largely autonomous factories, high incentive pay plans at all levels, and locations in right-to-work states. Taken together, all of these differences have allowed the company to produce large and fairly consistent positive economic profits during a time of massive restructuring for much of the rest of the industry.[13]

One characteristic of businesses, like Nucor, that succeed in Scenario V product markets is that they tend to be narrowly focused entrepreneurial enterprises. The vision and risk-taking mind-set required to enter or revolutionize these markets is not normally found or encouraged in larger, more established companies. The reasons for this will be amplified in Chapter 5.

Scenario VI: New Product Markets of Unknown EP Potential

This is the realm of businesses that create wealth in nascent or previously nonexistent product markets. Well-known examples include companies like Standard Oil, IBM, Microsoft, Kodak, and Xerox, each of which ignited and then dominated a profitable new industry where none had existed before. The profitability potential of product markets can only be guessed at before these businesses become established, and the guesses are usually wildly wrong.

One example of established companies trying to participate in new or emergent product markets is the research and investment major oil companies like BP have been putting into alternative energy since the early 1990s. From the perspective of the first decade of the twenty-first century, the future economics of various forms of biofuels, wind, solar, coal gasification, advanced nuclear, and hydrogen as efficient, cost-effective, clean, and widely available sources of energy are extremely hard to forecast. The future structure of these product markets, or even which ones will survive, is essentially unknowable. This does not mean that none of the large oil company efforts will succeed, but that the range of possible EP outcomes from these investments is huge and not necessarily encouraging. It is entirely possible that most of these new product markets will remain, as they have been, inherently unprofitable (i.e., sustained only by taxpayer subsidies) for most players in most markets. And it is highly likely that economically profitable players, if they do emerge, will be start-ups or smaller companies rather than the oil giants.

It is rare for a large established company to be a pioneer in Scenario VI product markets. Although we admire the entrepreneurial companies that have succeeded in extending the frontiers of technology and business in unique new ways, and would like to emulate them, the majority of these efforts do fail and the DNA required to "go where no man has gone before" is not widely distributed. For most large companies, funding start-ups with high odds of failure in product markets with unknown economics is usually, and rightly, a low priority. That is the realm of the true entrepreneur.

OFFERING CHOICES

Deciding which products and services to offer is probably the single biggest participation choice companies or business units make, and, of course, these decisions have a huge impact on economic profit. As is the case with all the major choices that shape strategy and drive profitability, there is no formula or set of heuristics that lead the CEO inevitably to the right answers. Nevertheless, there are some observations and examples that can be helpful.

When assessing the financial performance of products and services, a common finding is that the distribution of economic profits is highly skewed. A relatively few products generate high levels of EP, usually in excess of 100 percent of the business unit's net EP. At the other end of the spectrum, an average of around one-third of equity is employed in products and services that do not generate positive EP. Exhibit 4.2 shows an example of this characteristic distribution for a business unit in the medical devices and supplies business.

With an overall EP spread of 2.8 percent and earning an EP of $18.3 million on an equity base of $650 million, this business unit might appear to be on solid ground. But a careful look at the data reveals a very different picture. Of the nine product groupings, only four—Ophthalmology, Prosthetics, Cardiology, and Renal—are participating in economically profitable product markets, and of these four, only one, Ophthalmology, also holds a net competitive advantage. The top two product groups, Ophthalmology and Prosthetics, employ $140 million (22 percent) of equity and generate $22.6 million (123 percent) of the business unit's EP, with the majority of their profitability coming from favorable market economics rather than competitive advantage. For the business unit overall, approximately 90 percent of its economic profit comes from its participation choices and approximately 10 percent from its competitive position. Yet even its participation choices, with five out of nine product groups in breakeven or unprofitable product markets, appear to be far from ideal.

EXHIBIT 4.2 Product/Service Offering EP: Medical Devices and Supplies Example ($M)

Product Segment	Book Equity	ROE	ROE – COE Spread[a]	EP	ME[b]	CP[c]
Ophthalmology	$ 50	30%	20%	$10.0	25%	+5%
Prosthetics	90	24%	14%	12.6	24%	0%
Cardiology	75	16%	6%	4.5	18%	−2%
Radiology	145	13%	3%	4.4	10%	+3%
Respiratory	85	10%	0%	0.0	8%	+2%
Renal	65	8%	−2%	−1.3	12%	−4%
Hematology	20	5%	−5%	−1.0	7%	−2%
Pathology	55	2%	−8%	−4.4	0%	+2%
General Supplies	65	0%	−10%	−6.5	5%	−5%
Total	$650	12.8%	2.8%	$18.3	12.5%	0.3%

Notes:
[a] Assumes, for simplicity, that cost of equity is 10 percent in all cases.
[b] Market economics (ME): Total product segment average ROE.
[c] Competitive position (CP): Business unit ROE – total segment ROE.

Generally, the first place to look for the future drivers of EP growth is among the product groups already generating positive EP. In Ophthalmology, for instance, seeking ways to build on its strong competitive position and taking EP share from its rivals should have the highest priority. Prosthetics and Cardiology both enjoy positive EP, but only as a result of favorable product-market economics—neither one has an advantaged competitive position. For these two product lines it will be critical to thoroughly reassess their business models to determine how they can build at least some advantage that will enable them to grow EP share in the future. Radiology may be an example of a Scenario V type business, representing an opportunity to further build and exploit a strong competitive advantage against rivals who are wedded to less successful business models.

What should be done with the product groups that are generating negative EP? Each has a different set of challenges, and negative EP does not mean a product group should automatically be discontinued. The Respiratory and Renal units are both close to earning positive EP with at least some factors in their favor. They should be challenged to find new strategies that will generate positive and growing EP within one year, two at most. The situations of the last three product groups—Hematology, Pathology, and General Hospital Supplies—are poor and unlikely to be reversed. Basically, they are Scenario III businesses. Some of their products may generate positive EP in a few geographic markets or customer segments that could still be the basis of future growth. It is also possible that some of their products may be complements to profitable products and services in other segments, although this linkage can sometimes be overstated. With that said, it is likely that all three of these product groups—or significant parts of them—are candidates for downsizing sooner rather than later. Dramatically restructuring or exiting these product markets entirely would free up a substantial amount of equity capital that should be redirected to increase EP and create, rather than destroy, equity value.

Some Instructive Product Participation Cases

One of the most famous and successful offering choices ever made was Intel's decision, on a single day in 1985, to exit the large but unprofitable market for memory chips—a market the company had practically founded—and to concentrate all of its efforts on dominating the nascent market for microprocessors. In memory chips, Intel was competing against high-quality, low-cost Japanese manufacturers who were pricing to gain market share at all costs and who were, at that time, seemingly unencumbered with the need to earn the cost of capital for their shareholders. In this situation, Intel's leaders, Gordon Moore and Andy Grove, knew the product market in which they had built the company would not generate the profits needed for Intel to survive, let alone thrive. They could not know for certain what the future profitability or size of the microprocessor business would be—only that it was unlikely to be as bad as memory chips. In effect, they were looking at a decision to exit a Scenario III situation and build from a small base in a new Scenario VI situation. As it turned out, within a few years Intel as a company was making far more money than the entire memory chip industry from which it had exited: Intel's cumulative EP from 1998 to 2007 was *$28.8 billion*.[14]

Moore and Grove had made an inspired, courageous, and highly rational product participation choice, but one that few large public companies would have made. A typical public company would have been reluctant to shrink in size, to take accounting write-offs, to accept reduced earnings, or even to see its reputation suffer. Few executives would take such bold action, but Moore and Grove somehow saw that for Intel this was truly an existential participation decision.

An equally famous but far less successful offering choice made at almost the same time was the Coca-Cola Company's introduction of New Coke® in April of 1985. Here, the company made a decision rare in the annals of business: to completely and instantaneously replace its iconic and hugely profitable core product, Coca-Cola®, with a new, reformulated product—"New Coke." In other words, the company was trying to change a near-perfect Scenario II strategy into an absolutely perfect Scenario II strategy. But in what is now recognized as one of the greatest marketing errors of all time, the reformulated and rebranded product was a complete bust. Consumers may have preferred New Coke in blind taste tests, but they had such an emotional attachment to the original product that they were actually offended when the company tried to make the change—they wanted the Coke product they had grown up with. Within the first three months of its introduction, the company's cola sales were in free-fall, its bottlers were in revolt, and the negative publicity surrounding the product was withering. One of America's most respected companies, with the world's most recognized brand, was on the verge of collapse as a result of making a single change in its offering strategy. Faced with this impending disaster, the company's leadership, CEO Roberto Goizueta and president Don Keough, made the equally audacious decision to completely reverse course and reintroduce the "old" Coke, rebranded as Coke Classic®. Within a few short months the company had gone from making a disastrous offering choice to a future that would see annual EP grow more than tenfold over the next 12 years of Goizueta's leadership.[15]

Less spectacular but far more numerous are the examples of companies refusing to exit unprofitable product markets long after it was obvious even to most outsiders that future economic profits would not be forthcoming. In some cases, like the perpetually unprofitable U.S. airline business, there are powerful institutional and government forces preventing rational decision making. In just the short time from 1998 to 2007, the top U.S. airlines had accumulated *negative* economic profits of over $22 billion.[16] Why do executives decide to stay in an industry like this?

In the case of the airlines, the most obvious answer is that an exit decision is not about closing a single business unit but potentially about shutting down the entire company. It is natural that management, employees, and suppliers would try hard to avoid this outcome. But an equally important part of the answer is that the strategic option of industry restructuring and consolidation, which would help remove excess capacity and potentially improve margins and capital efficiency for the entire industry, is severely limited by

U.S. antitrust and foreign ownership laws and even by individual members of Congress. This makes participation choices almost bimodal—a company can stay in or get out, but a wholesale restructuring by the major players is likely to be stymied by regulators. Apparently the prospect that a few airline companies might earn decent returns on their capital is considered by some members of Congress and the Department of Justice to represent a grave danger to the American consumer.

Some small steps toward industry restructuring have been made in recent years, but they are indeed small, painful (almost always involving a bankruptcy filing), and slow. The determination to keep their companies alive, while faced with severe limits on options for consolidation and route rationalization, leaves airline CEOs between the proverbial rock and a hard place when it comes to changing participation strategies. Unless true industry restructuring is someday permitted, the prospect of earning a positive and sustainable economic profit by providing airline service in the United States will remain a near impossibility for the hub-and-spoke players and unlikely even for the more selective route players like Jet Blue and Southwest Airlines.

Although the offering options facing most companies are not as profound or difficult as those faced by Intel, Coca-Cola, or the airlines, they nevertheless constitute critically important decisions that will have an enormous impact on EP growth for years to come.

GEOGRAPHIC MARKET CHOICES

For a given offer, the economic profits available from participation in different geographic product markets usually vary widely. If a business unit participates in many different countries, odds are high that EP will be negative in some and enormously positive in others because each of these markets will have different customer buying behaviors, different competitive conditions, and different regulatory regimes. Exhibit 4.3 illustrates this range of outcomes for a branded consumer product line.

Clearly this business unit, as is common among consumer branded products, is economically profitable in most of the geographic markets in which it competes. As the data show, approximately three-quarters of its EP is explained by its strong competitive position, and approximately one-quarter of its EP is explained by its participation choices. A deeper look into its participation choices reveals that $1.235 billion, or 67 percent, of the equity invested in

EXHIBIT 4.3　Geographic Market EP: Branded Consumer Product Example

Country	Book Equity	ROE	ROE – COE Spread[a]	EP	ME[b]	CP[c]
Japan	$ 160	28%	18%	$28.8	22%	+6%
Brazil	75	22%	12%	9.0	15%	+7%
China	110	19%	9%	9.9	14%	+5%
United Kingdom	190	18%	8%	15.2	14%	+4%
Mexico	80	15%	5%	4.0	18%	−3%
United States	800	13%	3%	24.0	10%	+3%
European Union	230	11%	1%	2.3	7%	+4%
Canada	50	10%	0%	0.0	8%	+2%
India	50	6%	−4%	−2.0	2%	+4%
Russia	40	5%	−5%	−2.0	5%	0%
Rest of world	65	2%	−8%	−5.2	2%	0%
Total	$1,850	14.5%	4.5%	$84.0	11.2%	+3.3%

Notes:
[a]Assumes, for simplicity, that cost of equity is 10 percent in all cases.
[b]Market Economics (ME): Total segment average ROE.
[c]Competitive Position (CP): Business unit ROE – total segment ROE.

this business unit is in geographic markets with only breakeven or negative economic profits. Although its positioning advantage is strong enough to overcome this situation in almost all markets, it is still a red flag for the business unit when evaluating strategies for future EP growth.

For this relatively mature product, adverse changes in any of its major geographic market economics could cause total EP growth to slow or even decline rapidly. For instance, if the profitability of large U.S., Canadian, and European markets were to weaken further, a substantial amount of economic profit would be lost. This underscores the urgency of finding new strategies that can improve its already good competitive position in these markets. Obviously too, the faster the business can increase its share of EP in profitable markets like Japan, China, and Brazil, and the faster it can find new profitable markets to enter, the better.

Continued participation in Russia, India, and the rest-of-world product markets, all of which have poor market economics, is also highly questionable. For this company, the sustainable competitive advantage required to earn a positive EP in these markets is gigantic and may be asking too much of management. Because market economics seldom improve spontaneously, management should not look to that possibility for salvation. These geographies are clearly candidates for restructuring.[17]

General Considerations

Although there are no hard-and-fast rules for making profitable geographic market entry decisions, determining which of the six scenarios best characterizes the market is a good place to start.

Scenario I product markets (profitable, high entry barriers) are, by definition, difficult to enter profitably. This may be especially true for foreign competitors who enter with no local advantages and who may even face special trade or regulatory barriers. To succeed in these circumstances, the new entrant must have a highly advantaged business model that enables it to overcome the considerable obstacles to success. In addition, the new entrant must actually be allowed to pursue that business model in the new geography. Even a competitor as formidable as Wal-Mart has had difficulty entering countries like Japan and Germany successfully, in large part because the huge advantages of its core U.S. business model have, for legal and cultural reasons, been denied to it in these countries. On the other hand, Goldman Sachs has achieved enormous success entering new geographies despite facing sometimes entrenched local competitors and protectionist regulations restricting its activities. Also successful were Toyota and Honda in the United States. During the 1960s and 1970s when Japanese automobile manufacturers first entered the U.S. market, such success was far from assured. The "Big Three" of General Motors, Ford, and Chrysler were utterly dominant and still very profitable, and they enjoyed every conceivable local advantage. Yet by the early 2000s, the most profitable auto companies operating in the United States were Toyota and Honda, and the Big Three had ceded nearly all of their advantages and their economic profits to foreign competitors. So entry into Scenario I geographic markets can sometimes work out well, but the odds may be long.

To decide whether to enter Scenario II geographic markets (profitable, low entry barriers), rule number one is to look first at the success of the business unit's positioning strategy in its home market. If the business unit has a successful positioning strategy in its home market—that is, if it is able to consistently create new EP or gain EP share—then its odds for successful entry into other geographic markets with reasonably similar customer, competitor, and regulatory conditions will be good, though not guaranteed. The odds of a successful entry are even higher in this situation if the business unit is the first mover in the new geography.

Among the most successful examples of growing EP via geographic expansion in Scenario II markets have been companies with highly advantaged, repeatable, business models in their home markets, strong brand recognition, and little or no local competition—at least initially. For instance, the Coca-Cola product line has been successful at generating positive EP in nearly every country in the world in part because it was the first branded carbonated soft drink entrant into many of these markets. Other examples of first-mover companies that have generated enormous EP in this way are McDonald's, IBM, IKEA, Microsoft, and Exxon.

As the world's markets continue to become more integrated, and as emerging markets mature and develop strong economies with large middle classes and their own indigenous brands, the opportunities to take the world by storm as U.S. multinationals were able to do in the latter half of the twentieth century may be more limited in the twenty-first century. On the other hand, the number of consumers with disposable income is rising dramatically worldwide, as is their purchasing sophistication, so it will still be possible for new products and services with the right characteristics, like the Apple iPod® and iPhone®, to grow EP exponentially through rapid entry into new geographic markets.

It should go without saying that entry into Scenario III or Scenario IV (economically unprofitable) geographic markets without a strong positioning advantage will usually prove disastrous. As an example, retail banking in many countries outside the United States is an economically unprofitable business, and U.S. banks, even those that are well positioned in their U.S. retail markets, have usually not been able to earn adequate returns from their branch-based retail operations in other countries. Sometimes these Scenario III or Scenario IV entry decisions are made with an overly optimistic view that by bringing a new way of doing business, the local market economics can be significantly altered. Usually this is not a good bet. Unlike its offering strategy, where many variables are under the business unit's control, the structure of the local market is not so malleable. Changing customer behavior may prove impossible owing to strong cultural differences, and altering the local competitive landscape may be equally daunting. Local regulations and political practices, whether *de jure* or *de facto*, can also drastically limit the potential to earn positive EP. Thus, Scenario III and Scenario IV geographic markets are rarely suitable for entry.

Nevertheless, companies repeatedly make Scenario III and Scenario IV geographic entry choices. The sources of these errors are very much the same as we saw for choosing negative EP offering strategies. They include the drive for earnings and revenue growth, the desire for scale, alleged synergies with other parts of the business, and poor capital management practices.

What if a business unit is already participating in a Scenario III or Scenario IV geographic market without the large positioning advantage necessary to overcome the structural disadvantages? The decision here is whether or not to exit, and the answer is nearly always yes. Unless the business unit has a credible short-term, low-cost strategy for transforming local market economics while simultaneously improving its competitive position, it has little hope of earning an adequate return on the capital invested in this market and exit should become its "defender" strategy. Sale of the business may make the most sense if there are no proprietary brands or technology involved. Otherwise, an orderly exit becomes the most likely choice. Unfortunately, the cost of an exit in some country markets is extremely high, particularly in many EU countries where employment laws require multiyear payments to terminated workers. Here the business unit can find itself in a no-win situation, where continued participation yields negative EP and value creation, but exit could result in even more value destruction. On balance, the better choice is usually to exit and bear the extra apparent cost; the case for continued participation is probably optimistically valued, and the loss of capital discipline when the CEO is dealing with other restructuring choices may be significant.

All of these examples have assumed the business unit is evaluating a participation option based on a business model similar to what it follows in its home market. Of course, there are many other ways to participate outside the home market, including export, joint venture, and franchising. It can certainly be the case in a given geographic market that one of these alternatives could be EP positive, while others—including the home market business model—are not. As an example, whether owing to the local market's small scale or costly entry/exit barriers, an export model may generate positive EP from countries where setting up the integrated home market business model would not. In counties like Russia with limited property rights, politically controlled courts, and extensive corruption, a foreign business unit should lean toward asset-light participation whenever possible. The benefits of many years of positive EP participation can evaporate quickly if assets are seized or financial claims have to be abandoned owing to changes in the political winds.

A final observation on making geographic market choices concerns the role of acquisitions. For the most part, the examples of successful geographic expansion noted previously have been the result of organic start-ups. They involved comparatively few acquisitions related to the core product because each company had uniquely successful core product business models of its own. In these cases, there would have been few if any local firms to acquire that could have enhanced EP potential. In other cases, however, acquisitions can play a role in successful entry or growth of the core product outside the home market. Local market entry barriers, such as banking licenses or limited foreign ownership rules, might necessitate a "beach head" type of acquisition simply to be allowed to participate legally. Or the local supply or distribution chains may be inadequate to support the core product business model and have to be built up from a local acquisition.

Large-scale entry acquisitions are less likely to be successful. If the business unit is counting on its own advantaged business model to succeed outside the home market, a large local acquisition is more likely to impede than it is to help with the implementation of that model. This is in part what Wal-Mart experienced with its acquisitions of large retailers in Germany and Japan—owning the local businesses created as many or more problems than were solved, resulting in very unsatisfactory returns and, in the case of Germany, eventual exit. In addition to integration and possible negative synergies, the initial acquisition economics alone are often unfavorable to the buyer. So even if some product market benefit were to be gained, it might not be enough to offset the purchase premium that has to be paid to the local seller.

CUSTOMER SEGMENT CHOICES

One of the biggest problems managers face in making customer segment participation choices is the lack of good profitability information. Most companies have at least rudimentary data on product and geographic market profitability, but information on revenues, expenses, and capital by customer or customer group is more difficult to develop. In spite of this, acquiring good knowledge of customer profitability is critically important to making the right strategic investment choices.

One case that highlights the importance of making the right customer segment choices comes from a large U.S. wholesale banking operation that was serving a broad range of more than 1,000 large corporate and government customers with a standard array of products including deposits and payments, investment banking, loans, and credit card services. At the time, the bank was organized around geographic markets and had no individual customer or customer segment profitability measurement or reporting. The amount of attention lavished on a customer was based largely on the actual or potential

EXHIBIT 4.4 Customer Segment EP

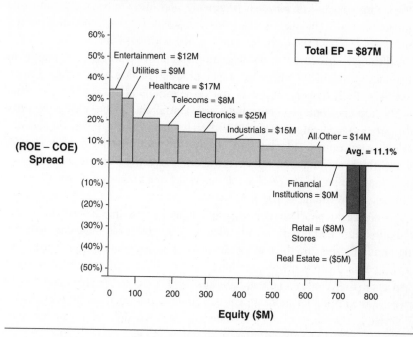

Wholesale Banking Payments Example

Entertainment = $12M
Utilities = $9M
Healthcare = $17M
Telecoms = $8M
Electronics = $25M
Industrials = $15M
All Other = $14M
Avg. = 11.1%

Total EP = $87M

(ROE – COE) Spread

Financial Institutions = $0M

Retail = ($8M) Stores

Real Estate = ($5M)

Equity ($M)

revenues or prestige that customer might bring to the bank. A detailed analysis of both product and customer profitability for corporate customer segments in one region of the United States yielded the profile shown in Exhibit 4.4.

Whereas the total EP for this geographic market was $87 million, the sources of EP varied from plus $25 million from the electronics segment to minus $8 million from the retail stores segment, and (ROE – COE) spreads varied from plus 35 percent for the entertainment segment to minus 50 percent for the real estate segment. Armed with this information, combined with the related product line profitability data, it is possible to tailor strategies to maximize EP growth for each segment. For instance, the bank could now see that its most profitable customers were being underserved with plain vanilla products and routine calling programs, whereas a much more high-touch and customized approach to these customers was not only affordable but essential to grow EP faster: A 1 percent increase in share of EP from these customers was worth about

$5 million. Among the unprofitable customers, some of which were very large companies traditionally considered good customers of the bank, one necessary change was to raise prices on certain products and services. With retail stores, for example, the prices for cash processing and lockbox products had to be increased, even if this meant losing some customers. In fact, almost all of the customers accepted these changes and stayed with the bank.

Although this may seem like an example of extreme differences in customer profitability within a single product market, the range shown here is entirely typical. What is not so common in this example is that such a large percentage of customers are so profitable. Often, only a minority of customers generates positive EP, thereby subsidizing the rest of the unprofitable customers. This situation, in turn, frequently results in the profitable, or potentially profitable, customers being underserved in some important ways. They may not be able to receive the precise product tailoring or service levels they would be willing to pay for.

A good example of segmenting profitability by customer needs is the Apple computer case mentioned earlier, where Apple appears to have captured the high-end PC users and the lion's share of total PC segment economic profits by offering a hardware-software combination that is viewed as superior in many respects to the Windows-PC combination. Apple's customers are willing to pay more, sometimes a lot more, to get the quality and functionality they desire. Meanwhile, the many other PC providers compete for high volume in customer segments that seem to yield little or no aggregate EP.

As was the case with the wholesale banking business, customer profitability analysis sometimes reveals that the highest-volume customers, those usually considered the most important and whom the sales force is given incentives to acquire and keep, are not the most economically profitable customers—and sometimes they are the least so. If a business is chasing revenue or earnings growth, it will almost never give up any customers, especially high-volume customers. But if it is seeking EP growth, a business will have to find ways to avoid or reduce the number of unprofitable customers, no matter how large they are, and to reconfigure its production and distribution capacity accordingly. Some of these customers will actually create more EP for the business if they are served by the competition.

Pursuing profitability-based customer segmentation will almost always yield large economic profit growth benefits to the company. A critical foundation to making the right customer segmentation choices is the economic fact base available to management to identify the biggest opportunities for serving the most profitable customers better and for serving the least profitable customers more efficiently or, in some cases, not at all. Of course, management needs a lot of other information about customers to understand their needs and to make the best choices, but without the profitability data, finding the Gold strategy will prove elusive.

 ## CORPORATE PARTICIPATION CHOICES

Most participation choices occur at the business unit level. But some important choices must come from the CEO and corporate center. Among these are the domain within which the corporation will participate, the best business configuration within that domain, whether and how to enter new businesses or exit existing businesses.

Domain Choices

Domain is defined primarily by the boundaries of the general offerings within which the corporation will allow business units to make their participation choices. These boundaries may be narrow, as in the case of a single general offering company like IKEA, or they may be very broad, as in a holding company like Berkshire Hathaway, with a spectrum of domain models in between, as illustrated in Exhibit 4.5.

There is no theoretical advantage to choosing any of these domain models; that is, none is inherently more or less likely to generate high EP growth. Empirically, there is some evidence that the hedgehogs with the more narrowly defined domains may do better than the foxes who participate in a broad range of businesses, but there are always notable exceptions. Companies typically operate with the expectation that individual business units will follow a narrow domain model, even if the company overall chooses a broad domain model.

Most companies begin operating in a narrow domain and then evolve from that core business to participate in broader or multiple domains over time. They

EXHIBIT 4.5 Corporate Domain Models

Narrow Product-Market Focus	Multiple, Closely Related Product Markets	Multiple, Loosely Related Product Markets	Multiple Unrelated Product Markets
Intel	ExxonMobil	General Electric	Berkshire Hathaway
IKEA	Wells Fargo Bank	Nestle	KKR
Southwest Airlines	Daimler-Benz	3M	Investor (Sweden)

may be driven by declining market economics in their original domain, or by a desire to increase earnings growth faster than possible in a single domain, or by following opportunities created by their own technologies or marketing prowess, or some combination of all of these. One contemporary example is the big pharmaceutical companies, almost all of which are expanding from their core domain, the discovery and marketing of proprietary prescription medicines, into new areas such as generic drugs, over-the-counter medicines, medical devices, and pharmacy benefits management. The desire to expand their domains appears to be driven more by concern about the declining attractiveness of their core business than about the inherent attractiveness of the domains they are getting into, so success in sustaining high EP growth is far from assured. In this case, CEOs may be trying just to slow the decline of earnings growth, believing perhaps that the phenomenal economic success of their original businesses is not likely to be repeatable.

Sometimes companies decide to shrink, rather than add to, their domains. Nokia is a good example of this type of domain choice. The company's nineteenth-century origins are the paper and rubber businesses, and the modern-day company was formed in 1967 by the merger of these two businesses and a wire cable company. Nokia's entry into the phone business came through a joint venture formed in 1979 with a Finnish television maker. At this point Nokia was participating in at least four or five distinct domains and was, in effect, a holding company. Then, in 1992, the company's new president and CEO, Jorma Ollila, made the decision to exit all domains except telecommunications and to focus in particular on mobile phones. This proved to be an enormously successful domain choice, with Nokia becoming the world's leading manufacturer of mobile phones by 1998. More important, the company was a prodigious generator of economic profits over the next decade, earning almost $30 billion between 1998 and 2007.[18]

Whatever is impelling the change, a CEO's main concern should be that the company's domain choices are driven exclusively by EP growth considerations. In general, the company should limit its domain to those offers and geographies in or very close to the northeast quadrant of the ME/CP Profitability Matrix, where favorable product-market economics and an advantaged competitive position allow for good EP and EP growth. One company that has done this very well over the years is 3M, which has followed its technology and innovation capabilities into literally hundreds of mostly small product markets, which it typically dominates. This rather unique approach to domain expansion, combined with a strong financial discipline, has allowed 3M to sustain ROEs in the range of 30 percent for many years.[19]

Changing domains is not just about participation choices but about positioning choices as well. The role of corporate positioning choices in determining domains is addressed further in the discussion of open and closed business models in Chapter 5.

Configuration Choices

Within a given offering domain, companies usually have a range of choices about how to configure their participation. A company may have several business units operating within the same general domain, each concentrating on maximizing its own EP growth. But because none of the business units has a perspective on the entire domain, it is possible that some potentially profitable participation options are being overlooked. Identifying and pursuing these options often requires the direction or intervention of the corporate center.

To illustrate, Exhibit 4.6 shows the total EP generated by all major players in U.S. retail financial services in 2002, organized by general domain (e.g.,

EXHIBIT 4.6 U.S. Retail Financial Services EP (2002)

Market EP by Need and Customer Segment (2002)

	Mass Affluent	Mass Market	Low Income	Small Business	Total
Credit G = 7%	$7–9 B	$7–8 B	$4–5 B	$(1)–0 B	$17–22 B
Liquidity and Payments G = 5%	$5–9 B	$3–5 B	$0–2 B	$3–5 B	$11–21 B
Investment G = 8%	$10–12 B	$(2)–0 B	$0 B	$0–1 B	$8–13 B
Total	$22–30 B	$8–13 B	$4–7 B	$2–6 B	$36–56 B

Source: Proprietary analysis for a major money center bank.

Credit) and by major customer segment (e.g., Mass Market). This is a rare product market in that almost any configuration is likely to result in positive economic profits for the average player.

Given this giant pool of EP, it would be tempting for any company to try to participate in as many of the boxes as possible, and that is exactly what many banks try to do—at least within their local or regional markets. But other configuration options are certainly possible. For instance, a bank could choose to try to dominate the consumer credit domain within its home market. This would require a radical rethinking of how credit products are typically packaged and serviced, but the prize could be an enormous slice of the available EP pie, potentially much larger than what would be available from the more disperse configuration typical of banks in these markets. The key point is that there are many configuration possibilities other than those most commonly followed, and it is part of the role of the center to identify and examine these options in cases where the business units are unlikely to have the perspective or bandwidth to do so on their own.

One company that has been working on a massive configuration change for many years is IBM. The company offers a broad array of discrete products and services, including computer hardware, software, information technology (IT) consulting, IT outsourcing, and financing. However, there has long been a recognition that the totality of what IBM can do to add customer value exceeds, at least in some cases, the sum of customer benefits from selling them individual products and services. At the frontiers of its capabilities, IBM is positioning itself as a brain trust with deep implementation skills, an intellectual partner able not only to help clients devise new solutions to difficult problems but to follow up with full implementation of the solutions as well, promising better outcomes at less cost than other options available to the client. IBM cites examples including solutions that bring significant efficiency and reliability improvements to urban traffic systems, power grids, telecommunications systems, and health care management.[20]

The claim of IBM to be able to bring these integrated benefits to customers is not new, and other companies are also attempting to compete on a similar basis. But the sheer scale of internal change IBM is making, from sometimes regional product and service silos to integrated global teams of experts organized as needed around specific client problems, is impressive. Such change can come only from the center, as the product and service silos on their own do not have the perspective, the ability, or the incentives to effect such huge changes. Indeed, when Lou Gerstner took over as CEO in 1993, some outside of IBM were arguing that the then-struggling colossus had to be restructured and individual pieces sold or spun off. Gerstner famously came to the opposite conclusion, seeing the potential for IBM's extraordinary resources to be reconfigured into a more valuable customer proposition.[21]

Two common configuration choices revolve around vertical and horizontal integration. In the case of vertical integration within a domain, like the oil and gas industry, the question is whether to be in nearly all activities of the value-added chain, from exploration and production through to chemicals and retailing, or to be more focused or specialized within a part of the domain; that is, is it more value-creating for the company to be fully integrated like an ExxonMobil or to be a more focused player like a Schlumberger, both of which are very profitable and well-managed companies? For ExxonMobil, which outperforms all of the other majors (and many niche players) in nearly every aspect of the vertical activity chain, vertical integration has been a winning configuration choice.[22] But for other major independent oil companies like Chevron and BP, it is less clear whether remaining vertically integrated will maximize long-term EP. Vertical integration can capture some valuable synergies, particularly early in the life cycle of an industry, but it can also create significant costs in the form of cross-subsidies from the more profitable to the less profitable parts of the company. And when vertically integrated companies find more focused competitors increasing their share of EP within different activities along the chain, or when some elements of the activity chain are clearly unprofitable for most players, then the economic argument for remaining vertically integrated becomes harder to sustain.

Horizontal participation choices focus on extending the company's domain into related product and geographic markets. An example has been the emergence of the megabanks like Citigroup, HSBC, and JPMorgan Chase, which participate in virtually all aspects of financial services, covering broadly retail or consumer finance, corporate finance and investment banking, and investment management. JPMorgan Chase itself has evolved from the merging of a number of large banks (Manufacturers Hanover, Chemical Bank, Chase Manhattan Bank, J.P. Morgan, BankOne, Bear Sterns, and Washington Mutual), each of which had somewhat different domain strategies. Now it is a megabank, participating in many countries and in nearly every aspect of consumer and corporate finance, including branch banking, mortgages, credit cards, debt and equity underwriting, mergers and acquisitions, money transmission, wealth management, and trading. The argument for this domain expansion is based on the exploitation of synergies, such as opportunities for cross-selling, additional IT scale economies, better market-making opportunities, and shared overheads. Unfortunately, this dramatic expansion of its domain has not yet proven especially profitable: The bank's average annual EP per share growth was minus 1.7 percent and total shareholder return was a modest 5.2 percent over the 1998–2007 period.[23] Having weathered the Great Recession far better than most of its competitors, however, the bank may yet prove that its broad financial services participation strategy will sustain a higher EP growth rate than the industry overall. Time will tell.

New Entry Choices

Entering new product markets is almost always a decision taken by the center, either because it represents a material change in the company's domain or configuration or because it entails a large enough investment to require CEO and board approval. New entry decisions really constitute two decisions: first, as always, determining whether the new entry opportunity offers a credible prospect for earning positive and growing EP over time; second, even if the opportunity is inherently attractive, determining the most profitable means of entry (*de novo*, acquisition, joint venture).

With respect to the first decision, the economic and strategic criteria for entry decisions have been addressed extensively in earlier sections of this chapter. However, knowing what the criteria are and actually enforcing them are two different matters. Once the new entry criteria are established, the center—and in particular the CEO—have a critical role in making sure they are actually followed. Too often the strategic myths creep back into the corporate dialogue, and instead of hard economic criteria managers revert to citing attributes, such as the potential size or rate of growth of the product market, that may have no relevance to the company's prospects for generating long-term EP growth. Sometimes, strangely, the less managers know about a new product market, the bolder their assertions become about the enormous opportunities not to be missed. Consider the many billions of dollars "old economy" companies invested in new Internet businesses in the late 1990s because managers believed they couldn't afford to miss the great wave of new transformational opportunities. The number of potential user "eyeballs" that might be attracted to a new Website actually came to be considered an important investment criterion, with predictable consequences. In the end, not all of this investment by well-established companies into new and largely imaginary product markets was wasted, but most of it was.

If a new product market has the potential for generating EP growth, the second question remains: What is the best way for the company to enter? Is a start-up better than a joint venture? Is a suitable acquisition available? Should export lead the way? Empirically, there are examples of success and failure for every means of new entry, so it is fair to conclude that the correct answer is, "It depends."

In theory, a company wants to enter a new product market by whatever means yields the highest value creation for shareholders, and this must always remain the acid test. In practice, however, the option that best passes the highest value creation test may not be obvious; sometimes, if entry barriers are high enough, there may not be any option that passes the test. To the extent that any generalizations are possible, they might include the following:

- If the company already participates in a profitable domain and has a positioning advantage in its home market, then entering new geographic markets *de novo* may well be the highest EP and equity value option. The examples cited earlier included McDonald's, Coca-Cola, and IBM.
- If the company participates in a profitable domain and has a positioning advantage in its core product or service group, then entry into new related products and services might be best achieved by making smaller acquisitions of undermanaged businesses. These businesses can then benefit from the superior business model and execution capabilities of the acquiring company. Emerson Electric and Danaher have pursued such strategies successfully for many years.[24] This strategy can be particularly successful in home or similar geographic markets—it is problematic if the acquired company is culturally distinct from the acquirer.
- If the company currently participates in an attractive domain but does not have a real positioning advantage, making a large acquisition to fix its disadvantaged position has fairly low odds of success. In these instances, the seller is in a far better negotiating position than the buyer and will tend to take the full economic gain of the combination, or more, in the purchase price. European banks attempting to enter the U.S. investment banking market, when they themselves had no real advantages to bring, lost billions of dollars trying to buy competitive advantage.
- If a company's principal domain is economically unprofitable and it is not favorably positioned, then entry into new domains is unlikely to be EP positive no matter what the means. During the 1960s and through the 1980s, there was a belief that a company with a low price-to-earnings (P/E) multiple could create shareholder value by acquiring another company, often in an unrelated industry, with a higher P/E multiple. As silly as this sounds (and is), some CEOs and investment bankers still harbor similar thoughts. But a poorly positioned and unprofitable

company like a General Motors could not create value by acquiring a strong company like a Cisco Systems, any more than kissing a frog will produce a prince.

Exit Decisions

Major exit decisions almost always have to be driven from the center. This is not an enviable task, and many CEOs shy away from what can be tough and emotional decisions, decisions that can have adverse effects not only on employees but on some customers and suppliers as well. Yet the intermediate and long-term health of the company demands that there be an almost constant pruning of chronically unprofitable products and services, geographies, and customer segments.

As noted earlier, in a typical large public company an average of about one-third of all equity capital can be imputed to economically unprofitable participation strategies. The adverse impact on the financial and strategic strength of the company is not limited just to the negative EP investments themselves. These value-consuming investments are being subsidized by the positive EP participation strategies, meaning the resources needed to maximize EP growth in the stronger parts of the company are being diverted to the weaker parts—a double whammy against value creation. As difficult as it may be, the CEO must be the enforcer and give the business units no latitude for keeping chronically negative EP products, geographies, or customers in the portfolio.

 CHAPTER SUMMARY

Participation choices largely determine the economic profit growth potential for individual business units and companies. By choosing to invest in economically profitable product markets, businesses give themselves the best opportunity to achieve superior economic profit growth. By choosing to remain invested in, or to enter, economically unprofitable product markets, businesses without a substantial competitive advantage will see their economic profits decline or remain suppressed below zero.

The primary choices of which products and services to offer, which geographic markets to serve, and which customer segments to serve, are made mostly at the business unit level. To make the best choices, business units need to develop a deep understanding of how much economic profit they are earning, or are likely to earn, from each product or service group, from each geographic market, and from each customer or customer group. Of special importance is the need to evaluate product-market attractiveness using quantitative financial measures rather than in purely qualitative indicators, which can prove to be quite misleading. Conventional nonfinancial indicators such as market growth rate, competitive intensity, and customer power do not always align with the actual economic profitability of product markets. Over-reliance on these nonfinancial indicators is likely to result in major participation errors.

Participation errors are not normally self-correcting, except in the very long term. Chronically unprofitable product markets do not turn themselves around spontaneously. Business unit heads making rosy forecasts for major performance improvements in those markets are being delusional. CEOs must act affirmatively to challenge such forecasts and ensure that the company's resources are not squandered in pursuit of illusory economic profits.

Corporate center participation choices pertaining to domain boundaries, the configuration of businesses within the domain, and product-market entry and exit decisions require the same high quality of information and capital discipline as the business unit choices. Overall, companies that are disciplined in making participation choices will not have difficulty in meeting the minimum performance threshold of earning at least a positive economic profit in every business unit and should enjoy at least average EP growth rates. If they are also able to make good positioning choices, the subject of the next chapter, they will achieve exceptional EP growth rates.

CHAPTER FIVE

Making the Right Positioning Choices

T HE OBJECTIVE OF POSITIONING choices is to maximize the share of economic profit a business captures over time. Pragmatically, this objective can be rephrased one of two ways, depending on the product markets in which the business is competing. In economically profitable product markets, the objective of positioning choices is for a business to grow its own economic profits at a rate faster than the competition. In economically unprofitable product markets, the objective of positioning choices is for the business to overcome the adverse conditions and earn at least its cost of capital, preferably much more. In either case, the business would be capturing an ever higher share of total economic profit and growing its equity value faster than its rivals.

In a multibusiness company, the goal of the corporate center is to help the business units earn higher economic profits than they could on their own. To do this, the company must understand the "affiliation benefits" that come from being part of the portfolio and how to leverage these benefits to make better positioning choices across business units. The role of the center will be elaborated later in this chapter.

Before turning to a more detailed examination of how good positioning choices are made, it is necessary to clarify how these choices are related to the concept of competitive advantage.

POSITIONING CHOICES AND COMPETITIVE ADVANTAGE

Positioning choices determine the degree to which a business will, or will not, enjoy a competitive advantage in the product markets it has elected to serve. In this sense, making good positioning choices and increasing competitive advantage might seem to be the same thing. However, the objective of positioning choices is to maximize share of EP in a product market, not to maximize competitive advantage per se. Pursuing some kinds of competitive advantages may contribute to achieving that objective, while pursing others may not. This is a subtle but important difference.

Competitive advantage is a powerful idea, but it is extremely important to recognize that competitive advantage is a means to an end, not an end in itself. In much of the strategy literature and in the minds of most executives, the presumed objective of strategy is to achieve and sustain a competitive advantage. But this is not, or should not be, the objective of strategy, which is to maximize the growth of economic profits over time. To maximize EP over time, making the best participation choices is usually even more important than holding a competitive advantage. Indeed, the value of a competitive advantage cannot even be determined without first knowing the underlying product-market economics. As was shown in Chapter 2, it is possible in some product markets for a business to earn positive and growing economic profits despite being at a competitive disadvantage (Big Dog), and it is also possible in other product markets for a business to earn negative and declining economic profits despite having a significant competitive advantage (PopulAir). Thus, the alignment between making good positioning choices and building competitive advantage is conditional, *subject to* an understanding of how management's choices impact EP growth.

Why is this being stressed? First, it is important to recognize that there are circumstances under which investing to build competitive advantage is unlikely to increase economic profit or equity value, *even if the intended advantage is achieved.* For instance, if a company in the unprofitable U.S. paper industry increases its competitive cost advantage by building a more efficient manufacturing plant, it may still be destroying value but slightly more slowly than its competitors—a Pyrrhic victory if ever there was one.

Second, it underscores the importance of being clear about what is meant by "competitive advantage," which has become one of the most loosely used terms in modern business. Perhaps the best-known example of this imprecision is the conventional wisdom that high market share (revenue or volume) is a competitive advantage. There are three problems with a statement like this:

- First, it is not profitability based. As noted earlier, high market share is not always synonymous with positive or growing EP. In some circumstances, such as Delta or American Airlines competing in the unprofitable U.S. airline market, gaining market share may simultaneously drive higher short-term earnings but also lower (or more negative) longer-term EP.
- Second, it conflates cause and effect. Even if a product market is economically profitable, a participant's competitive advantage is not measured by its share of volume or revenues per se. Market share is a by-product of advantage, not its source. The source of the advantage is in the combination of characteristics inherent to the business that enabled it to get and hold the high share in the first place.
- Third, it is an incomplete picture. High market share may reflect an underlying competitive advantage, but that is only one aspect of a participant's competitive position. Its current and prospective EP share will be determined by the "net" of all of its advantages and disadvantages. Having a particular competitive advantage, even a large one, does not mean that a business will have an overall, or net, advantage. In fact, whether or not a business actually has a net competitive advantage and how important that is can only be established by measuring the level and growth of its EP relative to the competition over time.

The graphic in Exhibit 5.1 lays out the specific connections between relative EP growth and the elements of competitive position.

EXHIBIT 5.1 Elements of Competitive Position

Sources of Competitive Advantage/Disadvantage	Components of Competitive Advantage/Disadvantage	Consequence of Competitive Advantage/Disadvantage
Business Model	Relative Offer Position	Relative EP Share and Growth Rate Over Time
Execution Capabilities	Relative Cost Position	
Special Assets		

The ultimate consequence of holding a competitive advantage or disadvantage is the share and growth rate of economic profit relative to the competition. If a business can consistently grow its share of EP, then it has a legitimate claim to having a net competitive advantage. If a business cannot grow its share of EP, then it cannot support such a claim: Even though the business might have certain specific advantages, these are being offset by other, larger disadvantages.[1]

The relative offer and cost positions of a business are the classic components of competitive position. Oversimplifying a bit, if a business can charge a premium price and still hold or gain volume share, then it has an offering advantage—customers clearly prefer its product or service to most others despite the higher price. On the production and delivery side, if a business can charge a lower price than rivals but still earn the same or higher EP per unit, then it has a cost (including capital costs) advantage—it can grow EP share while providing a better deal to customers. The combination of relative offer and cost advantages determines the net competitive position of the business and its potential to gain or lose EP share over time.

Superior offer and cost positions are frequently described as sources of competitive advantage, but they are manifestations of competitive advantage, not really its sources. To know that Intel can charge more than AMD for a microprocessor of similar specifications and still gain or hold volume share is to know that Intel has a competitive offering advantage, but it does not tell us why Intel has that advantage.

To understand the sources of competitive advantage we need to look at three primary drivers: the choice of business models, the choice of execution capabilities in which to specialize, and the choice of how to exploit any special assets the business may possess. Taken together, these are the key positioning choices a business must make. They largely determine the nature and scale of any offering or cost advantages a business may have, and they therefore also determine whether or not a business will be successful in competing for a growing share of product-market EP. The most important of the three will usually be the choice of business model, followed by execution capabilities and then special assets.

 BUSINESS MODELS

The concept of a business model can be difficult to pin down precisely, though in recent years there have been several thoughtful attempts to do so.[2] If the definition is too broad, one may miss the very elements of distinctiveness that explain why the model is successful or not. If the definition is too narrow, it can become so complicated and hard-wired that it is difficult to generalize or apply to other businesses. We need to know more than some vague generic characterization of the model (e.g., "be number one") but less than a full description of every aspect of the business (e.g., the complex mapping of organizational transactions and interdependencies). Here, business models will be described in terms of what gives them their distinctive shape or fundamental characteristics—their unique DNA.

A business model consists of the *dominant commercial and financial convictions* that management and employees live by. It may be thought of as analogous to a constitution, usually unwritten, comprising relatively few articles of faith that are deeply embedded, enduring, and not easily changed. These convictions are dominant in the sense that they tend to override or trump choices that would be at odds with their intent. Individually, these convictions may be a source of competitive advantage or disadvantage. Taken collectively, as a complete business model, they tend to be the most powerful drivers of the relative EP growth a business will enjoy within a given product market.

Dominant commercial convictions are essentially fixed, strongly enforced beliefs and practices that have a material impact on the offer and cost positions of the business. Examples of dominant commercial convictions would include Wal-Mart's "Everyday Low Prices," Intel's "Moore's Law," Southwest Air's 20-minute airport turnaround rule, and Nucor's autonomous plant operations. A complete business model typically includes several dominant commercial convictions. In the case of Wal-Mart, the business model might include commercial convictions that govern its choices about its store sizes and locations, its supplier relationships, its distribution configuration, its labor policies, its expense policies, and, most famously, its price point. Clearly these convictions are interrelated, driven in Wal-Mart's case by the determination to deliver a wide range of good-quality products at a lower price, but also at higher margins, than the competition. The details of how these convictions will apply to different product categories will vary; the supply and distribution chain for HDTVs is obviously different from the supply and distribution chain for fresh milk, both of which can be purchased in the same Wal-Mart stores. However, the dominant commercial convictions defining the business model must remain largely the same across the system for the whole to work together and for the price and margin imperatives to be met.

EXHIBIT 5.2   ExxonMobil Business Model

ExxonMobil has a consistent and straightforward business model that combines our long-term perspective, disciplined approach to capital investment, and focus on operational excellence to grow shareholder value. We identify, develop, and execute projects using global best practices that ensure project returns will be resilient across a range of economic scenarios. We operate our facilities using proven management systems to achieve operational excellence. As a result, we consistently generate more income from a highly efficient capital base, as demonstrated by our superior return on average capital employed. We deliver industry-leading financial and operating results that grow long-term shareholder value.

Source: ExxonMobil 2008 Annual Report, p. 19.

Dominant financial convictions are the embedded beliefs and practices that have a material impact on investment and divestment decisions. Typical examples would include revenue growth,. earnings growth, return on investment (ROI), return on equity (ROE), or internal rate of return targets. One company with deeply imbedded financial convictions is ExxonMobil, where capital efficiency considerations drive virtually every major decision. Indeed, the company even describes its financial convictions as its business model (see Exhibit 5.2).

The intensity and effectiveness of ExxonMobil's financial convictions can be seen in two observations. The first is that the company's published business model does not even mention its core commercial convictions, which are also deep. This may be because the company's commercial convictions are so strongly shaped by, or subordinate to, its financial convictions that—apart from its domain choice and strict safety standards—they would tend to be more flexible over time. The second observation is that ExxonMobil's business model is extremely successful. By adhering to the demanding financial convictions it has adopted, the company consistently earns returns on both total capital (ROI) and on equity capital (ROE) that average 10 percentage points higher than its nearest rivals among the major oil companies. And this is not just at the consolidated company level but within each major reporting segment: upstream (exploration and production), downstream (refining and marketing), and chemicals. In 2007, compared to its five largest independent peers, ExxonMobil generated 23 percent of the group's combined revenues—*but 33 percent of their combined EP.*[3] These are massive differences in capital productivity among companies that compete directly with each other in a mature industry.

Open and Closed Business Models

Nearly all business models consist of both commercial and financial convictions, but many are more strongly influenced by one or the other. To the extent that a business model is mainly driven by its dominant commercial convictions, it is a "closed" model: The big decisions pertaining to competitive positioning have basically been made and are not, for the most part, likely to change over the short or intermediate term. Companies adhering to relatively closed models, such as Southwest Airlines, tend to have narrow domains and look, at least superficially, much the same over long periods of time. They are more likely to emphasize organic growth and smaller "niche" acquisitions than to attempt transformational change with large acquisitions. Indeed, when they do make big acquisitions, they tend to integrate them poorly because of the inflexibility of their core business model.

In contrast, a business model more strongly driven by its dominant financial convictions is an "open" model: It is less committed to the specifics of a particular competitive positioning strategy than it is to achieving specified financial results. Open business model companies tend to have broader domains and may change their configurations quite dramatically over time. The evolution of the General Electric Company from a being a manufacturer of light bulbs, motors, and small appliances in 1892 to the broadly diversified conglomerate it has become is an example of an open corporate business model. For many years the company stressed expansion into almost any business it thought it could manage with high returns, based perhaps on the twin beliefs in its financial discipline and in the quality and depth of its management team.

Sometimes direct competitors adopt almost opposite types of business models, one closed and the other open. In the U.S. pharmacy sector, Walgreens and CVS/Caremark are examples of two companies that have generated positive and generally growing economic profits while pursuing very different business models for many years (see Exhibit 5.3).

In this competition, Walgreens has historically been very much the hedgehog, pursuing a fairly closed business model with strong commercial convictions, among them: growing organically rather than by acquisition, protecting and building the Walgreens brand (friendly, efficient, convenient service); building freestanding convenience stores rather than locating in shopping centers or strip malls; focusing intently on store-by-store productivity and profitability (profit per square foot is a key metric); being largely self-financing and debt free (except for real estate leases); and building onsite store locations for large company customers, partly as a counter to the incursion of pharmacy

EXHIBIT 5.3 Walgreens and CVS/Caremark Performance (1996–2007)

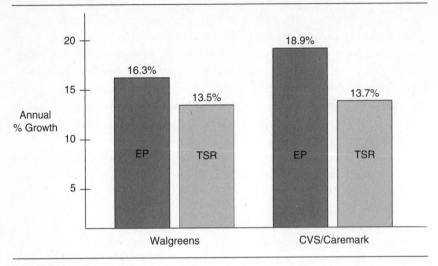

Source: Datastream.
Note: EP growth is per share.

benefits managers. These convictions have helped Walgreens achieve excellent operating performance and profitability through most of its existence.

CVS/Caremark, on the other hand, has played the fox, with a much more open and opportunistic approach to making its positioning (and participation) choices. Its core commercial convictions seem to be that scale and scope will be the big industry profitability drivers of the future, and its financial conviction is to seek scale and scope via acquisition whenever prospective sellers meet its financial tests. Thus, from 1997 to 2009, CVS made six large acquisitions and many smaller ones that not only expanded its overall domain into new areas like pharmacy benefits management (Caremark) and in-store clinics, but that have also influenced its positioning strategy in many ways. For instance, because it has grown so rapidly through acquisition, CVS/Caremark has inherited many different store formats and location types, making it more challenging for the company to achieve the same levels of merchandizing and operating efficiency as Walgreens with its more homogeneous store configurations. In recent years, CVS/Caremark has had to close many stores and reconfigure many others to achieve better store-by-store profitability.

But as CVS/Caremark plays catch-up on the sales and cost efficiencies of its stores, some would argue that it is now better positioned than Walgreens to compete in an industry where an increasing percentage of pharmacy sales will be driven through pharmacy benefits managers and other intermediaries, where prescription drug prices may increasingly be set or limited by government, and where customers can order and receive their prescriptions via the Internet and mail, eliminating the need to go into a pharmacy at all. In this new world, scale and scope—along with excellent operating skills—may be more important EP drivers than store locations, formats, and even brand strength.

As the battle for economic profit share continues to be a close one between these two capable competitors, the fox and the hedgehog may have to learn from each others' strengths to sustain their profitable growth performance. Meanwhile, a relatively new player, Wal-Mart, is applying its own core business model to the pharmacy business and seems to have found that there is still a lot of EP to be gained in this product market.

There is nothing inherently good or bad about choosing closed or open business models—there are many examples of success and failure with each. But they do have important differences that can provide management with a useful context when formulating or evaluating positioning options.

Closed Models: A Closer Look

Closed business models often arise spontaneously as part of an entrepreneurial vision, reflecting the beliefs and biases of a company's founder—sometimes lasting for many decades after the founder has left the scene. As one example, the Eastman Kodak Company held to essentially the same set of commercial convictions, originally established by George Eastman in 1888, for nearly 100 years, and earned enormous economic profits while doing so. Among the strongly held and most resilient convictions of its consumer business model were the following:

- A huge commitment to basic research and development to sustain its significant lead in silver halide and other chemically based photographic technologies (this research supported leading positions not only in consumer products but in graphics arts films, motion picture films, medical imaging films, and high-resolution reconnaissance films)
- A marketing strategy based on democratizing photography throughout the world by producing relatively inexpensive and easy-to-use cameras to stimulate ever higher sales of film and photographic paper
- A manufacturing strategy based on building proprietary engineering knowledge around the design and construction of high-speed film and

photographic paper-making equipment and processes (the famous Kodak Park)

- A retail strategy with strong incentives for consumers to use only Kodak products and Kodak-approved dealers and shops to develop their prints, slides, and family movies (capturing a "Kodak Moment")

Of course, even the remarkably successful Kodak business model eventually succumbed to new technologies, and the advent of high-quality and inexpensive digital cameras starting in the 1990s ended its phenomenal run. The company's attempts to create a new, sustainable, and economically profitable business model have yet to prove successful.

Closed business models are characteristic of many other iconic companies like Kodak, at least in their early years: IKEA, Home Depot, Nucor, Intel, Dell, McDonalds, Xerox, Wal-Mart, Southwest Airlines, and Coca-Cola were—and mostly remain—companies with relatively closed business models.

Closed business models have a number of characteristic strengths and weaknesses. Among their strengths are that they are virtually impossible for competitors with different commercial convictions to duplicate, and they can be phenomenal engines of profitable growth via self-replication in adjacent product areas and new markets. The reason competitors are unable to match a successful closed business model, even though some of its key elements may be well known, is that the underlying web of resources, skills, rules, processes, and people that it takes to execute the model properly is nearly invisible and would not, in any case, be replicable. It would be like trying to replicate an aircraft carrier while seeing it operate only from far away—the basic outline and purpose of the ship are evident, but hardly any of the intricacies of how it is built or operated can be seen or understood.

The greatest weakness of closed business models is their very orthodoxy or inflexibility. For a company to transition from a narrowly focused domain, often the legacy of the founding entrepreneurs, to broader or new domains can be difficult. When conditions in the product markets start to become less favorable, the dominant commercial convictions are so deeply ingrained that the new insights, behavior changes, and leadership necessary to change the existing model, and then to formulate and execute a profitable new model, are not usually present in the business. A successful company like Kodak has great difficulty being anything but Kodak, until it is no longer successful. Even a company as innovative as Intel has struggled for years to expand its offer beyond its spectacular success in the domain of microprocessors for personal computers (PCs), laptops, and servers. The results of its diversification initiatives have fallen well short of management's hopes, and it does not appear that Intel has been able to create much new EP growth or equity value from investing many billions of dollars in these efforts thus far. Andy Grove himself noted the difficulty of creating a second successful platform, even within the same general domain, when, in a compliment to Steve Jobs and Apple, he said, "There's no other company in technology that's started with a strong core business and developed another very strong one. The rest of us are lucky, or good, if [we're right] once."[4]

Open Models: A Closer Look

Companies with open business models come in many forms and are not as easily characterized as those with closed business models. The extreme form of an open business model is a private equity firm. The dominant convictions characterizing the private equity model are a set of financial tests applied to buying, refinancing, restructuring, and then later selling companies. There is normally no commercial coherence to the private equity firm's portfolio. Of course, the individual companies in the portfolio may themselves operate with closed business models, but their product-market positioning is only of secondary interest to the relatively short-term investment returns they might generate for the private equity partners.

A less radical and widely admired example of an open business model company is Berkshire Hathaway, which—perhaps as a reflection of the uniqueness of its visionary leader—is both an open model holding company but also a company dedicated to ensuring that each of the companies it invests in are strong EP generators. This is because, unlike the general private equity model, Warren Buffett does not buy companies or shares of companies with the intention of selling them. He is intensely interested in finding and then owning companies with highly profitable and typically closed business models (businesses that "we can understand").[5]

For more typical operating companies that do not see themselves as investment or trading vehicles, open business models have their own strengths and weaknesses that need to be taken into account. The greatest advantage of an open business model is that, properly employed, it continually highlights opportunities for profitable growth and profitable restructuring that might well be missed in a closed business model environment.

One of the best examples of an operating company that has followed an open business model for many years is the Walt Disney Company. When founded by Walt Disney in 1923, the company's initial focus was on producing animated cartoons for distribution in movie theaters—a new and untested business model based on the founder's conviction that there was a lucrative market for these costly-to-produce films. Disney pursued this closed model for more than 10 years, building on the phenomenal success of its main cartoon character, Mickey Mouse. In a major extension of that model, Disney produced its first full-length animated motion picture, *Snow White*, in 1937, and then followed with a further extension into live-action movies with *Treasure Island* in 1950. Along the way the main business model was bolstered by entry into the film distribution business (Buena Vista) and the music business, in both cases to protect Disney's own intellectual property, brand, and margins.

It could be argued that even at this point Disney was already following an open business model, expanding into related but distinctly different businesses, though there was a common thread of creating and controlling wholesome family-oriented motion pictures. But the next move, entering the emerging television business in the early 1950s, was a definite departure because the economics of this business were based on advertising, not ticket sales, and delivered to the home via a new medium of still unknown potential. Disney jumped in with both feet and had some of the most successful shows on early television, including the famous *Mickey Mouse Club*. Ultimately, this new platform would also include the Disney Channel and, via the acquisition of ABC/Cap Cities, ESPN and other cable network properties.

At the same time, Walt Disney made perhaps the boldest business decision of his career and entered the theme park business on a scale never seen before, opening Disneyland in 1955. While leveraging on many of the now established Disney characters, the theme parks again represented an entirely new business model, going beyond the film and TV entertainment businesses into the real estate and hospitality businesses with their own distinctive economics and drivers of competitive advantage. Disneyland was, of course, an enormous financial success and led directly to the later development of Walt Disney World, Tokyo Disneyland, and Disneyland Paris. Walt Disney World, in particular, is now a destination resort, with many hotels, restaurants, and other amenities designed to encourage people to spend entire vacations on the site.

From these platforms have grown many others that represent distinctive business models, including retailing (the Disney Stores), character and product licensing, cruise ships, DVD distribution, and live theater (e.g., *The Lion King*).

Had Disney remained a closed business model, it would still be an animated film studio with perhaps a licensing arm. It was able to pursue an open business model because of the expansive and brilliant business mind of its founder, and in later years because the company did adopt fairly stringent financial requirements that were applied to all investments. Not that Disney's rise has been a story of unbroken financial success—it has sometimes mirrored one of its own rollercoaster rides. Some of Walt Disney's early bets required investments that brought the company to the brink of illiquidity, though Disney himself always believed strongly in the financial potential of what he was doing and was almost always proved right. During the late 1980s and early 1990s when Frank Wells served as COO and Gary Wilson as CFO, the company's financial convictions were very strong and applied broadly across investments in existing and new businesses. These were years during which economic profits and the returns to the company's stockholders were exceptional by any standard. From 1984 to 1994, the first decade with Michael Eisner as CEO, Disney earned a cumulative economic profit of $3.2 billion and achieved a total shareholder return (TSR) of 29.4 percent. In the years following Frank Well's death in 1994, the company seemed to lose its financial discipline, starting with the highly priced acquisition of ABC/CapCities in 1995, and its EP and TSR performance went into a 12-year decline. From 1995 to 2005 when Michael Eisner retired as CEO, Disney earned a cumulative economic profit of negative $4.3 billion and achieved a TSR of only 2.9 percent.[6]

Another well-known example of an open business model, mentioned previously, is the General Electric Company. Particularly under Jack Welch, GE's CEO from 1981 to 2001, the company seemed to employ a set of financial convictions, for both organic growth and for acquisitions, that produced strong EP per share growth averaging 13.2 percent per year (very high for a company the size of GE) and excellent TSRs averaging 22.5 percent per year.[7] From 2001 to 2007, however, it appears that good financial discipline has played a subordinate role to pursuing grand strategic visions at GE. The overall corporate mind-set has remained "open," as it would have to be in a company with as many businesses as GE manages, but the same tough commercial and financial discipline Welch was famous for has not been in evidence. As described in Chapter 3, the financial objectives set by the CEO and board of directors during this period appear to have been overly focused on revenue and earnings growth and insufficiently focused on capital efficiency, which in turn contributed significantly to the company's poor EP growth and TSR performance during that period.

This is a constant danger of open business models—they require razor-sharp and unflinching financial discipline to execute successfully, and these are not traits that necessarily pass from one CEO to the next. In the private equity world, boards composed of major investors watch financial performance like hawks, and they react quickly to any hint of weakness in the performance of a business. In the world of large public companies, however, boards are often structurally incapable of playing such a strong role, and most CEOs would object if they tried. So with open business models like Disney's and GE's, the company's fortunes are almost entirely dependent on the financial acumen and discipline, or lack thereof, of the incumbent CEO and CFO.

Making Business Model Choices

Great business models beget great companies, but great companies do not necessarily create great new or regenerated business models. No aspect of doing business requires more creativity and conviction than formulating and executing successful business models. Creativity and conviction are not attributes than can be taught or emulated through following some preset formula or methodology—they are certainly not usually the by-products of a formal strategic planning process. So the odds of launching a successful new business model are inherently low under any circumstances, and certain characteristics of the corporate environment can make them even lower.

There is enormous randomness in the origination of business models, a reflection of the very high degree of risk inherent in launching any new commercial enterprise. In the entrepreneurial world, many, many new business models are tried that subsequently fail, with the enduring models representing only of small fraction of those attempted. And our ability to predict at their outset which models will succeed and which will fail is very limited, as evidenced by the venture capital investment model of evaluating hundreds of propositions, investing in only a few, and expecting that of the few only 10 to 20 percent will earn adequate returns. For an established corporation to invest in new business models with an expected failure rate of 80 to 90 percent or more would be unthinkable.

Adding to the inherent difficulties of creating new business models within established companies are two factors that represent additional barriers to success. First, there is usually an existing business model that, even if failing, has deep roots in the organization and that will inevitably act as a brake on making the radical changes needed to execute a new business model. Second, the risk-reward environment in established companies is hardly aligned with the kind of idiosyncratic thinking and risk taking that are required to create truly new business models. For an entrepreneur, trying a new business model has a huge upside—financially, in personal satisfaction, and in control over the business—and an unpleasant but acceptable (to the entrepreneur) downside—going broke and starting over or getting a conventional job. Of course, no established corporation offers its employees anything remotely like the entrepreneurial upside for championing a new business model, and few employees would accept the downside of a (likely) failure, including the possible loss of his or her position and a diminished professional reputation.

Under these circumstances, it could be argued that established companies should focus entirely on renewing, fine tuning, and extending their existing successful business models and not concern themselves with creating entirely new ones. And, indeed, this is mostly what established companies try to do. But business models, even great ones, do wear out, and when that time comes a CEO should certainly make the effort to reengineer the old model or create a new one that will enable a business unit to continue to grow EP faster than the competition. As noted earlier, there are no formulas, but there are some observations that can be helpful to making business model choices.

Review the Bidding

Before deciding an entirely new business model is needed, it may be possible to extend the existing business model many more years. For instance, closed models that have a history of great success can be undermined over time by a failure to adhere to appropriate financial performance standards. The models have produced such good EP growth results for so long that people forget that such outstanding financial performance is not guaranteed for all time; in fact, these models often start to show their age when relative EP growth begins to slow or flatten even as earnings remain prodigious. More and more investment is made, often in acquisitions, for each dollar of earnings. This pattern can be seen in the 1998–2007 decade at companies like Intel and Pfizer; both companies made enormous investments, including acquisitions, in "growth," but both ended the period with lower EP than they started with.[8]

By setting and enforcing high EP growth standards, companies with closed business models may force themselves into more creative thinking and risk-taking several years earlier than they otherwise would. This is exactly what happened at the Coca-Cola Company in 1981 when Roberto Goizueta was named CEO. The Coca-Cola business model was closed, its commercial convictions almost unchanged for nearly 100 years. Although the brand remained among the most recognized in the world, performance by almost any measure was flagging. Had the old model lost its power?

The core of the model was the "system," consisting of the parent company and its exclusive bottlers—a model that was repeated in many countries throughout the world. The key features of the model are shown in Exhibit 5.4.

EXHIBIT 5.4   The Coca-Cola Company Business Model

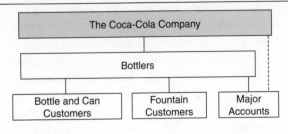

The Coca-Cola Company
- Creates/owns the brands
- Owns the formula/syrup
- Sets quality, positioning standards
- Does national marketing
- Sets competitive tone

◄ Contract ►

The Bottlers
- "Own" territories/customers
- Own production/distribution assets
- Distribute finished product to retailers
- Do local promotion and pricing
- Compete for local market share

This is the high-level business model for carbonated soft drinks. Although the model is similar in most countries, important details, such as the bottler contract terms and the role of third-party distributors (not shown), do vary—as does the product mix.

Many thought this business model, while still profitable, might have run its course as an engine of high growth for the company. But Goizueta had the opposite view—he believed the model had been undermanaged and could, with three changes, continue to drive the company's growth for a long time. His first change was to shift growth aspirations. To reenergize the marketing effort the new CEO coined the phrase "share of stomach," a metric he used to show that globally Coca-Cola products held only 1 to 2 percent share of what people drank every day, meaning there had to be enormous upside for the company to grow. His second change was to introduce economic profit as the key measure of performance at all levels down to individual product sales. This showed everyone in the organization that volume growth also meant high EP growth, reinforcing the message that the company was far from reaching any limits on its potential to produce exceptional financial performance (the market economics and the company's competitive position were, of course, ideal for this type of pedal-to-the-metal strategy). His third positioning change, which came a bit later, was to begin to revitalize the bottler organizations to gain their full participation in the new growth efforts. So while leaving the basic structure and many elements of the "old" business model in place, Goizueta was able to see its full potential and create the new commercial and financial convictions necessary to redirect the entire organization to the best EP growth and shareholder value creation of its existence.[9]

For open business model companies, the problem of economic profit decay can often be traced to a lack of focus on commercial convictions. Management may focus so heavily on achieving short-term financial results that it may fail to see when a business unit is losing competitive advantage over time. This occurs, for instance, when a business unit is participating in profitable markets where the weakness of its competitive position is masked for a time by the generally attractive market economics (e.g., Big Dog). Here again, the key early warning metric is not necessarily declining earnings or even ROE, but declining relative EP growth. Once management sees this signal, it is probably time to reinforce or modify the current business model before it slips into the disadvantaged zone.

In neither the closed nor open business model cases does the slowdown of relative EP growth, or loss of EP share, tell management what the problem is, only that there is in fact a business model problem that should be addressed sooner rather than later. In an ideal circumstance, the early warning signals will cause management to dig deeply into the underlying issues, revisit the fundamental convictions of their business model, and find effective choices that allow for evolutionary rather than revolutionary changes so the existing models can continue to produce outstanding EP growth for many more years.

Plan to Type of Business

The challenges posed by revitalizing an existing business model or creating an entirely new one may vary considerably depending on the market economics and competitive position of the business. Recalling the ME/CP Profitability Matrix, reproduced here as Exhibit 5.5, the business model changes required for each unit may range from constant modification to a complete and immediate overhaul. The CEO should set strategy formulation expectations accordingly.

Profitable and advantaged units like High Octane and Smart Shop will generally need to make only incremental changes to their business models in order to continue to maximize their share of EP. They must certainly make constant innovations in their offer and continually improve the efficiency of their supply chain, but with respect to their core convictions they will be in the "if it ain't broke, don't fix it" mind-set. Their primary concerns will be watching for and reacting to significant or unexpected changes in market economics or the appearance of new, more successful, business models that could challenge their advantaged positions. Wal-Mart, for instance, may have as much or more to fear from Amazon as from Costco or Target. When these types of threats

EXHIBIT 5.5 ME/CP Profitability Matrix

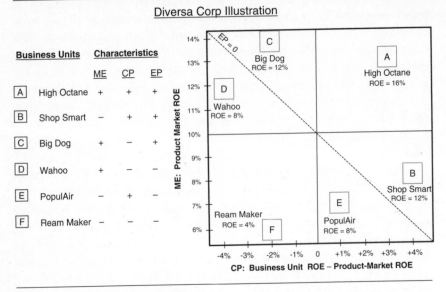

Diversa Corp Illustration

Business Units	Characteristics		
	ME	CP	EP
A High Octane	+	+	+
B Shop Smart	−	+	+
C Big Dog	+	−	+
D Wahoo	+	−	−
E PopulAir	−	+	−
F Ream Maker	−	−	−

Note: Cost of Equity = 10% in all cases.

occur, or are projected to occur, then a complete review of the current and possible alternative business models is clearly mandatory.

For businesses like Big Dog and PopulAir, a CEO should require that the units look immediately for options to substantially modify their current business models or to create new ones. Because it is earning an acceptable ROE and a positive EP, a business like Big Dog might be allowed to coast for a number of years without addressing the fundamental shortcomings of its model, but this would be a mistake. With the passage of time, that business unit is likely to drift into the unprofitable Wahoo space unless corrective action is taken. PopulAir is already generating negative EP, so creating a new or much better business model is urgent. And although its existing model is competitively advantaged and there are positive elements to build on, it must still make what will probably be significant changes to move into consistently positive EP territory.

When challenged to formulate new or better business models, businesses like Big Dog and PopulAir often plead for more time, not to fundamentally change their business models, but to lower their costs or improve their offer to a point of matching the "best practices" of their advantaged competitors. They will submit strategic plans showing their financial performance improving dramatically in three to four years as their proposed efforts to match the competition begin to pay off. These forecasts are fantasies. Simply trying to match best practices will almost never move one of these business units into an advantaged position. Odds are high their competitive problems are more basic and that at least some of their underlying commercial and financial convictions will need to be changed before they can improve their position significantly.

Finally, with units like Wahoo and Ream Maker, only a radical revamping of their business models could profitably improve their competitive positions, and nothing short of that effort should be accepted in their strategic plans. They are well past any possibility of making a comeback to positive EP based only on incremental performance improvements. First, the CEO should insist that they execute a complete restructuring of all irreversibly unprofitable products, customers, markets, and activities. Only then would it make sense to try to formulate a profitable new business model. Alternatively, the best outcome for these units might be a sale to an advantaged competitor that can apply its own superior business model to the acquired business unit. When this happens, it is a win for both companies.

Apply Four Tests

It is a near certainty that new business model proposals will look better in PowerPoint presentations than the business itself will look on future income statements and balance sheets. So when a new, or significantly revamped, business model is proposed, how should a CEO evaluate the proposition? Forecasting the odds of success of new business models always carries a lot of uncertainty, but for business units serving established product markets there are four tests that can improve the odds of making good choices: Proposals should be well grounded, reverse engineered, contrarian, and flexible.

Well Grounded. The proposal should reflect a deep and objective understanding of product market economics and of competitors' business models (i.e., how they grow their EP at above or below average rates), as well as the weaknesses in our own model. If product market economics are still favorable and seem likely to remain so but the business unit is losing EP share, then the weakness will be in one or more of the current model's commercial convictions: for example, a commitment to providing an expensive product attribute that cannot actually garner a premium price, or a commitment to vertical integration when the product market is disaggregating, or a commitment to a distribution system that is too costly or inefficient. If product-market economics have turned unfavorable, then the business unit's participation choices, not just positioning choices, have to be reviewed. For the business unit to justify continued participation in an economically unprofitable product market, its new business model will have to confer a very large positioning advantage or it will not earn a positive EP.

Reverse Engineered. One excellent source of ideas for new business models is to reverse engineer the factors that would have to be true for the business to sustain positive and growing EP and then to determine what the business would have to do to put those factors in place. As one example, a large but unprofitable glass container producer realized that, given the intense competition and poor pricing structure in its markets, the only way it could ever earn a positive EP would be to eliminate almost half of its total costs, including capital costs. Using a reverse-engineering approach to generate options, the management determined they would have to restructure the entire U.S. factory configuration, reducing the number of factories by 30 percent, while simultaneously increasing factory utilizations and losing almost no production capacity. In addition, their new business model would have to abandon several of the long-standing core convictions that had lead to the proliferation of too many plants in the first place, including a conviction that the company had to serve 100 percent of a customer's glass container needs, a conviction that shipping distances had to be kept under 200 miles to maintain profitability, a conviction that the sales force had to be paid based on volume (versus profitability), and a conviction that any volume priced above variable cost should be accepted. It was not just the physical configuration of the business that had to change, it was essential that deeply held beliefs and ingrained behaviors change as well. Otherwise, executing a profitable business model in this product market would be impossible.

Reverse engineering a business model has several benefits. It maintains a rigorous focus on the true economics of the business and limits digressions into strategic platitudes. It is also a source of many important insights into what the new core convictions of the business will need to be. And it certainly focuses the mind on the priorities for change, and scale of change, that will have to be achieved for the new model to fulfill its potential. At the same time, reverse engineering can help determine which elements of the current business model do not need to change because they can continue to support good EP growth.

Contrarian. A business model that captures a disproportionate share of EP will almost always be contrarian in its origins (though it may become conventional over time). Holding key commercial and financial convictions that depart, sometimes radically, from the conventional wisdom among incumbent competitors is essential to growing EP share faster than those competitors. Generally, both the offering and cost positioning of a new business model will have to be built on convictions that seem to competitors to be ill conceived, impossible to execute, or otherwise unlikely to succeed. Such was the case in the early days with companies like Apple, Dell, Disney, Nucor, and Southwest Airlines. Inevitably, creating and implementing new business models does require taking a lot of risk, and the more contrarian they are the riskier they may seem. But that can be a mistaken assumption— new business models that are not contrarian are far less likely to sustain superior EP growth in the long run.

Flexible.   Given the high failure rate of new business models, it is important that they be designed and implemented with the expectation that at least some of the commercial or financial convictions that characterize the model will have to be modified or changed entirely in light of actual experience, especially during the formative period of the first few months or years. This does not mean that every new business model proposal has to come with a Plan B, but with an expectation that there could eventually be a Plan B or a Plan C. A good proposal should at least acknowledge the likelihood that changes will need to be made to achieve the promised performance of the new model, and it should include some preliminary ideas for options that might need to be evaluated.

Stay Out of the Way

Trying to create and execute a new business model in close proximity to an existing model is like trying to run fast enough to escape the gravity of Jupiter. Jupiter always wins. The company needs to try to create a "zero gravity" environment, as far away as possible from the influence of the current model, for a truly new business model to have any chance of success.

New business models are a big threat to the old model. The new business model is likely to cannibalize sales from the old business model, as, for instance, book publishers experience with electronic distribution taking sales from hard copy editions. Elements of the cost structure from the old business model may be hard to eliminate, acting as a drag on expected performance. And frequently, people invested in the old model are unable or unwilling to change their convictions, making it difficult for them to perform well within in the new model. Thus, setting up a new model to "incubate" inside of or close to the business unit it is designed to transform is problematic. That would be like expecting the Dell PC business model to emerge from within the old IBM PC business—their basic convictions and execution capabilities are not only different, they are at almost complete odds and could not coexist. Delta Airlines' attempt to match Southwest Airlines and Jet Blue with its own low-cost carrier, Song, is another example, somewhat like trying to mate an elephant with a gazelle—the gazelle will not fare well.

One solution for allowing new business models to develop outside the gravitational pull of the old models is to set them up as entirely new business entities that are not only staffed and funded separately but that are also geographically, culturally, and perhaps even legally separate from all other business units. In the early 1950s, Walt Disney created WED Enterprises solely for the purpose of housing what would become Disneyland in order to build an organization that could focus on an entirely new business model free from the influence and practices of the established film business. In addition to the benefits of getting away from the influences of the old model, this type of separation can lead to the new business model becoming profitable more quickly. It will have its own income statement and balance sheet, its own customers and suppliers, and its own leaders and staff. The need to achieve stand-alone financial success will be felt more powerfully than if the new model were buried inside another business unit. This separation is no guarantee of success, but it may increase the odds that a good business model will emerge.

Acquisitions: A Special Case

Acquisitions are special cases that automatically present major business model reengineering challenges. CEOs must decide before buying another company how the inevitable conflicts between the incumbent and new business models will be addressed, otherwise the odds of a successful integration will be very low. At one extreme, the acquired business can be treated as a new and independent business unit, allowing it to retain its legacy business model and continue to find its own path to maximizing EP growth: This appears to be the choice the "big pharma" company Roche has made with its acquisition of the bioengineering company Genentech.[10] At the opposite extreme, the acquired business can disappear entirely, being subsumed into the business model of the buyer: This is typically the case when a large bank acquires a smaller bank. The third approach is to modify both the buyer's and seller's business models into something new. One buyer famous for this approach is Danaher, which thoroughly reengineers each newly acquired business into the "Danaher Business System" as quickly as possible:[11] The result is a still separate business, but one with much stronger financial convictions and execution capabilities. The best choice of how to manage acquired business models will be specific to the circumstances, but buyers with a clear and well engineered rationale for their choice will have the best chance of seeing EP accretion from the transaction.

 ## EXECUTION CAPABILITIES

Execution capabilities are not usually the foundation of positioning strategies but important enablers of strategy. They consist of the distinctive knowledge and skills required to fulfill the performance potential of a business model. As such, their impact on EP growth will be a function of the participation and business model choices management has already made. The highest value of execution capabilities is to increase the resiliency and longevity of great business models. The combination of a superior business model and the right execution capabilities creates an almost unassailable competitive position.

Execution capabilities do not exist in a vacuum. They are elements of an interactive network, or system, of institutional knowledge and skills that is essential to deliver a particular business model. Some of the individual capabilities may even be generic, like inventory management, but when combined and applied to executing particular activities, they can become distinctive, even unique, sources of competitive advantage. And whereas many of the individual elements could be identified and emulated by competitors, the complete system of capabilities usually cannot be. The real power of execution capabilities lies in the intricate, subtle, and detailed ways in which businesses configure their knowledge and skills. These deep interrelationships are truly proprietary, unique to the business model, and cannot easily be decoded or emulated.

Every good business model requires distinctive capabilities to achieve its potential. From product conception to customer delivery and service, there will be points in the activity chain where a business must have unique or superior skills that enable it to execute its business model successfully As an example, a key conviction of Intel's microprocessor business model is the need for manufacturing leadership (i.e., volume, quality, and cost leadership) in a product market that sees the introduction of major new products approximately every 18 months. This means that the company must also add new manufacturing capacity, either by building new plants or reengineering older ones, every 18 months. Microprocessor manufacturing facilities are enormously complex and expensive to build, and Intel has established and maintained a clear advantage in the multiple skills required to have the right capacity, in the right places, at the right time for each product cycle. In terms of its business model, this means only Intel can reliably supply many large customers with the volumes of chips they require on a timely and cost-effective basis. The sophistication, experience, training, and dedication required to accomplish this is virtually impossible for competitors to match.

As noted, however, execution capabilities are valuable only in relation to the business model in which they exist. Intel's manufacturing prowess is a competitive advantage because it participates in a profitable product market and its entire microprocessor business model has a net competitive advantage. If Intel were a laggard in chip design, for instance, having its superior manufacturing skills would not be as meaningful because it would always be behind in the product introduction cycle anyway. And as Intel moves into higher-volume but lower-margin chips for consumer electronics other than personal computers, the picture may change dramatically: Some of these consumer product markets may not even yield positive EP, or Intel may not be able to establish a superior business model in those product markets, or it may encounter competitors whose manufacturing skills for these lower margin products are equal to or better than its own. Any or all of these factors could negate the value of Intel's existing manufacturing capabilities when competing in these new markets.

Three questions will be explored briefly here: (1) How should the right execution capabilities be chosen? (2) What is the role of "best practices"? and (3) What is the significance of "core competencies"?

Choosing the Right Execution Capabilities

How do companies with great business models choose which capabilities are the most important to develop and how do they determine how these capabilities must interact to build the strongest possible competitive advantage?

Very little study has been done on this question, but it is likely in most cases that these choices are made by trial and error. Business models seldom spring up wholly formed. They begin with one or two core convictions and then evolve into a more complete commercial idea as the leaders get feedback from customers, employees, suppliers, and investors. Experience becomes the teacher. The same pattern is probably true for choosing the most important capabilities needed to execute the business model. Once the more promising elements of the business model are identified and adopted, the organization is more or less driven to figure out how to execute them. The process is actually somewhat spontaneous.

For example, when Richard Santuli conceived of the business that was to become NetJets (originally Executive Jet Aviation), he had developed mathematical models to determine the basic requirements (minimum number of aircraft, number of crews and support staff; airport locations; turnaround times; operating costs; pricing, ownership and financing options, etc.) for making a private network of fractionally-owned executive jets work, operationally and financially. On paper, he had a basic business model, but he could not know at the outset exactly what the key capabilities were that would be necessary at each part of the activity chain to make the model work. How would enough pilots of the caliber and experience he required be hired, trained, kept current in their skills, motivated, and retained? How would the aircraft be serviced properly to assure both safety and customer availability requirements were met? How would potential customers be located and convinced to buy into this fairly radical new idea? These capabilities are all elements of NetJets's competitive positioning advantages today, but for the most part they have been worked out over time by employees at all levels of the company as the strengths and weaknesses of the business model itself were identified and addressed.

The adaptive and often spontaneous nature of identifying and developing key execution capabilities is not a weakness but a strength of the selection process, making it even harder for competitors to sort out what exactly the capabilities are and how they fit together. Adaptive and spontaneous do not have to mean random or unrigorous. As ideas for new or improved capabilities emerge from all levels of the organization, they can be screened starting with just two questions: Is the new or changed capability essential to the successful execution of a profitable business model, and is it a novel capability that must be invented in-house or can it be acquired from outside? If a capability is essential to executing the business unit's Gold strategy, then of course it must be acquired or improved as the case may be. The more distinctive the business model itself, the more likely the capability will have to be developed in-house, making it proprietary and adding to the strength of the business unit's competitive advantage over the longer term.

The Question of Best Practices

There is a constant danger of defining execution capabilities too broadly, to include nearly all of the important activities needed to operate a business whether or not they are mission critical to the business model. For instance, many companies aspire to the standard of achieving "best practices" in a wide range of activities like sales force productivity, inventory turnover, manufacturing efficiency, customer satisfaction, and the rate of new product introductions. "Best practices" usually means the most efficient performance levels found among competitors or similar companies, though some best practice pursuers expand their comparison groups to include all exemplars regardless of industry.

Achieving best practices usually, not always, leads to some improvement in competitive position and economic profit, particularly if the business has fallen into sloppy habits and allowed significant inefficiencies to creep into its everyday behaviors. But achieving best practices is not necessarily a game changer. Even the highest levels of efficiency cannot alter the underlying forces of market economics or add to the long-term EP growth potential of a poor or mediocre business model. For example, from the 1970s to the 2000s General Motors, Ford, and Chrysler continued losing ground in volume and economic profitability to Toyota and Honda in the U.S. conventional automobile segment, despite catching up on the quality and reliability of their cars. The U.S. companies had successfully adopted *kaizen* and other superior Japanese production processes. But these new execution capabilities were not enough to restore consistent profitability or stop the losses of market share—the U.S. companies were still pursuing commercial and financial business models that were very different from, and inferior to, the Japanese business models.

Another factor can dampen the hoped-for profitability improvements from pursuing best practices: competition. In most industries, new efficiencies are quickly competed away, primarily in the form of companies giving price concessions or spending more to enhance their offers in order to keep customers and maintain or gain revenue share. This is why in mature product markets, average return on equity does not typically rise over time even as general productivity improves—the benefits are largely given to customers rather than shareholders.

These realities notwithstanding, companies must certainly strive to achieve excellent operating efficiency—constant efficiency improvements are essential to remaining a serious competitor over time. It is important to keep in mind, however, that these improvements alone are usually not sufficient. To be among the best-performing competitors usually requires much more.

The Question of Core Competencies

The concept of leveraging a company's "core competencies" has had an almost exalted place in strategic mythology since it was proposed in a famous *Harvard Business Review* article in 1990.[12] In essence, the article holds that a company should structure its organization and base its corporate strategies around proprietary technologies with the potential to yield multiple products that can achieve large or dominant global market share. The article does not address profitability considerations. There appears to be an underlying assumption, for which no evidence is offered, that by achieving large scale and market share a company will necessarily enjoy good financial performance.

Many companies attempt to identify their core competencies as a foundation for formulating growth strategies (though few have gone to the extreme of actually trying to organize around them). This exercise tends to produce lists of capabilities that the company's leaders feel they execute better than most and which can therefore be the basis of a growth strategy. The main problem with this approach to leveraging core competencies is that knowing how well a business compares to others in terms of its technology or operating prowess is not the same thing as knowing whether or how that business generates economic profits. The pursuit of strategies that leverage the kind of core competencies defined in the article has never been shown to necessarily yield good EP growth. Indeed, many companies cited as exemplars of the core competency mind-set, like NEC, have not enjoyed good financial performance at all.

There is a different interpretation of core competencies that can be useful to the CEO, and that is the five core competencies of strategic management. If a company builds exceptional capabilities in selecting its performance objectives, in making its participation and positioning choices, and in making its organization and risk management choices, then it will almost certainly achieve higher rates of EP growth than its rivals and continue to do so as long as it maintains those advantages. When defined in this way, building core competencies is something every CEO and company should be striving to do.

 ## CORPORATE POSITIONING CHOICES

At the corporate level, positioning choices are those that involve leveraging the company's "group affiliation benefits." Group affiliation benefits comprise opportunities to improve business unit competitive positions through the sharing of knowledge, capabilities, and resources distinctive to the corporation. These group benefits may confer increased economic profit growth opportunities across business units through mechanisms the business units would not usually create or have access to on their own—for instance, access to debt capital with an investment grade credit rating. Therefore, positioning choices based on group affiliation benefits typically arise in, or are driven by, the corporate center.

Group affiliation benefits can be classified into two types, operating and strategic. Group operating benefits include most of what are commonly called "synergies" that exist within the portfolio; among them are increased purchasing power, lower-cost distribution, production scale economies, lower-cost debt, and greater regulatory clout. Group strategic benefits include the ability to share successful business models, execution capabilities, and special assets across the portfolio. Both types of affiliation benefits will be examined more closely.

Group Operating Benefits

Group operating benefits arise mostly from the scale and scope of the total company: They are the inherent benefits of membership in the group, shared more or less proportionally by all of the business units. Business units will rarely see their choice of Gold strategies impacted by group operating benefits because these efficiencies, to the extent they exist, affect all strategies in essentially the same ways. When the company uses its purchasing power to negotiate lower occupancy or energy costs, all units benefit. If the company credit rating is changed from A to AA, all units benefit from lower borrowing costs. If the company can use its power in the distribution channels to introduce new brands more quickly and efficiently, this benefit is shared by the various units using those distribution channels. In all of these cases, the company's unit economic costs are lower than the individual business units could achieve on their own.

Larger multibusiness companies can identify and exploit many opportunities to leverage group operating benefits. Viewed in isolation, operating benefits can be significant sources of cost advantage to the business units, and most corporate centers work hard to capture them. This is the basic rationale behind many centralized functions such as purchasing, real estate management, information technology, treasury, and human resources. At the same time, however, there are quite strong forces at work that can mitigate or even erase these benefits. The first is the force of competition, and the second is the impact of group operating *costs*.

As is the case with achieving best practices, competition tends to transfer many of the gains from capturing group operating benefits to customers rather than directly to the bottom line. Most group operating benefits are generic and can be captured equally well by most competitors. When a business unit within a large company is competing against business units in other large companies, they may all enjoy similar group operating benefits, meaning these benefits are not necessarily conferring an outright cost advantage on any of the players. When this happens, competitors tend to use their similarly lowered cost structures to fight for market share, either lowering prices or adding features (costs) to their offers without raising prices. This behavior, which is perfectly natural in competitive markets, gives most of the increased efficiency from group operating benefits to customers. Of course, this does not mean that these benefits have no value to the company. Companies still need to work to capture their group operating benefits or they may actually fall behind the competition.

Affiliation with a large company confers not only benefits but also costs on a business unit, and these costs—sometimes called diseconomies of scale or scope—can be significant. Stand-alone businesses or units within smaller corporations have several advantages over business units that are embedded in large companies. One key advantage is speed and autonomy of decision making on all matters, whether operational or strategic: The larger the company, the more meetings and time it takes to get decisions made and the less accountability there is for the outcomes. It is difficult to put a price on the costs of bureaucratic decision making, but an interesting perspective on the trade-off between the value of autonomy and the forced adoption of group operating benefits was voiced by a plant manager at Nucor: "We are honest-to-God autonomous. That means we duplicate efforts made in other parts of Nucor. The company might develop the same computer program six times. But the advantages of local autonomy are so great we think it is worth it."[13] This is one of Nucor's key commercial convictions, a part of their intensely profitability-driven business model, and it turns conventional wisdom about group operating benefits completely on its head. Others might do well to emulate this thinking.

Another large offset to group operating benefits is the degree to which business units inside of larger companies are almost always forced into a system of costly cross subsidies. Business units like High Octane, Big Dog, and Shop Smart are forced through inappropriate target setting and inefficient resource allocation processes to fund business units like Ream Maker, Wahoo, and PopulAir. This has a huge negative impact on the company's economic profits and EP growth. Whether such practices come under the heading of diversification, portfolio balance, smoothing earnings, or any other euphemism, cross subsidies invariably diminish business unit competitiveness and economic profit across the entire portfolio. They are a powerful negative synergy.

On balance, CEOs should certainly try to capture the added efficiencies that can come from group operating benefits, but they should also be wary. Unless the company is organized to eliminate or severely limit the offsetting costs of group affiliation, the net effect on the company's total competitiveness and operating performance may well be neutral or negative.

Group Strategic Benefits

The objective of leveraging group strategic benefits is to transfer or extend, if possible, sources of competitive advantage from individual business units or the corporate center itself to other business units in the portfolio. These sources of competitive advantage include business models (or elements of business models), execution capabilities, and special assets. Transferring or extending these benefits successfully will have a direct impact on a business unit's choice of Gold strategies and the rate at which it is able to grow economic profit.

By their nature, group strategic benefits are distinctive to the company and cannot be matched by competitors easily or quickly. Therefore, a greater percentage of the economic rewards from leveraging strategic benefits can be retained by the businesses rather than being fully passed on to customers, as they might have to be in the case of operating benefits. But although group strategic benefits are generally more valuable than operating benefits, they are also harder to capture. Unlike operating benefits, which pass to the business units automatically, strategic benefits must be individually identified and proactively transferred from one business unit or the corporate center to other business units. The business units themselves are usually not in a position even to see how they might benefit from sources of competitive advantage elsewhere in the portfolio, so they are not able to take the lead in transferring or extending these benefits—that initiative must come from, or be facilitated by, the center.

Leveraging Business Models

When a company's portfolio includes business units like High Octane or Shop Smart, with highly advantaged business models, the CEO should be raising the question of whether any elements of those models could be transferred to other business units or extended to new markets. The potential to leverage these models into sources of higher economic profit growth for other business units will be influenced, among other factors, by whether the exemplary model is closed or open.

In a closed business model, commercial convictions are so closely tied to the competitive conditions faced by one business in its chosen product markets that they are not usually transferable to other business units competing in different product markets. The specific commercial convictions that drive the success of General Electric's jet engine business, for instance, would have little overlap with the specific commercial convictions necessary to succeed in GE's electrical distribution businesses. It would do no harm at all for the leaders of these units to observe each other's business models and possibly take away some new ideas, but the distinctive commercial convictions of the jet engine business would be of limited value to other GE businesses.

Despite the natural limitations of transferring closed business models across the portfolio into unrelated businesses, extending successful closed business models into new geographic markets can be, as noted in earlier chapters, a source of tremendous economic profit growth. For companies like Coca-Cola and McDonald's, such extensions have been spectacularly successful. Although these extensions could in theory be achieved by a single business unit expanding from local to global markets, in practice the corporate center usually plays a very active role in pushing the expansion as a matter of corporate rather than business unit strategy. The center is much better positioned than a home-market business unit to address the many challenges of geographic expansion. In addition, the original business model inevitably has to be modified to some extent to suit local market conditions, and these modifications can be made more easily and successfully in what are really new business units that are separate from the original unit. The Coca-Cola business models in Germany or Brazil have many similarities to the original U.S. business model but also many differences dictated by local market conditions. They may share the same bones, but each needs to formulate its own local market Gold strategy to maximize economic profit growth.

Open business models, characterized more by the strength and efficacy of their financial convictions, are more easily transferable across business units because they impose a general management discipline rather than a unique solution set characteristic of closed models. Whether this financial discipline originates in a business unit or the center, it will need to be imposed by the center if it is to be transferred across the portfolio.

An interesting example of leveraging a corporate financial discipline to shape a business unit's commercial business model is the Touchstone movie studio built by the Walt Disney Company. Starting in the early 1980s, Touchstone, which was a very small player in the film industry, began making R-rated movies for the first time. As a participation choice, this would not appear promising because the market economics of R-rated movies are generally weak: Many R-rated movies struggle to make an accounting profit and, as a segment, they do not appear to be economically profitable.[14] Disney entered this segment with several important commercial and financial convictions, creating an entirely new business model.

Commercially, the Touchstone movies were almost all adult comedies and very much on the soft side of the R ratings, avoiding hard-core sex or violence, meaning they could attract audiences closer to those for PG-13 movies where the market economics are somewhat better. Financially, the movies were held to strict budgets (uncharacteristic of Tinsel Town) that assured they would be profitable if they attained even modest popularity—absolutely no big-budget films were allowed. This financial model, which set an ROI minimum translating to positive EP for each movie, then dictated how much could be spent on scriptwriters, actors, directors, and crews. To meet these financial constraints, Jeffrey Katzenberg, who then headed the studio, negotiated contracts with well-known and very capable professionals like Richard Dreyfus, Danny DeVito, and Bette Midler who were, for various reasons, not then at their peak earning power. Of course, no one knew if such a radical departure from Hollywood's customary practices would work, but it did work and very well. Nearly 90 percent of Touchstone's movies over the next decade generated positive earnings, and the studio was transformed from an also-ran into a market leader and genuine moneymaker.[15]

While leveraging business models should always be explored as a potential source of growing economic profit, it is usually not as easy as it might appear to be. A common error in making strategic choices is to overestimate the potential benefits from transferring or extending business models. Indeed, too much of what passes for corporate strategy falls into this trap. Even the Coca-Cola Company, with all of its success in replicating, with modifications, its original carbonated soft-drink model in countries all around the world, has stumbled when trying to extend that model, or elements of it, into other beverage categories such as bottled water and noncarbonated fruit drinks where the market economics and sources of competitive advantage are very different. Microsoft, with one of the most profitable business models of the late twentieth century, has struggled mightily to transfer elements of that model into new product markets with only limited success.

Corporate strategies are laced with grandiose plans to extend business models into new markets or adjacent businesses, often without a good understanding of the underlying economics or necessary commercial convictions to be successful. When IBM, for instance, entered the personal computer market in 1981 with the IBM-PC, expectations were that Big Blue would be able to transfer elements of its successful mainframe model to the new business unit.

The new product was well received, the advertising was award winning, and a new population of home and office computer users was created, but the product line was not a financial success for IBM.

Part of the reason was that IBM misread the sources of value added in the product, which turned out to be in the microprocessor (made by Intel) and in the software (from Microsoft). Compounding this error was IBM's belief that apart from the microprocessors it needed to be vertically integrated in hardware components, a core conviction (ultimately to be changed) of IBM's mainframe model that transferred to the PC. But vertical integration was not a cost-efficient activity chain for the home and small office markets, where pricing was far more sensitive and margins much lower than in the business-to-business segments. Within a few short years it became apparent to other PC providers such as Compaq and Dell that it was far cheaper to purchase the individual components of a PC from various suppliers and assemble them into complete machines under a common brand. This not only undermined the vertical integration model, but it meant almost anyone could enter the PC business, and many did. Thus, IBM's PC model, as successful as it was in many respects, failed its most important test of generating economic profits and creating value.

Despite the challenges, CEOs should look for ways to cross-pollinate good business model ideas across the portfolio. In general, voluntary knowledge transfers between business units will be more easily accepted than dictates from the center. This was, in part, the thinking behind GE's "boundaryless" program in the 1990s, where Jack Welch was pushing knowledge sharing across lines of business and functions to leverage the enormous intellectual capital at a company like GE and to generate more creative commercial ideas throughout the company. It is also the philosophy behind knowledge transfer at Nucor, where each production facility is considered an autonomous profit center and is free to use, or not to use, whatever ideas it can learn from other facilities—provided it continues to earn its required 25 percent ROI.

Leveraging Execution Capabilities

At the business unit level, critical execution capabilities tend to be so particular to the business model they support that attempting a wholesale transfer of these capabilities across multiple business units would not normally make any sense. There may, however, be areas of special expertise, representing the collective wisdom of the company, which are nurtured and promoted by the center on behalf of all the business units. A well-known example would be the Procter & Gamble company's deep expertise in marketing consumer-packaged goods, accumulated over many years and actively leveraged by the center to be available to all business units. Ideally, this special expertise allows many of Procter & Gamble's business units to formulate Gold strategies with higher economic profit growth than they would have been able to achieve on their own.

Another company that has been extremely successful at leveraging group execution capabilities is the Danaher Corporation, a tool, instrument, and equipment manufacturer. Danaher has the doubly rare distinction of being able to make consistently profitable acquisitions while also being able to manage a portfolio in which most of its more than 50 business units have earned substantial economic profits. During the period 1998 to 2007, Danaher's EP per share grew at a compound annual rate of 18.6 percent and its average annual total shareholder returns were 18.9 percent.[16]

Danaher is a multibusiness operating company, but its origins as a private equity firm may explain its insistence that every unit in the portfolio earn at least a 10 percent after-tax return on invested capital, which for most of the Danaher businesses would be just above the cost of capital. Newly acquired businesses are required to reach this threshold within three years, with goodwill fully accounted for. A critical factor in achieving these impressive levels of performance is a body of shared execution capabilities known as the Danaher Business System. The objective of the system, which is based on the conviction of continuous improvement, is for every employee to discover and adopt the most efficient practices at all points of the activity chain, including manufacturing processes, general business processes, acquisition integration, sales and marketing processes, product innovation processes, and people management processes. More than 50 training courses are conducted with employees of every business unit and at every level of the company to transfer detailed knowledge of how Danaher's businesses are able to continually improve efficiency and effectiveness in all of these areas. The courses embed not only knowledge of how to improve processes but a deep understanding of and commitment to Danaher's performance objectives and rigorous performance management practices, without which the courses alone would not have much impact.

The Danaher Business System is managed both centrally and within business units. The center has created the Danaher Business System Office, a group of executives who largely reside in the business units with the mandate to ensure that the business system is successfully adopted and employed by the businesses, especially those newly acquired. This commitment by the center reinforces the fact that adopting the Danaher Business System is not optional. It is not just a series of courses that people take and forget about. The system itself is the way business is conducted throughout the organization, a core commercial conviction that must be embedded in every business unit's Gold strategy.[17]

Many companies have training courses and try to teach best practices, but few seem to be able to combine managerial disciplines, capabilities development, and sheer persistence, which have produced the concrete results seen at Danaher. One example of the effectiveness of the Danaher Business System is the company's ability to transform its many acquisitions into economically profitable business units. The company typically makes 10 to 20 acquisitions a year,[18] following a rigorous acquisition screening, targeting, and pricing process (another aspect of the Business System). Each acquired business is immersed in the Danaher Business System with the intention of raising its sustainable return on invested capital, including goodwill, by several percentage points and of increasing its rate of profit growth as well. It is easy to set such goals, but difficult to achieve them, especially on a repeatable basis in businesses that typically do not compete in product markets that yield economic profits easily. That Danaher is able to accomplish this year in and year out with many different kinds of businesses is testament to its ability to transfer execution capabilities as a matter of course, and not simply on an ad hoc basis.

Neither Procter & Gamble nor Danaher would be so successful at leveraging execution capabilities across their portfolios unless the business units were, at least for the most part, also pursuing superior business models. The combination of profitable business models and specialized know-how that can be shared across multiple businesses is truly a virtuous circle, with constant positive feedback and opportunities for improvement being fostered by the experience of seeing good results getting better and better relative to the competition.

Leveraging Special Assets

As used here, the term *special assets* refers to specific property rights, either in the form of owned assets or legally enforceable claims, which meet two requirements: (1) they are proprietary to the company and (2) they are, or have the clear potential to be, a critical positioning element in a Gold strategy. Among the more common types of assets that may become "special" are discoveries and inventions, artistic creations, manufacturing processes, brands, networks, land and mineral rights, and government grants, subsidies, or transfers. A characteristic of most special assets is that they are (or would be, if permitted) salable—they have a discoverable market value to others.

Special assets come in many forms. Perhaps the best example of a company with a proprietary claim that is central to its business model is the Saudi Arabian national oil company, Aramco. Aramco's special asset is the exclusive right to explore for, develop, and produce oil and natural gas in the world's largest known hydrocarbon reserves. Aramco can and does bring in other partners to help with these tasks, but no other company can access these resources except through the national company. It would be hard to imagine having a bigger positioning advantage in a profitable product market. Other examples of special assets include Disney's rights to the commercial exploitation of its animated characters, Pfizer's patent rights (for a limited time) on a blockbuster drug like Lipitor®, and the Coca-Cola Company's access to and influence over its exclusive bottler network.

Special assets can increase economic profit growth in three ways: first, as an essential element of a single business unit's Gold strategy; second, across the portfolio as part of multiple business units' Gold strategies; and third, outside the portfolio when shared with or sold to third parties. Within a single business unit, the specifics of how a special asset should best be exploited for competitive advantage is unique to its business model—generalizations are almost impossible. However, some limited generalizations about leveraging special assets across the portfolio and about sharing them with third parties outside of the portfolio can be made.

Within the portfolio there may be several business units whose Gold strategies require access to a special asset such as a brand, a patent, or an artistic creation. Disney has done a particularly good job of leveraging the value of its animated characters across its film, theme park, music, and retail businesses. Daimler-Benz has successfully leveraged its Mercedes-Benz marque across multiple product segments, including conventional sedans, luxury cars, SUVs, buses, and trucks. And most technology companies leverage their key product patents across multiple business units whenever possible. In these cases and most others, the corporate center, rather than a single business unit, usually has to own the special asset and actively seek opportunities to leverage it in business unit Gold strategies across the portfolio.

Just having a strong brand or other special asset, however, does not ensure that its value can be transferred from one business unit to another. In some cases the asset simply doesn't fit the Gold strategy of another line of business. Eastman Kodak discovered this when it tried to leverage its Kodak brand onto products like photocopiers, VCR tape, and alkaline batteries. The Kodak brand may have helped these products marginally, but not much—none were ultimately successful. IBM had a similar experience when the IBM brand was extended onto what became the ThinkPad® laptop computer. The IBM moniker may have helped the company to gain market acceptance, but again the ultimate outcome was disappointing profitability for the company. In extreme cases, attempts to leverage special assets can have disastrous consequences because there is always a danger that even a strong brand can be damaged by an unsuccessful association, as was the case, for instance, with Coca-Cola and the introduction of New Coke®.

Overall, the center's role in leveraging special assets within the portfolio would normally include four tasks, starting first with maintaining an inventory of assets that meet the criteria and second with ensuring the company's legal claims to these assets are sustained and protected from improper use by others. Third, the center will be looking for opportunities to leverage the use of the assets in more business units, being careful to assure there really is a fit—even a great asset will not necessarily fix a poor business model or overcome unattractive market economics. Finally, the center will want to protect special assets from being devalued through overuse or association with a failed strategy.

The center also needs to evaluate the EP growth potential special assets may have outside the portfolio. In evaluating this potential, companies have three options to consider: retaining the assets for their exclusive use, sharing the use of special assets with others, or selling them outright.

For many companies the second option seems to be the best, making the special asset a part of its own Gold strategies while also finding ways to share the asset with others. Disney has an extensive range of licensing agreements for its animated characters that adds significantly higher economic profit than it could achieve by limiting their use to Disney-originated projects only. Aramco does bring in partners because the expertise and experience required to develop its fields properly does not all reside in-house, adding to its economic profit stream by accelerating development and production and by increasing the percentage of reserves that can ultimately be recovered. Virtually all pharmaceutical companies license at least some of their drugs to be manufactured or distributed by others, especially to attain global coverage that they are not staffed up to do themselves, again seeking to earn a greater economic profit than they could with their Gold strategy alone.

Companies that hold special assets entirely to themselves usually do so because the assets cannot in any meaningful sense be shared. This would be the case with most brands, whose value is unique to the company that owns them, or with some technologies whose commercial value to the company could be diminished greatly if they became available to competitors. At the other end of the spectrum, companies sell assets all the time, but usually these are not special assets, which, by definition, would be embedded in Gold strategies. It would be very unusual for the outright sale of a special asset to have a higher value to the company than the combined benefits of the Gold strategies and third-party sharing agreements the asset supports. When special assets are sold outright, it is often a financing rather than a strategic decision: A company may be selling the crown jewels in order to sustain itself through a difficult period.

 CHAPTER SUMMARY

Positioning choices are major determinants of economic profit growth, although they are not, as is sometimes suggested, the be-all and end-all of business strategy. Positioning choices will determine the offer and cost advantages or disadvantages a business unit enjoys relative to the competition and the share of economic profit it will achieve in a particular product market over time. As long as a business is growing its share of economic profit, it can be sure it is pursuing a superior positioning strategy and justifying its claim on the company's resources.

The most important positioning choice is the business model, or combination of deeply held commercial and financial convictions that actually determine how the business will compete and what share of total product-market economic profit it will earn. Great business models often have their origins in entrepreneurial start-ups. These are usually closed business models that prove to be exceptionally profitable in a narrow domain, laying the foundation for what may become a large and prosperous company. Over time, the company may adopt a more open business model, applying a set of financial convictions to direct its growth into new areas.

Execution capabilities are also an important, but secondary, consideration in making positioning choices. Capabilities alone are not usually at the basis of positioning choices because they alone cannot overcome a poor business model or assure good economic profit growth. But having the right execution capabilities is a critical complement to a good business model, making it more profitable, less easily matched, and of longer duration than it otherwise would be.

CEOs have to constantly review and refresh the good business models they inherit, and they must also ensure that poor business models are overhauled or discarded. They must also pursue opportunities to extend business models and execution capabilities, as well as special assets, across the company's portfolio in order to create Gold strategy options that would not otherwise be available to the business units. Leveraging these strategic affiliation benefits can be a proprietary and significant source of additional economic profit growth.

CHAPTER SIX

Making the Right Organizational Choices

HE CEO'S PRIMARY ORGANIZATIONAL goal is for the enterprise to be consistently better than the competition at growing economic profit. This is an enormously ambitious objective, and one that is difficult to achieve. It requires a lot of time, effort, investment, tough decisions, and tireless reinforcement to reach a point where one company, at the level of each of its business units, can consistently outperform most or all of its peers. Some very successful companies, like ExxonMobil, Berkshire Hathaway, and Goldman Sachs, are recognized by their peers as having a unique combination of organizational skills, disciplines, and even confidence that sets them apart year in and year out in their ability to make good choices and outperform the rest. But the relatively small number of companies that seem to have this recognizable institutional advantage is evidence of the hard work it takes to build and sustain it, and, indirectly, of how easily and quickly such an advantage can be lost.

There is no single formula for creating an organization that can sustain superior economic profit growth. This chapter puts forward some important principles and guidelines that are consistent with that goal and that are broadly applicable to companies in different industries. These ideas have been proven to work well in many companies, but in each case they had to be tailored to the realities of a company's unique situation. All companies have their own institutional legacies and their own combination of executive personalities and capabilities that will inevitably influence what goals they will pursue and how successful they will be in achieving them. So making changes to better align a business organization with the CEO's paramount goal is only partly a matter of science—much of it is art.

 ## THE INSTITUTIONAL IMPERATIVE

Every business organization is in a constant state of conflict between preservation and performance. At the performance end of the spectrum is the drive to find and execute Gold strategies, and at the preservation end of the spectrum is the institutional imperative. The institutional imperative is the inward-looking tendency to want to preserve or marginally expand on existing strategies, resource commitments, power structures, and pay levels. It is the group manifestation of the agency problem—just as many individuals seek to gain maximum personal benefit (power and money) with minimum personal risk (peace of mind), so does the group seek to make its own existence as comfortable as possible.

The institutional imperative is not a static or benign force that simply impedes progress by cramping innovation and decision making. It is a dynamic force that can push an organization into making consistently poor choices with respect to growing economic profits, choices that in the short run may seem to benefit stakeholders other than investors, but that in the intermediate and long run sap the organization of its ability to perform at a high level. The institutional imperative drives companies to adopt toothless performance objectives, to pursue underperforming business models, to keep assets with poor returns, to expand into markets with unattractive economics, to build "competitive advantages" lacking economic benefits, to tolerate bloated corporate functions, and to reward mediocre or poor executive performance.

Every CEO has to deal with the institutional imperative. A few may even give into it, conceding that the self-interested objectives of the institution will generally be allowed to trump the hard work, superior creativity, and execution necessary to achieve great performance. But most CEOs recognize that defeating, or at least beating back, the institutional imperative is essential to achieving excellence. There are three manifestations of the institutional imperative that CEOs especially need to overcome: strategic myopia, cross-subsidies, and lack of transparency.

Strategic Myopia

When formulating strategies, business units tend to look at only a small number of options, or sometimes no true options, to their current strategies. This failure to produce robust options is strategic myopia, seeking progress within only a narrow band of possibilities not too different from what the business is doing now. Typically, this is all that is expected of business units and is reflected in the annual planning ritual that produces "status quo plus 10 percent" type plans. These plans are not grounded in rigorous strategic analysis but are merely a negotiated budget with added strategic bells and whistles. The businesses are not tasked to examine deeply the economics of the products they sell or the markets in which they participate, or to put forward new business models, or to recycle unproductive capital; in other words, they are not tasked to formulate their Gold strategies. In essence, they are tasked to underachieve, and, within the dictates of the institutional imperative, they are willing to comply.

Cross-Subsidies

One of the most enduring and damaging corporate belief systems is that the business units have interdependent capital requirements. This belief system is anchored in the concept of capital scarcity, or more prosaically in capital budgeting. In a typical capital budgeting cycle, the CFO declares that the company has, say, $1 billion available for fixed capital additions next year, the business units submit initial plans calling for $1.5 billion of new fixed capital, and then the negotiations begin as the units battle with each other and the center for the "scarce" resource of company capital. This process almost always results in underfunding the business units with the best prospects for growing economic profit and overfunding those with the lowest prospects. In other words, the businesses with the best prospects subsidize the rest of the portfolio at the expense of maximizing economic profit across the board.

This phenomenon will be examined more closely in a later section, but the institutional imperative dimension of the problem arises from the belief that every business unit somehow "deserves" to keep the capital is already has and to add to it each year. This belief is grounded in a preservation mind-set, not a performance mind-set. Business units only deserve the amount of capital necessary to maximize economic profit growth, which may be much more or much less than they currently have or would get under typical capital budgeting schemes. The right amount of capital for a business unit is unrelated to what is in the corporate checking account or to what other business units may require to pursue their own Gold strategies.

Lack of Transparency

This problem has been referenced throughout the book. The CEO cannot achieve his or her economic objectives without having excellent information at the business unit level, and the business unit heads cannot formulate or execute their Gold strategies without even better information at the level of products, markets, customers, and activities. But institutional instincts work against providing this very high degree of information quality and transparency at all levels of the company. Good information invites good, probing questions about the business plans from the CEO and also allows for good reward-for-performance management, two outcomes that some managers may see as having more career downside than upside. Many managers also have a strange sense of entitlement to information about "their" businesses, because information truly is power.

These and other institutional behaviors significantly degrade the quality of strategy formulation and execution and represent one of the biggest organizational challenges to the CEO. There are actions a CEO can take to improve the odds of success, measures that over time can alter the institutional DNA. Among the most important of these actions are embedding the right governance practices, executive processes, and executive capabilities within the organization.

 ## GOVERNANCE PRACTICES

The term "governance" is normally used to describe the relationship between a company and its shareholders, with the roles and responsibilities of the board as the primary focus of attention. But there are also internal governance practices that can have a big impact on the performance of the company, particularly the division of labor between the board, the center, and the business units.

Roles and Responsibilities of the Business Units

As the building blocks of economic profit and equity value, the business units bear the bulk of responsibility for driving EP growth through superior strategy formulation and execution. To fulfill this responsibility properly, certain governance principles and practices need to be embedded in the organization:

■ Business units should be defined so as to be essentially independent of one another. This can be fairly simple to accomplish in companies that hold a diversified portfolio of businesses, or much more challenging to accomplish in companies with portfolios containing many related businesses sharing common production and distribution assets and operating across multiple geographies. Even in these complex situations, however, it is usually possible to define business units and their supporting cost centers in such a way as to be able to manage them relatively independently.[1] This does not mean they are fully free to do whatever they please. There are definite constraints on how the business units must manage company assets such as brands and technology, or company policies such as employment and safety. But within those constraints, each business unit should be able to pursue its own Gold strategy.

■ Business units require full, pro forma income statements and balance sheets, as well as a wealth of EP related data on their markets, customers, and competitors. This requirement will be addressed more fully in a following section.

■ Business unit heads should be held directly accountable to the CEO for the EP growth performance of their units. Even in companies with matrix management involving regional and functional inputs into business unit strategy and execution, it is important to keep accountability for EP performance as narrowly defined as possible. Once accountability for EP growth becomes shared, or goes outside the line directly to the CEO, it rapidly becomes diluted and is of little consequence. Of course, the business unit heads need to delegate responsibility to their own executives for different aspects of performance within their organizations, but they themselves should remain fully and solely accountable to the CEO.

Roles and Responsibilities of the Center

The *center*, as defined here, is the CEO, his or her direct reports apart from the business unit heads, and their respective staffs. The center always includes the CFO, and, depending on the company, may also include a chief operating officer and heads of strategy, technology, marketing, human resources, and legal functions.

The center has a responsibility, at a minimum, not to subtract from the total equity value of the company by creating costs that exceed the economic benefits it delivers. If a center function is not directly helping to drive EP growth or is not legally mandated, it should be eliminated or devolved to the business units. Many companies tend to accumulate more resources in the center than they need, thus lowering overall EP and equity value. The negative impact on EP and equity value can arise not just from incurring excessive expenditures to run the centralized functions but also from the inefficient information management and decision making that comes with any unnecessary bureaucracy.

To help the company maximize profit growth over time, the center needs to help the CEO perform certain tasks especially well:

- Setting performance objectives
- Assuring the availability of high-quality information
- Approving business unit strategies (including funding and targets)
- Addressing performance variances
- Leveraging affiliation benefits
- Selecting the best business unit and functional leaders

For setting the right performance objectives, approving strategies, addressing performance variances, and selecting business-unit and function-unit leaders, the CEO is ultimately accountable and should take direct responsibility with appropriate support from the center staff. In the case of assuring high-quality information, the CEO and business unit heads should set the requirements, though other executives would normally lead the execution. And with the leveraging of affiliation benefits, the respective roles of the CEO and other executives would depend on the magnitude and nature of the opportunities specific to the company.

The substance of each of these tasks is addressed elsewhere in this book. Here the point is that the center needs to take responsibility for the design and execution of these tasks because they normally transcend the scope of what business units can do on their own and because they are so valuable in their own right. Executing these tasks properly would result in a large increase in equity value of almost any company, exceeding by orders of magnitude the costs of operating the center itself.

The track record of how well corporate centers manage these tasks is mixed. In most cases these are not even the tasks the center is designed to accomplish. The typical center is a collection of functional units, or "silos," with mandates to standardize policies and practices, assure regulatory compliance, handle financing needs, and try to save costs through exploiting scale economies. This traditional structure is, as it was designed to be, mostly administrative rather than strategic in its purpose. As just one example, in the traditional center, there is no single group with the responsibility, knowledge, and resources to create and maintain the kind of strategic database and analytical tools that support maximizing EP growth. An alternative approach for organizing the center to better accomplish the most important tasks is suggested in Appendix IV.

Roles and Responsibilities of the Board

Boards of directors can execute their responsibilities for a company's financial and strategic performance primarily through the exercise of three powers: the power to approve performance objectives, the power to appoint the CEO, and the power to ask good questions.

Approving Performance Objectives

It is the board's responsibility to support and reinforce the CEO's objective of maximizing EP growth over time. This means the board should assure that the proper EP thresholds and targets are being observed for all business units and that there are no material cross-subsidies occurring within the company. It also means that the board should take the lead in eliminating the use of inappropriate metrics, such as earnings growth, as performance objectives.

This may seem a more intrusive role than the conventional expectations of a board, but unless the board can assure the CEO is using the right performance objectives, it cannot have much influence on the quality of strategy formulation and execution throughout the company. The board cannot have the requisite knowledge to know whether the business units are actually pursuing Gold strategies, but directors should have sufficient line of sight into business unit and company performance to know whether the required and actual performance levels are consistent with what would be expected from excellent strategies.

Appointing the CEO

Choosing the right CEO is by far the most important responsibility of any board. Among the many qualifications a board may be looking for in a chief executive, one should be paramount: Can the individual lead the company to exemplary economic profit and equity value growth? Unfortunately, there is no list of CEO capabilities, personality types, or career tracks that can reliably predict how well a prospective CEO will do in that job.

When Roberto Goizueta was appointed CEO of the Coca-Cola Company in 1981, he was a Cuban-born engineer in an Atlanta-based marketing company who had catapulted, as much to his surprise as anyone's, over several layers of management into the top job. Yet, as noted previously, he subsequently led the company to achieve the highest levels of economic profit growth and value creation in its history. Clearly, the Coca-Cola board had made an inspired choice. Yet after Goizueta's death in 1997, the board's next choice for CEO proved almost as disastrous as its earlier choice had been brilliant. And with directors like Warren Buffett, the Coca-Cola board was certainly looking for a CEO who would be a good value creator. If they got it wrong, it could happen to any board.

But getting it wrong does not mean a board has to live with its mistake. Here, boards vary widely in their willingness to change CEOs. In the Coca-Cola case, once it realized its error, the board acted quickly and appointed another CEO. Other boards seem frozen with fear of looking bad or not sticking with their leader, sometimes despite years of evidence that the CEO's strategic management choices are not going well and that the company is not generating good EP growth. Making a complex and difficult decision that doesn't work out as hoped is certainly forgivable, but refusing to correct it is not.

Asking Good Questions

Directors of public companies cannot begin to understand the operating details of the many businesses and activities that drive EP growth, nor would it be realistic to expect them to have such knowledge. However, boards do have a strategic oversight role and so must, at a minimum, be in a position to ask good questions of the CEO and other members of the top management team. The goal is not for every director to understand or approve of every strategy, but for the board to have the ability to judge whether the company's overall strategic management is at a high standard. Directors want to be in a position to ask informed questions about the company's major performance objectives, participation choices, positioning choices, organization choices, and risk management choices. In other words, the directors should be in a position to know whether the CEO and management team have the right priorities and whether they are able to make consistently good strategic management choices.

Directors must not only ask good questions, they must be firm in their insistence on getting good answers. For example, during the U.S. stock market's love affair with Enron and other companies in the power trading business in the 1990s and early 2000s, a director at one of Enron's larger competitors was troubled by a curious fact. The accounting treatment of the forward delivery contracts that were driving the reported earnings growth of his company seemed at odds with economic reality. Forward delivery contracts, in this case for the future sale of electricity at specified quantities and prices, must by definition be zero-sum transactions. Based on what actually happens with electricity prices over the life of the contract, one party will ultimately make money and the counterparty will lose the same amount of money on the transaction. Yet based on "fair market" accounting rules at the time, when a new forward delivery contract was sold it was possible for *both* the supplier and the customer, using different assumptions (favorable to themselves) in their respective discounting models, to book an initial accounting profit on the transaction. On a larger scale, and so long as the market was growing rapidly, this meant that the total reported earnings arising from these types of contracts were far higher than they could possibly be in reality.

The director's question was simple: "If we are making so much money on these deals, who is losing?" This question went right to the heart of the specious nature of what the executives at Enron and other power trading companies were touting as a new paradigm, a business model so sophisticated and complicated, they claimed, that only the rarest of human beings—certainly not mere board members—could possibly understand it. But it was not only board members who were bamboozled. In this particular case (and at other similar companies), it was clear that few members of top management understood the economics of these contracts and neither did the salespeople who were paid enormous sums to sell them. They did not have answers for "who is losing?" or other straightforward questions about the economics of the power trading business.

Unfortunately, once this ignorance became apparent, the board did not react by questioning whether the company should be in a business that the management did not fully understand and for which the reported earnings, although conforming to accounting rules, were almost certainly overstated. This would be an extremely awkward discussion with a CEO who was committed to the business. Yet the director was only asking for a compelling answer to a simple—but deeply insightful—question. If directors cannot ask these kinds of questions in the expectation of getting honest and accurate answers, then there is little point in having board oversight. In this case, responding properly to the director's question might have saved the company from taking subsequent huge losses and the CEO from losing his job.

Being in a position to ask these important questions is harder than it seems for individual directors. For one thing, modern regulatory practice, at least in the United States, is deliberately designed to ensure that except for the CEO, directors are "independent," meaning as a practical matter that they begin their tenure almost wholly ignorant of the companies they serve. For another, many CEOs prefer not to have the directors as well informed as they would need to be to ask penetrating questions—another manifestation of the institutional imperative. To be fair to CEOs on this point, it is hard work keeping board members informed, and many directors do not wish to play such an activist role in board meetings anyway. But a confident CEO will want as much help and support as possible from the board and will be more than willing to take on the challenge of answering tough questions from well-informed directors.

 ## EXECUTIVE PROCESSES

Many manifestations of the institutional imperative are embedded in and reinforced by the key processes the CEO relies on to manage the company, including the processes for information management, strategy formulation, capital management, control, and compensation. For example, poor information quality and low transparency are literally built into most executive reporting systems, uneconomic cross-subsidies are virtually assured in the way that both operating and capital budgets are prepared, effective strategy formulation is blunted by strategic planning processes that are mired in mythology and subordinated to the budgeting process, and executives are often paid to reach goals that have little or nothing to do with growing economic profit.

The creation and maintenance of good executive processes is a challenge to every CEO, though not one that always has great appeal. It requires enormous effort to overcome the inertia of the embedded systems that people already understand and know how to manipulate, and changing process does not light up many CEO agendas. But for most companies, if executive processes are not changed, it will not be possible to consistently formulate and execute Gold strategies. We will look here briefly at the key design principles that should prevail in aligning executive processes with the CEO's objectives.

Information Management

Any company committed to maximizing economic profit growth needs to be able to measure, or at least make reasonable estimates of, EP and its drivers at multiple levels: for the company overall, for each business unit, for competitors' businesses, for major product and service lines, for geographic markets, for customer segments, and sometimes even for specific activities in the supply chain. Exhibit 6.1 illustrates, at a very high level, the kind of information business unit heads and CEOs would like to see on a regular basis.

To achieve this level of sophisticated measurement and reporting can be an enormous, time-consuming, and sometimes contentious undertaking. On an ad hoc basis, EP estimates can be patched together from existing information sources and systems. But for a CEO and management team to have continuous access to good-quality EP information, new capabilities and systems usually need to be created. For a large company with multiple businesses, creating these capabilities and systems can take several years to complete; however, the return on this investment begins to accrue early in the design stage as executives build their understanding of the financial and strategic drivers of EP growth and start to think more deeply about its implications for their businesses.

At the heart of an EP-based information system are two questions: How much EP are we generating (or, in the case of forecasts, expected to generate), and what are the EP drivers?

How Much EP Are We Generating?

The first question can be broken down into three smaller parts: for each unit we are measuring (i.e., business unit, customer segment, product line, or geographic market), what is its contribution to earnings, how much equity capital should be imputed to it, and what cost of equity should be used to determine the capital charge? Typical management reporting systems answer none of these questions, nor are they designed to. Conventional reporting systems are designed to align with the budgeting process and often go no further than business unit operating income, with limited or no balance sheet information. These scraps of financial information are totally inadequate to the task.

Specific EP measurement issues will be different at every company and they cannot all be covered here. However, there are some general guidelines for building an information system based on measuring, reporting, and understanding the three elements of economic profit:

EXHIBIT 6.1 Big Dog Strategic Overview

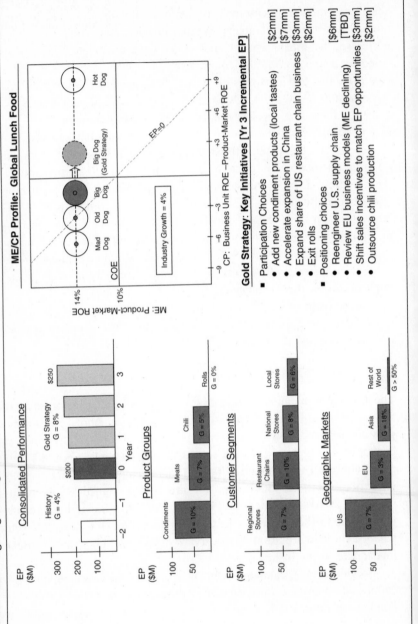

ME/CP Profile: Global Lunch Food

Industry Growth = 4%

ME: Product-Market ROE

CP: Business Unit ROE –Product-Market ROE

Gold Strategy: Key Initiatives [Yr 3 Incremental EP]

■ Participation Choices
- Add new condiment products (local tastes)   [$2mm]
- Accelerate expansion in China   [$7mm]
- Expand share of US restaurant chain business   [$3mm]
- Exit rolls   [$2mm]
■ Positioning choices
- Reengineer U.S. supply chain   [$6mm]
- Review EU business models (ME declining)   [TBD]
- Shift sales incentives to match EP opportunities   [$3mm]
- Outsource chili production   [$2mm]

Consolidated Performance

History G = 4% | Gold Strategy G = 8%

Product Groups

Condiments G = 10% | Meats G = 7% | Chili G = 5% | Rolls G = 0%

Customer Segments

Regional Stores G = 7% | Restaurant Chains G = 10% | National Stores G = 8% | Local Stores G = 6%

Geographic Markets

US G = 7% | EU G = 3% | Asia G = 18% | Rest of World G > 50%

Do Not Sacrifice the Good on the Altar of the Perfect. Measuring economic profit, especially below the level of a business unit, will almost always require making difficult allocations and accepting approximations for each of its elements. For instance, to measure the earnings contributions from product and customer groups, management will have to have guidelines for the allocation of items like shared revenues, shared costs, imputed interest charges, and even taxes. Management will also have to adopt fairly standard methodologies for deciding how much equity to impute and what cost of equity to apply to different units. There are better and worse ways to make these judgments, but the goal is to have reasonable, grounded estimates of economic profit, not false precision.

As an example, when analyzing customer or segment profitability, management needs to know that Customer Segment A generates approximately twice as much economic profit per customer as Customer Segment B, and why. It usually does not need to know the exact EP per customer (even if this were possible to determine, it probably would not be cost effective to do so). At the product and customer level, EP estimates that are within plus or minus 10 percent of the hypothetically exact EP per unit are usually good enough—and light years ahead of the information limitations managers normally have to work with.

Do Not Be Overwhelmed by Interdependencies. Many efforts to create good EP data and forecasts are hampered by the presumption that interdependencies between measurement units are greater than what they really are or, where the interdependencies do exist, that they cannot be resolved without internecine warfare breaking out between units. Some companies find it difficult even to determine revenues, let alone costs and assets, by product, market, and customer. In these situations it is almost always the organizational structure that is at odds with the underlying economics of the business.

For instance, formulating and executing Gold strategies for large customers of business-to-business companies requires estimating economic profit by customer. But if a customer is being served in several geographic markets, or is buying from more than one operating unit, or is being served through multiple channels (or all of the above), capturing and analyzing all of the information necessary to measure EP can be difficult. Different groups within the company feel they own the customer and customer data, whereas others may point out the difficulty of estimating manufacturing and distribution costs by customer. Yet to make the best decisions about how to serve the customer while simultaneously trying to grow EP from the relationship, these organizational and measurement difficulties must be overcome.

In these more challenging instances, it may be necessary to create an information system that does not follow existing organizational lines but follows products, markets, and customer lines. In fact, the process of creating the information system may cause management to rethink the organizational boundaries. The measurement issues may be a symptom of a deeper problem, which is that the existing organization boundaries themselves are actually impediments to good strategy formulation and execution.

Do Not Be Overwhelmed by Financial Wizardry. For some, economic profit measurement has simply become too complicated to be useful. Many books and articles have been written on just the accounting adjustments necessary to estimate "true" EP, and many others have been written on the various esoteric approaches to estimating the cost of equity capital. As good as much of this work is, it goes far beyond what managers need to know or worry about in building their own EP measurement and reporting systems. In fact, if managers become too engaged in the measurement wars, it is unlikely they will ever reach the pragmatic consensus necessary to build a good information system.

As an analogy, an executive needs to measure economic profit in much the same way a track or swim coach needs to measure time trials with a reasonably accurate stopwatch. The coach does not need to understand Einstein's theory of the space-time continuum, or to understand how an atomic clock runs on the oscillations of a Cesium atom, or to know anything about the inner workings of a stopwatch. The coach needs to know the athlete's time, whether his or her performance is improving or slowing down, and by about how much. This is just what an executive needs to know: the level of EP, whether it is increasing or decreasing over time, and by about how much. An executive does not need to have a deep understanding of the capital asset pricing model, options pricing theory, the 100-plus pages of rules for fair market accounting, or the differences between a traditional IRR and CFROI calculation. None of these arcana are needed to identify or implement the Gold strategy.

What Are the EP Drivers?

Market economics is usually the biggest factor impacting a business unit's ROE and EP, so it would normally be the first "driver" to estimate. For businesses with publicly traded competitors, the task can be relatively straightforward, but in many cases the competition is found in business units of large companies or in private companies where detailed profitability information is not easily available. Often it is possible to piece together a reasonable estimate of competitor profitability from indirect sources such as industry and trade publications, government data, former employees, and customers. Of course, qualitative factors of product-market attractiveness should also be analyzed, being careful always not to rely on this approach exclusively because it can be misleading.

Estimating the second key driver, competitive position, relies on much of the same information and analysis as estimating market economics. Modeling a business unit's own activity chain and looking for differences between that and how competitors appear to design, produce, and deliver their products can also yield a lot of new insight into ROE and EP growth differences. Again, the goal is to determine the major differences between the business unit's and competitors' offer and cost positions to a reasonable level of accuracy, not to seek exactitude.

With reasonable quantitative estimates of market economics and competitive position in place, the third EP driver that must be examined closely is the business model itself. The CEO and business unit management must understand which commercial and financial convictions are helping to earn a positive and growing EP and which are not. Objectivity in this effort can be difficult to achieve because engrained beliefs and behaviors have to be questioned, but without such objective questioning the real internal drivers of EP growth will never be properly understood. And without that understanding, Gold strategies cannot reliably be formulated.

Strategy Formulation (Creative Construction)

How can executives increase the odds of creating Gold strategies? The evidence is clear that it is not by doing strategic planning as practiced at most companies. When we think of enormously successful business strategies—like Apple, IKEA, Microsoft, and Amazon—almost none originated as the product of a formal strategic planning process. For the most part, these super strategies are the largely unpredictable results of the creativity and risk-taking of entrepreneurs, with their (initially) meager fortunes on the line, or of particularly gifted CEOs who followed their own strategic convictions.

Of course, just being creative and willing to take risks, especially with other people's money, is certainly no guarantee of coming up with a great strategy. Venture capitalists, who specialize in finding the next Big Idea, work on the model of needing to make only one or two successful investments out of ten in order to earn a satisfactory return on their equity. As noted earlier, this would be a hard approach for any public company CEO to sell to the board, and it would never work. The conditions that fuel entrepreneurial success and failure are impossible to replicate inside a publicly traded company. The huge range and variability of outcomes in such a model would unnerve investors and managers alike.

Given the limitations of conventional strategic planning and the impracticality of an entrepreneurial free-for-all, is there a third way for established companies to formulate great strategies? There is a third way, which we may call *creative construction.*

Creative construction is the constant search for higher EP growth options within a set of rules. Essentially, it is a process of continuous informed questioning and of making continuous adjustments to better information and new insights. This is done primarily through regular meetings between the CEO and business unit heads. It rarely requires a complete strategic plan, is not a creature or a captive of the annual budgeting process, and does not culminate in an annual PowerPoint presentation to an exhausted (from sitting through all the other business unit PowerPoint plans) CEO.

The process of creative construction is grounded in having timely, high-quality EP information of the kind shown in Exhibit 6.1, but at an even more granular level with detailed information on product, customer, activity, and geographic profitability. From this data set it is possible to begin an informed search for higher-value options. The search has two components, compliance and growth. The compliance part of the search is to determine whether current performance is within the rules, and, if not, to ensure there are specific initiatives under way to get into compliance rapidly. The growth part of the search is to formulate and test new options for growing EP even faster over time.

Examples of the issues to be addressed in the compliance part of the creative construction process would include the following:

- Ensuring all products, markets, and segments are earning a positive EP (meeting the minimum financial threshold).
- Ensuring that product-market EP growth rates meet or exceed the rate at which our competitors are growing EP (meeting the strategic threshold).
- Ensuring that the business is meeting or exceeding current EP growth targets (executing the Gold strategy as promised).
- Ensuring quick and effective action is being taken to address compliance shortfalls, including those that arise because of new external factors

such as changes in customer needs, government regulations, competitor strategies, or interest rates. Compliance requires fixing, not just discussing, problems.

As noted in earlier chapters, the biggest drivers of EP growth are participation choices and business model choices, and these would typically be the focus of the growth part of the creative construction process. Consider these examples:

- If tasked to double the equity value of our business unit over the next five years, what participation and positioning changes would be required?
- If tasked to increase our share of EP in the most profitable customer segments by 50 percent over the next five years, how would we do it?
- Where are there new opportunities for participation in profitable product markets we are not serving currently, and how should we enter them?
- If tasked annually to withdraw 10 percent of our capital from the least profitable parts of the business and then to reinvest those funds in the most profitable parts, where would we begin?

The issues and questions that drive the creative construction process are evergreen, meaning strategy formulation should be a continuous, not a batch, process. Thus, the compliance and growth questions should be the basis of issues-based meetings, held at least quarterly, directly between the CEO and each of the business unit heads. This keeps the CEO continuously informed of the important issues and also allows the CEO, through friendly but well-informed and firm questioning, to push the business units both to deliver on their performance promises and to constantly seek higher growth EP strategies. There would seldom be a need for a business unit to develop a totally new strategic plan, though in cases where product-market economics are rapidly deteriorating or where a business model is clearly not working, a complete rethinking of the business might be in order.

Capital Management

The golden rule of capital management is to fund all the Gold strategies, but only the Gold strategies. This rule seems sensible and simple enough in theory, but it can prove challenging for the CEO to follow in practice. Powerful elements of the institutional imperative are arrayed to force other, less successful, outcomes. Strategic myopia makes it almost impossible even to identify the Gold strategies, cross-subsidies reflect practices that ensure continuous funding for not-so-golden strategies, and the lack of transparency makes it difficult for the CEO to know whether capital is being properly invested.

To attain good alignment between the CEO's paramount objective and the way capital is invested within the company, two conditions must be met. First, the company must follow good information management and strategy formulation practices along the lines already described. Otherwise the CEO will be flying blind in terms of understanding the investment levels required to maximize EP growth. Second, as noted in an earlier section on cross-subsidies, the company must abandon the common practice of allowing largely artificial funding considerations to influence strategic choices rather than having its strategic choices determine the right funding levels.

As an example of the contrast between normal corporate practice and what is being recommended here, suppose Diversa Corp's CFO makes a one-year financial projection for the company overall and concludes that, allowing for targeted debt levels, dividends, and working capital requirements, there will be $5 billion of additional equity "available" for investment. At the same time, the six business units submit the most recent update of their strategy projections which, when consolidated, indicate a need for $7.5 billion of additional equity investment. What will prevail, the CFO's suggested $5.0 billion capital budget or the $7.5 billion funding the business units are asking for?

The initial answer, or first line of defense, is often the CFO's $5 billion capital budget limit. The underlying phenomenon here is that CEOs and CFOs typically use the artificial limits of the projected capital budget to impose a discipline on business unit investment demands, the thought being that because business unit heads will game the system by asking for "too much" capital, the center needs a mechanism to pare back the requests to what is "affordable." In a bizarre kind of Kabuki dance, the center is saying, "We don't believe your financial projections and will use the bludgeon of the capital budget to cut back your requests" and the business unit (and functional) heads are saying, "We know you won't believe our projections; therefore, we are inflating them so that by the time you cut us back we hope to get about what we think we need." So the units and the center iterate their way to a negotiated solution and usually end up at a number, in this case, of between $5 billion and $7.5 billion.

But this mind-set has nothing to do with maximizing economic profit or equity value. There is no way the business unit heads or the center could know how much capital is too much or too little or what is or is not affordable without first having agreed on what strategies will maximize EP over time. Some business units, like Ream Maker, need to formulate a whole new business model and probably disgorge rather than receive capital. Other business units, like High Octane, may be able to justify proportionally much more capital growth than the others because of long lead times to production combined with having the high returns to justify that investment.

What if each Diversa Corp business unit was actually pursuing its Gold strategy—what would be the "right" amount of additional equity to invest next year? The answer in this case is that neither the CFO's projection nor the business unit requests are close to the correct level of new equity investment that would be consistent with maximizing economic profit over time. This is illustrated in Exhibit 6.2.

Given the current status of Diversa Corp, with a consolidated EP of zero and three business units failing to meet even the minimum financial threshold of earning their cost of capital, the company's equity allocations need to change dramatically from what they have been in the past. In this case, the consolidated one-year new equity requirement to support the Gold strategies is actually a *negative* $3 billion. The typical capital budgeting and earnings growth–driven approaches produce completely meaningless estimates of how much new equity Diversa Corp should invest in the coming year. In fact, following either one of the top-down approaches (or trying to find a compromise between them) assures that the business units will stand almost no chance of ever formulating or executing their Gold strategies.

What Exhibit 6.2 also shows implicitly is that strategy approval should mandate capital approval. This is the essence of aligning capital management with maximizing economic profit growth. Through regular creative construction meetings with the business unit heads, new strategies, or changes to strategies, are being reviewed and approved by the CEO throughout the year. As the CEO and business unit head agree on compliance or growth changes, the capital requirements of the new strategy must be approved simultaneously. This means companies do not even need a separate capital budget or a capital budgeting process. A continuously updated consolidation of the approved center and business unit strategies will already include approved capital levels. In the Exhibit 6.2 example, the "right" amount of new equity for the next year is negative $3 billion, with each business unit understanding how and why its capital levels have been approved by the CEO.

What if Diversa Corp were in an entirely different situation, with six profitable business units like High Octane and Shop Smart, and found that the consolidated Gold strategies required $10 billion of new equity investment in the coming year—$5 billion more than is "affordable" from internally

EXHIBIT 6.2 Big Dog Strategic Overview

Source	Proposed New Equity Investment	Rationale
CFO/Center Starting Point	**$5.0B**	A simple estimate of internal funding capabilities represents difference between earnings ($7.5B) and dividends paid ($2.5B), or the change in book equity.
Business Unit Starting Point	**$7.5B**	Represents the case where the CEO has set a top-down 10% earnings growth target. Business units will want a similar 10% increase in capital (from $75B to $82.5B for the total company).
Gold Strategies Requirements		
• High Octane	$2.5B (+25%)	Significant upward shift in market economics justifies new investments in deep water and other difficult sites.
• Shop Smart	$3.0B (+15%)	Excellent business model supports expansion in challenging markets. Growth rate of 15% deemed the maximum manageable.
• Big Dog	$0.5B (5%)	Growth initiatives actually require nearly $1B of new equity, but half expected to come from within the business unit by reengineering U.S. supply chain.
• Wahoo	$0.0B	Required to achieve positive EP before receiving further investment.
• PopulAir	−$1.5B (−10%)	Restructuring unprofitable routes.
• Ream Maker	−$7.5B (− 60%)	Required to restructure (exit negative EP markets, products, and customers) and to develop a new business model.
	− $3.0B	

144

generated funds? This is a tactical question, the answer to which depends on whether the CEO and CFO see legitimate capital demands exceeding internally generated funds for a short time or a long time. If this is a short-term situation, then it is probably easiest and cheapest to increase borrowing by $5 billion, and if it is a long-term situation then the company may choose to issue new equity as well. Either way, the capital markets almost always stand ready to raise funds for economically profitable growth (2008–2009 proving to be exceptions, not the rule, on external capital raising limits).

Control

For a CEO, the key control questions for business units are whether the Gold strategies are working and the EP and revenue growth commitments are being met. For the most part, provided the company can reliably produce updated information as shown in Exhibit 6.1, frequent meetings with business unit heads will provide CEOs with timely input on these questions and give them an opportunity to offer guidance and approve changes if needed. For example, if a business unit's EP or revenue growth is falling behind target levels, a logical series of questions follows: What is the source of the shortfall, is it internally or externally driven, is it temporary or likely to be permanent, what immediate actions can be taken to get back on track, and what are the longer-term strategic and financial implications?

This process of honest, well-informed inquiry and options evaluation is an essential part of creative construction. In fact, for the CEO, the strategy formulation process and the primary control process are really one in the same, linked by the common objective of maximizing EP growth over time, reliant on the same information base, and managed through the same ongoing dialogue between the CEO and business unit heads. In any particular strategy review meeting, the discussion may place more emphasis on compliance issues or on questions about future growth options, but there is no need for any forced or artificial process separation in addressing these two closely linked issues.

As is the case with strategy and capital approvals, the CEO should not assume interdependencies in the control of business unit performance. Each business unit is tasked to meet its EP growth and revenue commitments based on the approved Gold strategy, and each should be treated independently for control purposes. Thus, using Diversa Corp as an example, if PopulAir is falling short on its commitments, perhaps causing the company overall to miss its performance goals for the year, this should have no impact on the CEO's demands of Big Dog, Wahoo, or any of the other business units. Even if the company misses its overall annual EP target, it will create more shareholder value by keeping the other business units on-strategy than it will by asking the other business units to deviate from their Gold strategies in order to make an annual corporate goal.

Another implication of this approach to controlling performance is that top-down, across-the-board initiatives to reduce costs, however well-intentioned, usually yield unintended consequences. In the case of Diversa Corp, for instance, what would a company-wide initiative to reduce costs by 5 percent mean? There would probably be a general presumption that this belt-tightening edict applies to all of the business units more or less equally, but as we have seen there are enormous differences between the units and their profitability positions. Shop Smart is clearly a well-managed unit participating in a tough market, and it may already be keeping its costs at exactly the level they need to be to execute its most profitable strategy—what purpose is served by imposing further cost reductions that would likely be offset by lost revenues? On the other hand, Wahoo, which is earning negative EP in a profitable product market, might need to reduce its costs by 20 percent (and probably make a lot of other changes as well) in order to become just an average competitor. So what does the top-down 5 percent cost reduction goal mean for Wahoo—is it permission to continue on at a somewhat improved, but still negative, level of EP? Rather than mandating cost cuts from the top down, it is usually better for the CEO to enforce the proper EP thresholds and targets for individual business units and let them determine, legally and ethically, how to meet their commitments.

The seamless integration of strategy formulation and control described here is, unfortunately, not typical corporate practice. At most companies the principal control mechanism is not the strategy formulation process but the annual budgeting or operating plan process, the Trojan horse of the institutional imperative. The annual budgeting/planning process embodies all of the attributes a CEO intent on maximizing EP would want to avoid: the imposition of top-down performance targets, a very short-term outlook, an absolute assumption of interdependencies across units and functions, a presumption of capital limits, an annual (batch) rather than an evergreen (continuous) process, projections with minimal linkage to market economics and competitive position, and numbers generally disconnected from any concept of Gold strategies.

But if there is no centrally driven annual budget production, how is a CEO supposed create a total company financial plan for the coming year? The company's overall financial plan—the big picture outlook—should be based on a point-in-time, bottom-up, rollup of the projected income statements and balance sheets for currently approved business unit and center strategies. These consolidated company numbers would be used primarily for communication and administrative planning, but not for profitability control, which occurs within the regular strategy reviews between the CEO and the business unit heads. There is nothing to be gained, and much to be lost, by superimposing an additional expensive, time-consuming, and often contentious top-down budgeting or annual planning process on top of a good bottom-up strategy formulation, approval, and funding process.

Does this mean there are no budgets? No, it means that budgets or annual plans should be the servants of strategy, not surrogates for strategy. Budgets have a perfectly legitimate and useful role in controlling expense and investment levels, *once investment levels and EP targets have already been decided by the approval of the Gold strategy.* At the business unit and center function levels, executives certainly need expense and investment growth plans encompassing the details of how they will meet their performance commitments. But there is no need for the CEO even to see, let alone review, these budgets or plans—they are at a level of detail far below what is necessary to monitor EP drivers and growth rates. And at the overall company level, at least for multibusiness companies, the very concept of a company "budget" or detailed annual plan is problematic. What would it mean, and what would the CEO use it for?

The one clear need for a consolidated company projection would be for financial planning. The amount of funding needed would be determined by the Gold strategies, but the sources and kinds of funding are decisions that need to be made at the center. Other center functions, like IT and human resources, might also need a consolidated forecast of the levels and kinds of new resources or capabilities they will need to add to support the business units in the coming years. These are all legitimate planning needs, but they are not strategic or control needs. As soon as an overall, or top-down, company plan or projection becomes a control mechanism, there is a great danger that some or all of the business units will actually be driven away from their Gold strategies.

Compensation

"Pay for performance" is considered a key objective of virtually every executive compensation plan. Although this is a laudable objective, it must also be recognized that creating a perfect pay for performance executive compensation process is not achievable. Crudely put, individuals want to be paid as much as possible regardless of performance, and shareholders want executive pay to be tied closely to the company's financial performance. At a philosophical level, these are seemingly irreconcilable goals, reflected to some extent in the difference between the impersonal nature of the capital markets and the more benign nature of the labor markets. No plan can be expected to fully bridge this divide.

At a pragmatic level, too, there are many obstacles to attaining perfect alignment between company and individual performance. No universal system of financial incentives or rewards is right for all people under all circumstances. Executives have widely different motivations and different perceptions of their true worth to the company. And linking individual responsibility for specific outcomes can be difficult: Outcomes, whether good or bad, may not be known until some time after an executive has changed roles. These and other factors will cause even the most sophisticated efforts to link executive pay and performance to fall short of the ideal.

This does not mean companies should completely abandon the idea of pay for performance, which is a powerful economic concept and one that appeals—at least in the abstract—to most people's sense of fairness. But it does suggest that executive compensation plans should not be overengineered to try to achieve greater linkage than it is realistic to expect. Sticking with a few design principles is more important than having a lot of complicated objectives or rules.

For senior executives, most notably business unit heads, whose primary responsibility is to deliver EP growth, pay for performance must be strongly aligned with that objective. How should CEOs create this alignment?

Most U.S. and many European public companies have executive pay plans that include four basic elements: an annual salary (typically 50 to 75 percent of annual compensation), an annual bonus payment for meeting specified performance targets (typically 30 to 100 percent of base salary), a "long-term incentive" payment often consisting of stock options or some other form of company equity, and perhaps participation in an overall profit-sharing plan as well. Companies that utilize this basic plan architecture need to consider what modifications might be necessary to give EP growth the appropriate weight in each element of the plan. Some guidelines for modifying the elements of a typical executive pay plan so as to conform with the principles of good strategic management would include the following:

Reinforce the Gold Strategies

For determining the annual bonus element, CEOs should use the same EP growth and revenue growth targets to assess individual executive's awards as are used to assess business unit performance. For example, meeting Gold strategy EP growth targets might be weighted as one half of the potential bonus, meeting Gold strategy revenue growth targets might be weighted as one quarter of the potential bonus (payable only if the EP targets are also met), and achieving other nonfinancial goals might be weighted as one quarter of the bonus award. In this way, the quality of Gold strategy formulation and execution becomes the primary factor that determines at least three quarters of the variable pay component for executives with accountability for EP and revenue growth.

For determining the long-term incentive element, economic profit growth should certainly be the primary and perhaps the only metric used to determine the amount of the payout, at least at the business unit level. If a business unit is not meeting or exceeding its multiyear EP growth objectives, the rationale for a variable payout over and above the annual bonuses all but evaporates. Perhaps the size of this award could also be influenced by a business unit's gain in EP share over time.

If there is a general company profit-sharing pool, "profit" should be redefined from earnings to economic profit. Paying out "profit sharing" when the shareholders have not, in fact, received a true profit is a significant source of misalignment between the interests of owners and management. Owners are entitled to earn at least the minimum required return on their capital before management can claim to have produced enough "profit" to share among themselves and other employees.

Do No Harm

This is the corollary of the first principle: do not induce or reward actions that can diminish or distract attention from economic profit growth. One common error is larding up business unit pay plans with multiple, often conflicting objectives. This widespread practice can create as many problems as it tries to solve.

An analogy might be when governments use the tax code to manipulate social and individual behavior: It is hugely inefficient and often unfair, it always yields unintended consequences, and after a time it loses credibility with many of the people it is supposed to motivate. For a company, even seemingly laudable top-down goals (i.e., reducing costs, gaining market share, improving customer satisfaction, building teams) can prove to be a major distraction from delivering on the Gold strategy performance commitments at the business-unit level. In basketball, for instance, players are not paid for how well they dribble, how well they pass, how coordinated they are, or the quality of their body art.

They are paid, ultimately, for their overall contribution to winning games. Similarly with business unit heads, where winning might be defined as consistently growing EP faster than the competition, trying to incentivize presumptive subelements of that objective through an annual bonus plan may actually reduce the odds of longer term success.

It should go without saying that bonus payments of any kind should be negated, regardless of EP and revenue growth performance, whenever actual harm to employees, customers, or the company itself results from an executive's actions or inactions. Meeting the company's health, safety, legal, or ethical standards should not be optional, and failure to do so should be costly to those accountable.

Keep the "A" Team

An effective compensation program will ensure that proven top performers are not lost because of insufficient financial reward for their work. That's how the Boston Red Sox lost Babe Ruth to the New York Yankees, a decision from which it arguably took Boston 80 years to recover. However compensation plans are constructed, total pay for the best performing executives will have to be high enough for them to stay with the team.

At the CEO level, existing compensation practices seem to satisfy almost no one except the CEOs themselves. In the U.S. in particular there are endless examples of CEOs receiving extraordinary compensation while their companies perform at mediocre or worse levels and shareholders suffer with poor returns. To say that this is a problem that defies a solution is an understatement. Few business topics over the past several decades have attracted more passionate attention in the form of academic studies, editorials, management conferences, testy shareholders' meetings, and even government intervention.

Despite what the severest critics might think, setting CEO pay is not in any way a straightforward exercise for the boards entrusted with that responsibility. As much as the directors might wish, they cannot ignore external market levels of pay, which inevitably set limits on what they can do. They might, however, reconsider some of the basic architecture of typical CEO pay so as to establish a much clearer link between pay and performance at this ethereal level. A proposal for how this might be accomplished is set out in Appendix V.

Following these general compensation principles for senior executives will not guarantee superior company or individual performance, nor will it guarantee that all participants will think that the outcomes are always fair and equitable.

But it will go some way toward offsetting the agency problem and help assure that the company's executive compensation practices are not simply sinecures or actual obstacles to the achievement of superior performance.

EXECUTIVE CAPABILITIES

There are a few general attributes that define a great executive, starting with the ability to lead and motivate teams of people to achieve challenging goals. Other essential attributes include personal integrity, fair-mindedness, decisiveness, and the ability to adapt to new or changed circumstances. Gauges of these critically important qualities are variously incorporated into the executive review, development, and promotion processes of most companies and will not be further elaborated here. The focus here will be on three additional attributes or capabilities necessary to drive superior EP and equity value growth.

The three specific attributes and capabilities the CEO and business unit heads would ideally share are a deep understanding of the economics of the business, the discipline to make the right participation choices, and the ability to create superior business models.

Deep Understanding of the Economics of the Business

It seems axiomatic that the head of a business unit would have a profound and detailed understanding of the underlying economics of the products, markets, and customers of the business as well as a good understanding of the profitability dynamics of the most important competitors. In smaller, more focused companies, many executives, particularly those who have "grown up with the business," do have at least a strong intuitive grasp of what drives their economic profits. But in large multibusiness companies, executives with this granular level of understanding are, in fact, a small minority.

The reasons for this pervasive lack of deep understanding are found more in the nature of large companies and their management practices than in any shortcomings of the individuals themselves. Among the most important of these reasons are the following:

- The business units are often large and complex entities, with possibly hundreds of products, thousands or millions of customers, hundreds or thousands of employees, hundreds of suppliers, and operating in many geographic markets. There is just a lot to know.

- The financial and strategic information available to the business unit head is, for reasons described earlier, woefully insufficient for gaining a quick and accurate understanding of how, where, and how much economic profit is being made and lost throughout the business unit. An executive who wants to have this information cannot normally access it from existing reports or processes.
- The career track for successful executives in large companies typically entails a series of two to four year assignments in different functions, regions, and business units, allowing enough time to become familiar with these entities but usually not enough time to gain the deep knowledge and experience necessary to formulate and execute the best strategies.

So an executive has a lot to know, limited access to high-quality information, and a relatively short tenure within which to learn and take action. Under these circumstances, it is impressive that so many executives manage to perform as well they do. But improvements can be made. Where possible, business unit boundaries should be drawn so as to minimize matrix management and allow for increased insight and accountability for performance. Measurement and reporting processes must be created to provide access to the high-quality information all executives need for good decision making. Finally, big companies should rethink the traditional executive career path. There will always be trade-offs between the need for breadth and depth of experience, but sometimes breadth can be overrated. Who would be the best choice for CEO: an executive who, over 25 years, has held a dozen positions throughout the company but never one long enough for the CEO and board to know how good a value creator he or she really is, or an executive who, over the same time period, has held only five or six positions but who has managed business units through good times and bad and has proven he or she can consistently deliver exceptional EP growth over extended periods of time?

The Discipline to Make the Right Participation Choices

Making good participation choices is inherently a radical activity, involving constant challenges and changes to the status quo: Products, markets, and customers that no longer add equity value must be continuously repositioned or restructured, and new ones with good potential to grow EP must be added. Because the process can be so disruptive, when tough participation choices are being made, the forces of the institutional imperative are likely to respond like the body's immune system does to a disease, sending out killer cells to find the foreign agent and to stop it if possible. For example, an executive radical enough to constantly push for exiting unprofitable product markets or to favor investment in a new technology that would cannibalize existing products is in danger of being labeled "not a team player"—the modern institutional equivalent of inviting the killer cells over to make a meal of one's career.

But making the right participation choices is an essential competency that the CEO should foster in all executives. Participation choices are often the biggest driver of EP and EP growth potential, so they must be at the heart of the creative construction process. And getting participation choices right requires even more than having excellent information and the analytical skills to evaluate options. It requires executives who are willing to act on the information and analysis, even in the face of enormous resistance from the organization.

This seemingly obvious point is made because so often, even with sufficient information, executives—including CEOs—do not act to change participation strategies when they should. General Electric, for instance, was in denial for decades about the need to radically restructure or divest NBC/ Universal, despite the generally dismal economics of the U.S. entertainment industry and GE's lack of any compensating competitive advantage.[2] Similarly, General Motors sustained a commitment to its Saturn division for over two decades during which the unit rarely if ever earned an economic profit. Only the terms of a government bailout ultimately forced GM to abandon Saturn. These are only two high profile examples from a list that would include many thousands of ongoing participation choices that, however attractive they might have seemed at one time, should have been remediated long ago by business unit leaders and CEOs.

It is relatively easy to see the errors companies make in failing to restructure capital efficiently. Much harder to know is the price paid when companies underinvest in potentially positive EP products, markets, and customers. One common reason for missing good investment opportunities is that they are viewed as too small or immaterial in relation to the size of the business unit or the company (i.e., not big enough to "move the needle"). But a company like 3M is an example of how enormous EP, $3.1 billion in 2007, can be generated by participation in a great many small products and markets.[3] Economic profit is earned at a small scale, one product at a time, one customer at a time. Participation opportunities that can add profitable new products, customers, or markets should not be overlooked based merely on size.

Another example of a tough participation choice is when to do nothing, like deciding not to participate in a new product area when competitors are jumping in with both feet. How many U.S. bank CEOs would like to take back their decision to actively pursue the subprime mortgage business between 2000 and 2007? Yet during that time period, the peer (and political) pressure for banks to enter or grow that business rapidly was enormous. Similarly, think of the financial carnage that would have been avoided if U.S. utility CEOs had not allowed their companies to be drawn into the smoke and mirrors game of futures trading as exemplified by Enron. The suggestion here is not that it is possible for executives to make error-free participation choices. It is that executives should not allow the momentum of the madding crowd to become a substitute for a thoughtful understanding of the underlying market economics and sources of competitive advantage that are the foundation of sustainable EP growth.

Making the right participation choices requires an executive, at least at times, to make unpopular calls, to buck the system, and to take business and personal risk. All of this requires a determination and discipline to do the right thing, but it should not require self-sacrifice in the form of becoming the target of institutional antibodies. The CEO must make it clear to the organization that making good participation choices, and correcting or avoiding bad ones, are among the highest priorities of the company and that efforts to achieve those ends will be rewarded, not penalized, at all levels.

The Ability to Create Superior Business Models

This is the rarest of business skills, the one capability more than any other that separates entrepreneurial icons like Henry Ford, Thomas Watson Sr., Walt Disney, Sam Walton, Steve Jobs, and Bill Gates from even the most highly regarded executives like Alfred Sloan, Walter Wriston, Andy Grove, Roberto Goizueta, Lou Gerstner, and Jack Welch. There are good reasons for this. For one thing, it is easier (though far from easy) to build a new business model from scratch, as entrepreneurs do, than to transform an existing poor or mediocre business model into a great one, as professional executives may have to do. Taking Wal-Mart from a start-up and building it into a great company was a spectacular achievement, but it would be harder still, and in some ways even more impressive, for any group of executives to transform the Sears/K-Mart of 2010 into a company rivaling Wal-Mart's success. Similarly, transforming an AMD into an Intel would, in some respects, be even more impressive than what Andy Grove and Gordon Moore achieved in building Intel in the first place.

So, in a corporate environment where few true entrepreneurs are to be found, how can a CEO elicit the creation of more good business models or business model improvements from individual executives? There is no obvious or easy answer. Certainly it would help, as part of the creative construction process, for the CEO to require executives to regularly reevaluate their business models and to initiate changes whenever EP growth falls behind the competition. This challenge would motivate executives to build strategy formulation skills they would never attain if they were being held to a less demanding objective. It might also help to extend the tenure of business unit heads to four to five years so they have time enough to assess the current business model, evaluate options, execute to completion, and live with the results of any major changes.

Evaluating an executive's potential to create superior business models should not be based simply on qualities such as intelligence, energy, or even leadership. At the end of the day the CEO will have to look to outputs, actual achievements, as the best indicator of whether an executive has the requisite skills. Perhaps the most realistic goal is to build a small cadre of executives who have proven their ability to move business units from average or below-average EP growth to above-average EP growth for a sustained period in their chosen product markets. These individuals have shown that somehow (it may not be possible to generalize exactly how) they can alter existing business models for the better. They should be recognized, rewarded, and put in positions where their unusual skills will benefit the company the most.

 ## CHAPTER SUMMARY

All companies face the task of overcoming the institutional imperative, a kind of regression toward the mean that arises from making safe choices and yielding mediocre performance. This bias toward preservation rather than performance is embedded in companies' governance practices, executive processes, and executive capabilities, actually limiting rather than enhancing the potential for profitable growth and value creation. Where this is the case, changing these practices, processes, and capabilities should be one of the CEO's highest priorities.

Among the CEO's organizational priorities are ensuring that the corporate center is a value-creating and not a value-consuming entity, that management reports contain the EP and EP drivers information necessary to formulate and execute Gold strategies, that the company's capital is invested only in Gold strategies, and that executives are challenged and rewarded for making good participation choices and creating good business models. The CEO's ultimate goal is to have a single effective process of creative construction throughout the company, where excellent information, rigorous examination of the facts and available options, and disciplined decision making are the foundation for a continuous collaboration between the CEO and a cadre of business unit and functional leaders who are proven value creators.

CHAPTER SEVEN

Making the Right Risk Management Choices

THE EARLY YEARS OF the twenty-first century have not been kind to the companies, particularly large financial institutions, that supposedly led the world with their intricate and sophisticated practices for managing risk. The carnage inflicted by the most destructive financial tsunami since 1929 is evidence enough that what passed for risk management before 2007 comprises a set of unreliable and dangerous practices we do not want to see continued. Nearly all of Wall Street's math PhDs, traders, bankers, hedge fund managers, private equity funds, credit rating agencies, and so-called asset managers, not to mention the world's major regulatory authorities, missed seeing or properly preparing for an event that triggered the crippling and, in some cases, even the collapse of many large and well-known companies. If all of these "experts" could not get it right, what are CEOs supposed to do to protect their companies from financial calamity?

In particular, what can CEOs do to avoid the implosion of the company's economic profits? To address this question, CEOs have to make important choices in three areas most likely to affect the resilience of the company's economic profits:

- *Portfolio choices*—deciding on the acceptable boundaries of market economics and competitive position for the business units

- *Balance sheet choices*—deciding on the optimal levels of cash, debt, and equity to support economic profit growth
- *Ethical choices*—deciding on the standards for information management and process integrity needed to sustain and protect economic profit growth

These choices, which encompass strategic, financial, and reputation risks, are the subject of this chapter. But they are not the only elements of risk of concern to the CEO; others include execution risks and systemic risks.

Execution risks are usually specific to particular business units and companies: For pharmaceutical companies, there are huge risks in the search for safe and effective new drugs; for technology companies, there are risks of missing an entire product cycle; for consumer products companies, there are risks of product tampering or contamination; for oil refining companies, there are enormous casualty and safety risks; and for banks, there are risks of mismanaging credit quality or interest rate spreads. Because execution risks are so company- and industry-specific, there is no general management framework that can be applied to them. These risks must be addressed in the context of a single industry or perhaps even a single company.

Systemic risks include political risk (e.g., expropriation), macroeconomic risk (e.g., recessions), capital market risk (e.g., credit freezes), and natural disasters (e.g., earthquakes) that can have a large negative impact on the economic profits of many companies or business units simultaneously—regionally, nationally, or globally. Predicting the magnitude, timing, nature, duration, and likelihood of these events is nearly impossible and therefore they are difficult to totally protect against. The best protection will come from making good portfolio and balance sheet choices, as will be elaborated later in this chapter.

CLARIFYING "RISK"

In statistical terms, risk is uncertainty, or a probability distribution of outcomes, whether those outcomes are good or bad. Virtually every business decision, from hiring a new employee, to running a new advertising campaign, to building a new factory, to entering a new market, involves some uncertainty, some range of probabilities or outcomes. Any of these decisions and the hundreds or thousands of others made every day in a large company can work out to be better than, worse than, or about as expected. Continuously taking all of these risks in a way that produces good economic profit growth over time is the essence of what successful companies do.

At the enterprise level, the CEO wants to ensure that the aggregated risks the company is taking are justified by the likelihood of earning higher economic profit in the future. It is not so much the absolute level of risk but the amount of risk relative to amount of economic reward that is of concern to a CEO. In financial terms, this can be described as making investment and divestment decisions that have an expected net present value greater than zero. If all probable outcomes of a decision have been properly taken into account (a big "if"), then a decision with an expected net present value greater than zero indicates the reward is worth the risk.

In common business usage, the term "risk" has come to be synonymous with bad outcomes only. For instance, bankers talk about the risk of loan default, not the risk of repayment, and pharmaceutical executives worry about the risk that a new compound will fail in clinical trials, not the risk that it will succeed. Understood in this way, there are many risks that could legitimately concern a CEO, such as the risk of insolvency, the risk of a damaged brand or company reputation, the risk of an unproductive research and development effort, and the risk of expropriation of the company's assets. Any one or more of these risks may be top of mind at a particular point in time, but sitting above all of these specific risk issues is a more general and, ultimately, a more important concern: *the resiliency of the company's economic profit stream over time.* Specifically, the CEO and board will want to protect against the major risks that the company's EP growth rate will stagnate or decline, because this is a sure sign of serious and potentially more damaging problems to come.

Risk management, like strategy, has its own set of myths that need to be set aside. Two in particular are myths about volatility and about the past as prologue.

Volatility alone is not the measure of business risk. A lot of earnings or EP volatility does not mean a business is necessarily risky, and a small degree of volatility does not mean a business is necessarily safe. This may be counterintuitive to many executives who mistakenly believe that the stock market rewards companies that have more predictable earnings with a higher P/E ratio. What CEOs should worry about is not so much the absolute volatility of EP but the volatility of EP in relation to its average or expected magnitude. For example, a business unit with an average ROE of 5 percent and low volatility is still a bigger threat to the company's future EP resilience than a business unit with an average ROE of 25 percent that varies by 5 to 10 percentage points in any one year—the latter will likely still be earning its cost of equity even in a poor year, while the former is a steady drain on economic profit and equity value even in a good year.

Management's predisposition for steady outcomes is embedded in the institutional imperative, which prizes predictability and low (downside) volatility. One reason for this is that executives strongly prefer predictability in their own compensation, which often is tied to meeting earnings targets—so absolute volatility for them personally *is* risky on a year-to-year basis. This is a serious disconnect between capital market and labor market perceptions of risk and can lead to naive and misplaced efforts to control volatility rather than enhance EP growth.

The past is not always prologue. For something as complex as the world of business, statistical risk models built using historical data have very limited predictive power. Virtually all of the forecasting models used by financial institutions, credit rating agencies, and government regulators before 2007—most of which relied on probabilities calculated from historical data—failed to predict anything like what happened to financial markets and companies in 2007 and 2008. A crystal ball would have done as well. This does not mean that companies should exclude quantitative analysis as part of their risk management efforts, but this analysis should not blind them to the possibilities that product-market economics can change rapidly and in unpredictable ways, that a new competitor's business model can quickly overwhelm older entrenched models, or that rare external events ("Black Swans"[1]) can alter the economics of the business dramatically over a short time period. Eternal vigilance and common sense can be more important in managing risk than over-reliance on esoteric number crunching.

 SETTING RISK THRESHOLDS

There are two bad economic profit growth outcomes the CEO should focus on, starting at the business unit level. The first and worst is when EP falls to or below zero. The second is when EP is still positive but its growth rate has slowed significantly or even turned downward.

The Risk That EP Will Fall Below Zero

Some risk management methodologies focus on threshold events like earnings falling below zero or the equity value of the firm falling to or close to zero. These are certainly outcomes to be avoided, but for pragmatic managerial purposes, these threshold levels are much too low. By the time earnings have fallen below zero or the value of the company or business unit has fallen to or near zero, it may be too late to reverse the damage. The company or business unit is already under water and must struggle merely to survive.

The minimum risk threshold CEOs should set for every business unit is an economic profit of zero. If EP falls to zero, at least the business unit is still earning its cost of capital and usually has time to take steps to correct its problems and resume its course of higher EP growth in the future. Further, this threshold is exactly the same as the minimum financial threshold for making strategic decisions. Having both strategic decisions and risk management decisions based on the same minimum standard reinforces the message that falling below an EP of zero requires urgent remedial action, whether that means fixing execution problems, refining or changing the strategy, or possibly even changing business unit leadership.

Estimating the mathematical probability that a business unit or company will experience negative economic profits over a future time period is a dark art for which common sense is often a better substitute. Two initial observations are useful when trying to assess the rough probabilities that a business will fall below the minimum EP threshold over the short or intermediate term:

- For businesses that participate in very negative EP product markets, like airlines and paper manufacturing, operating below the zero-EP threshold almost all of the time is the norm. There is very little uncertainty to be managed in these businesses. In terms of their expected returns on equity and their ability to self-finance, there are only two outcomes—bad and worse. Not only will a majority of these businesses fail to create shareholder value, but there is no balance sheet strong enough to protect most of them from eventual takeover, restructuring, or insolvency.
- For businesses participating in profitable product markets, the best protection against deteriorating EP growth is to have an advantaged competitive position. Generally, the greater the competitive advantage a business has, the more resilient its EP will be. As one example, ExxonMobil has achieved a level of competitive advantage that translates into an ROE that is consistently 5 to 10 percentage points higher than its nearest large rivals, meaning that in the inevitable event of cyclical profitability declines, ExxonMobil's economic profit should remain well above zero even if the EPs of its largest rivals do not.

The Risk That EP Growth Will Stagnate or Decline

When a company with a profitable history experiences flat or declining economic profit over a period of years (after allowing for the effects of industry cycles), it is usually a sign of serious underlying issues that should be addressed well before EP actually falls to zero. Key market economics may have changed, old business models may no longer be advantaged, the company may be trying to buy earnings growth, strategy execution may be getting sloppy, or there may be too little restructuring of underperforming assets. Often it is a combination of these factors that must be addressed in a clear-eyed and firm way by the CEO. Left unchecked, they can put the company into a long period of stagnation or even failure.

As we saw earlier with the example of the General Electric Company, years of stagnating EP were sending a signal of underlying weakness in the business unit strategies. Once the systemic shock of frozen credit markets hit in late 2007, even this titan of American industry and finance was so weakened that it became dependent on taxpayer bailouts to keep it solvent. In effect, the General Electric Company has become basically a quasi-state entity, with the credibility of its balance sheet and much of its revenue dependent directly or indirectly on government largess. The CEO now seems less like the leader of an exemplary commercial enterprise and more like a potentate from a small nation, schmoozing with world leaders, going from government to government asking for handouts or seeking special treatment for GE's products and services.

Assuming this scenario is not the aspiration of most CEOs, they will want to set the minimum risk thresholds for their business units well above an EP of zero. Signs that EP growth is falling below the target expectations of the Gold strategies should always be a stimulus for action, not just to address immediate profitability issues but also to reduce the risk that a longer-term trend in EP decline may be underway. When a business unit is unable to meet its EP growth targets, whether because of deteriorating market economics or a weakening competitive position, the sooner action is taken, the more secure the long-term EP growth of the business will be. Through the process of creative construction and its related control elements, the CEO will want to use the business units' and company's EP growth commitments as the hair trigger for initiating corrective action long before outcomes that may be simply disappointing in the short term become enterprise threatening in the long term.

PORTFOLIO CHOICES

The elements of making the right participation and positioning choices have been addressed in the context of *strategic* decision making, but how do these choices affect risk management? The answer is that the criteria for maximizing

EP growth over time and the criteria for making the right portfolio risk-reward trade-offs are, or should be, exactly the same. At the company level, the more capital a company has invested in business units with advantaged positions operating in product markets with favorable economics, the lower the odds of an overall EP implosion. Conversely, the more capital a company has invested in business units serving unprofitable product markets without a compensating competitive advantage, the higher the odds are the company will experience stagnating, declining, or even negative EP.

The challenge for the CEO is to define the strategic boundaries within which business units must fall to meet their risk threshold requirements. Exhibit 7.1 illustrates this using the ME/CP Profitability Matrix.

The Green Zone contains business units, like High Octane and Shop Smart, that enjoy high and (usually) growing economic profits. In addition, because of their advantaged competitive positions, their economic profits are

EXHIBIT 7.1 Portfolio Choices

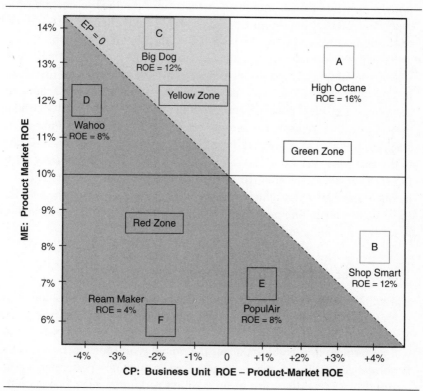

likely to be more resilient than those of most of their competitors. This creates a virtuous circle, in which the business units that consistently create the highest average EP and equity value growth often expose the company to the lowest risk of poor EP performance. This may seem like a paradox, because higher rewards are normally associated with higher, not lower, risk. But in the case of business strategy, the factors that drive higher rewards—good market economics and a highly advantaged competitive position—also lower the odds of EP declining rapidly or falling below zero. Therefore, the Green Zone truly is the risk-reward sweet spot for portfolio choices[2] (for an important qualification, please see endnote).

The Yellow Zone contains businesses that are profitable but competitively disadvantaged; they rely entirely on market economics to keep their economic profits positive. The Big Dog unit is an example of this type of business. The danger here, of course, is that EP could easily slip into negative territory with even a modest worsening of market economics or competitive position. For both strategic and risk management reasons, businesses in the Yellow Zone usually need immediate attention to their business models and execution capabilities so that improvements can be made while the businesses are still relatively healthy and have the potential to improve their position.

The Red Zone holds the negative economic profit businesses that already violate the minimum strategic investment and risk management thresholds. In this zone, risk increases as rewards decline. Whether their negative EPs are mainly a result of poor market economics or a weak competitive position, these businesses represent a serious threat to the company's longer-term viability. In an ideal company, there would be no established business units in the Red Zone (start-ups and some acquisitions could be temporary exceptions). The process of creative construction should drive constant adjustments to strategy and capital restructuring in order to minimize the odds that these value-consuming and highly risky businesses would never be allowed to evolve or remain in the portfolio.

The Impact of Portfolio Diversification

Many CEOs believe that having a more diversified portfolio of businesses will reduce the odds that the company will suffer a catastrophic financial event. The general concept is that in years when some units perform badly others will perform well, thereby reducing the volatility of the company's overall performance. Thus, in the aggregate, the company's performance (unfortunately, CEOs usually just mean earnings performance) will be smoothed and the odds of seriously bad outcomes will be reduced. But is this belief true? In some specific circumstances it may be true, but for the vast majority of companies it is not true. And, as far as equity investors' perceptions of risk are concerned, the argument that company diversification translates to higher value is unconvincing.

The one circumstance where having multiple business units in the portfolio can lower the odds that the company's EP will decline or go negative is if all of its business units are in the Green Zone and if their economic profit streams are somewhat uncorrelated. In this case, the company's EP resilience will be very high and its EP volatility, relative to competitors at least, very low. Here again we see the virtuous circle: The strategic choices that maximize EP growth are also the choices most likely to minimize enterprise risk over time.

In the more typical circumstance, companies have portfolios of businesses falling into all three risk zones. In these cases, higher diversification and risk reduction do not go together. In fact, the best way for companies in this more common situation to reduce risk is to *reduce* diversification by restructuring the business units in the Red Zone and possibly even some in the Yellow Zone. The result of this restructuring would be to increase the company's EP growth potential and its future EP resilience simultaneously, even though it may have fewer or smaller business units and a less diversified portfolio (though unlikely, it is even possible that the company's EP volatility could increase after restructuring the Red Zone units, but this volatility should be more than offset by the increase in average future EP).

A commonly cited benefit of acquisitions is that they can help diversify a company's portfolio of businesses and thereby reduce earnings volatility and risk. But unless the acquired business is in the Green Zone *and* the acquisition price is at or below the seller's intrinsic value (think of this as the Warren Buffett test), it is likely that the acquiring company will experience higher, not lower, risk of EP weakness in the future. Acquiring businesses that fall in the Yellow or Red Zones, particularly when control premiums are paid, only adds to the future risk of EP shortfalls for the acquiring company.

But doesn't the smoothing effect of portfolio diversification translate into higher stock prices? There seems to be little evidence that it does.[3] Equity investors can create portfolios of stocks to suit their own risk-reward preferences, mixing and matching businesses in different industries, in different geographic markets, with different competitive positions. So to the degree investors see benefits from diversification, they can usually achieve those benefits for themselves. They have no reason to award a higher valuation to a company simply for having a diversified portfolio of business units. There is even some evidence of the opposite effect, that highly diversified companies have stock prices below what might be expected on a comparable P/E basis—the so-called conglomerate discount effect.[4] Whether this effect is real and what explains it are still debatable, but there is certainly no evidence to support the opposite view of some CEOs that diversification can result in a "conglomerate premium."

There can be one financial benefit to companies that have diversified portfolios of at least reasonably good businesses, and that is a lower cost of debt. This can arise because each business unit is, in effect, guaranteeing the debt of every other business unit, which lowers the overall credit risk of the company. But while this benefit is real, for nonfinancial companies the actual EP impact from a lower interest rate alone is usually modest. If this diversification benefit is to be exploited, it will come in the form of increased borrowing, the merits of which will be addressed in the following section.

 ## BALANCE SHEET CHOICES

After portfolio choices, a company's balance sheet is the second, and by far the lesser, bulwark against economic profit meltdown. It is possible to expect too much of this second line of defense, as the near collapse of even some seemingly well-capitalized companies, like GE and AIG, has shown in recent years. Poor strategic choices will overwhelm even the strongest of balance sheets, sometimes with amazing speed. Still, when combined with sound portfolio management, the balance sheet can increase the resilience of EP in some important ways.

For nonfinancial companies, the two major balance sheet choices impacting economic profit are how much excess cash to carry (liquidity) and how to manage the capital structure, or mix of debt and equity (leverage), of the company. If the risk of insolvency was the CEO's only concern, then the more cash and the more equity on the balance sheet, the better. But balance sheet choices are complicated by the fact that using more cash and more equity, while perhaps lowering the risk of insolvency, will—at least for normally profitable companies—also lower EP. Conversely, using less cash and less equity (i.e., more debt) will normally increase EP. This trade-off between profitability and risk is the chief dilemma of managing the balance sheet: There is no known "optimum" combination of excess cash and equity financing. At the end of the day, these trade-offs are matters for the considered judgment of the CEO, the CFO, and the board.

Excess Cash

As used here, excess cash consists of the immediately available cash and cash equivalents (primarily short-term government notes) on the balance sheet that exceed the ordinary cash operating needs of the company. At a minimum, these would be the "last ditch" or "rainy day" funds available in the event that the company's normal sources of short-term funding—bank lines, commercial paper, supplier credit—were to dry up for a period of time. In this sense, excess cash is a form of self-insurance against temporary illiquidity.

For public companies with normal access to the capital markets, a reasonable case can be made that they should carry little or no excess cash. The main argument for this position is that (1) excess cash usually earns a return less than the cost of capital (i.e., the company's borrowing costs exceed the government's borrowing costs) and is therefore not a good investment for shareholders and (2) the extreme circumstances under which the excess cash would be needed, however infrequent, are likely to be so dire that the amount of cash required to see the company through unscathed could exceed the rainy day fund by orders of magnitude. The argument, in effect, is that carrying excess cash has a high opportunity cost for shareholders and is unlikely to provide enough protection in the situations where it is really needed.

But what worries CEOs and CFOs may not be these extreme cases of illiquidity in the markets so much as somewhat less extreme but more common adverse events such as industry down cycles, raw material price spikes, or economic recessions. In these events, customer demand may fall, margins may be squeezed, or credit availability may be somewhat reduced for a time. Does carrying excess cash provide cost-effective protection in these situations? It may for some; indeed, for companies in cyclical industries, like commodities and autos, there may be enough predictability to the general frequency, duration, and size of these periodic events that higher cash balances might really fall within the "ordinary operating needs" of the company.

Many factors would affect a decision on the amount of cash to hold to help see a company through these normal swings in profitability and internal cash generation, including the range of expected profitability levels, the mix of fixed and variable costs, the minimum required levels of reinvestment and maintenance, the degree of flexibility in existing credit facilities, the relative financial strengths of competitors, and the degree of customer power. For companies in the Green Zone of Exhibit 7.1, the amount of excess cash required to manage through most normal cycles is likely to be low or zero because they are very profitable and tend to be largely self-financing. Also, they are the last companies that would lose access to the capital markets. At the other extreme, the Red Zone companies would tend to need large amounts of excess cash to handle industry or macroeconomic cycles because they have such low profitability and do not to have good access to the capital markets when credit is tight. The irony, of course, is that the companies that actually do carry a lot of excess cash—because they can—are often Green Zone companies that don't need the extra protection. And the Red Zone companies that suffer most in tough times, like airlines, cannot always accumulate the cash cushion they would like to have.

In addition to the opportunity cost to shareholders, high levels of excess cash can pose another potential problem for the CEOs of nonfinancial companies—loss of financial discipline. As one example, large cash balances can create a desire by some executives for the treasury function to become a profit center, seeking "excess returns" from investing in securities carrying greater risk and return than more pedestrian government notes. Although almost all public companies protect against this temptation by placing strict limits on the types of investments in which their cash balances can be invested, there can be expensive lapses as Bristol-Myers learned when it took a $270 million write-down on auction rate securities in 2007. Managing excess cash as a profit center is not what shareholders are paying the management of nonfinancial companies to do. It usually increases rather than reduces enterprise risk and is not a reliable source of long-term EP growth for nonfinancial companies.

Another argument in favor of carrying excess cash is that it is a potent competitive weapon. It signals to the competition that the cash-rich company has the war chest to seize any opportunity, to launch a devastating competitive attack at any time, or to withstand any competitive assault, whether it be in the form of a price war, increased spending on technology and innovation, or adding new production facilities. This argument is not strictly about risk management but about positioning strategy—the use of excess cash as a fundamental element of competitive advantage. This argument may have merit in limited circumstances. For instance, this is a possible rationale for the very large cash positions that companies like Microsoft and Intel, both known as fierce competitors, have historically carried. On the other hand, as both of these companies have also shown, the mere existence of such huge cash hoards may feed the temptation to make acquisitions, the majority of which have not had a noticeable economic benefit.[5] Even though many acquisitions are paid for using company stock rather than cash, the mere existence of these enormous war chests can stimulate the desire to venture with other people's capital.

Overall, it is difficult to make a general case for nonfinancial companies that the benefits of carrying excess cash will exceed the opportunity cost to shareholders of having their money tied up in relatively nonproductive uses. And for those tempted to try their hand at hedge fund management or who see the funds as a honey pot for making unprofitable acquisitions, carrying excess cash can dampen long-term EP growth even more.

Capital Structure

For companies outside of financial services, capital is defined here as total assets minus non–interest bearing liabilities, meaning it is the portion of the balance sheet comprising the interest-bearing debt and equity obligations of the company.[6] The key questions for the CEO and CFO are, for a given set of portfolio choices, how will capital structure decisions impact (1) the size, (2) the growth rate, and (3) the variability of economic profit over time? There are general answers and company-specific answers to these questions.

Capital Structure Impact on Economic Profit: General Choices

The general answer to the first question, how will capital structure decisions impact the size of economic profit, is that increasing the amount of debt relative to equity will normally increase the (ROE – COE) spread the company earns, and therefore economic profit will increase as debt replaces equity. A simple example of this effect is shown in Exhibit 7.2: For a company growing even at a modest 4 percent per year, this increased economic profit of $50 million would translate to an increase in its equity value of around $834 million—certainly a significant impact from changing capital structure alone.

For U.S. companies, the positive economic profit and equity value effect from substituting debt for equity arises solely because of the way corporate tax laws are written. As long as interest payments are treated as tax deductible to the company but dividends are not, this leverage effect will play a material role in how capital structure decisions get made. Even if company executives choose to ignore the tax effect and maintain low leverage, private equity and hedge fund managers may put pressure on management to increase debt levels—or perhaps even try to take the company over and do it themselves. This underexploited tax benefit was one of the factors that triggered the leveraged buyout movement in the United States in the 1980s, and it has continued to fuel the growth of private equity investing for decades.

Answering the second question, what is the impact of capital structure decisions on the sustainable growth rate of EP, is more complicated and will depend on the particular circumstances of each company. In the Exhibit 7.2

EXHIBIT 7.2 Impact of Capital Structure on EP

	No Debt Case	$1 Billion Debt Case
Debt	$ 0 B	$ 1.000 B
Equity[a]	$ 5.000 B	$ 4.000 B
Total Capital	$ 5.000 B	$ 5.000 B
Earnings[b]	$ 1.000 B	$ 0.950 B
ROE[c]	20%	23.75%
COE[d]	10%	10%
Economic Profit[e]	$ 0.500 B	$ 0.550 B
		$13.167 B[f]
		+$ 1.000 B[a]
Equity Value	$13.333 B	$14.167 B

Notes:

[a]$1 billion of equity replaced by $1 billion of debt, with replaced equity returned to shareholders.

[b]Assumes interest rate of 7.5% on $1 billion of debt and a tax rate of 33%: after-tax interest = $50 million.

[c]ROE = Earnings/Equity.

[d]Cost of equity (COE) = 10% in both cases. This is before consideration of the increase in COE that comes from increasing leverage (lowering interest coverage). In this case, with interest coverage = 20x, the effect on COE would be quite small. However, as interest coverage ratios decline, the effect on COE would become correspondingly higher and more meaningful.

[e]Economic Profit = Equity (ROE − COE).

[f]Equity Value calculation assumes constant EP growth of 4% in both cases.

example, the decision to increase leverage is implicitly assumed not to affect the choice of the best strategy for the business: Its Gold strategy is expected to generate 4 percent economic profit growth under either capital structure scenario. Put another way, the capital structure choice does not impact the choice of which assets to hold on the left-hand side of the balance sheet: Participation and positioning choices remain the unchanged. Therefore, the equity value impact of changing capital structure is a one-time event and future EP growth will be unaffected.

However, if changing capital structure would, in and of itself, also cause a business unit or company to change its choice of Gold strategies, then, of course, longer-term economic profit growth would be affected—in these circumstances, capital structure is actually an essential part of the business model. As will be noted in a following section, in some industries the use of some debt may be necessary just for a company to be able to earn its cost of capital: Competitors in these industries could not execute a Gold strategy using equity financing only.

As to the third question, what is the impact of increasing leverage on economic profit resiliency, the answer is that it depends. If a company's operating income and interest payments are largely uncorrelated then adding debt will put EP increasingly at risk as debt increases and interest coverage falls. As a rule of thumb, if average interest coverage (operating income/interest expense) falls below a multiple of five or six times, a nonfinancial company may be entering into the serious caution zone. If operating income and interest payments are highly correlated (as would be the case with most banks, for instance), then debt levels can become quite high before additional EP variability becomes a serious threat. As recent events have proven, however, even banks can get it wrong.

Capital Structure Impact on Economic Profit: Company-Specific Choices

The fundamental capital structure challenge for the CEO and CFO is how to balance the profitability benefits of using more debt with the higher risks that come with that choice. There is no scientific solution to striking this balance—it is ultimately a question of informed judgment.

Making that judgment can be thought of as making a series of four choices: how much debt is needed to meet the company's normal operating requirements; how much debt is needed (on occasion) for bridge financing; how much debt is mandated by industry specific conditions; and, on top of the debt levels required by the first three considerations, what additional discretionary debt, if any, should the company carry?

Operating Debt. Operating debt requirements are the periodic borrowings necessary to bridge short-term mismatches between cash inflows and cash outflows, most typically the timing differences between the outflows to pay for the labor and materials that precede the receipt of payments for products sold. For most companies this borrowing is short term and self-liquidating and is covered by bank lines of credit and supplier credit. It is not normally a source of significant risk to future economic profits.

Bridge Financing. Bridge financing is the occasional short-term borrowing needed to make an acquisition or a particularly large capital outlay. By definition, bridge financing is not part of the company's normal, or targeted, capital structure, and it is usually repaid within a year or two through increased retained earnings or the issuance of new equity or long-term debt. However, because it can cause a significant short-term spike in debt levels and is subject to some refinancing risk, the decision of whether and how much bridge financing to use is an important one. If the newly acquired assets prove to be less profitable than had been expected or if the future refinancing options are fewer or more costly than expected, then bridge financing can sometimes add considerably more risk to EP than was initially assumed. The commercial real estate industry experiences this problem with some regularity.

Industry-Specific Debt Requirements. Some industries have evolved such that most competitors carry permanently high levels of debt (and relatively low interest coverage) as a matter of course: real estate developers, construction companies, commercial banks, and airlines are examples. One big driver of these permanently high debt levels is that the average company in these industries could not expect to earn its cost of equity and a positive EP unless it matched its competitors' debt levels. Carrying high levels of debt, often secured by the underlying assets, is an attempt by these companies to minimize the dollar cost of equity in order to squeeze out a positive economic profit.

As long as a company in this type of industry is pursuing a business model similar to those of its competitors, it will have a hard time escaping the need to also match their debt to equity capital structure. In industries with high financial leverage that are usually economically profitable, like retail banking, it should be possible for a participant with competent management to earn positive economic profits even if it follows a conventional business model. But in industries with low or negative economic profits and high debt, there is no long-term financial engineering solution to avoiding periodic EP implosions. The only long-term solution for these businesses, if there is one, is to raise profitability and lower leverage by adopting a radically different business model from the competition, as Nucor, which carries much lower average levels of debt than its competitors, was able to do in the U.S. steel industry.[7]

Discretionary Debt. Once a company determines its appropriate average operating debt, bridge financing, and industry specific debt requirements, it can model its economic profit growth and variability to determine whether any additional debt would offer a positive risk-reward trade-off. For companies already in the Red Zone from Exhibit 7.1, the answer is emphatically *no*—these companies are already at high risk of periodic default or restructuring and there can be no long-term EP benefit from adding even more debt to their capital structure.

For companies in the Yellow Zone, the picture is more complicated. If they happen to compete in industries with permanently high debt, adding more debt would not be wise because they are already at a competitive disadvantage and therefore more vulnerable to experiencing financial distress if industry economics should deteriorate. But even if competitors' debt levels are not high, these Yellow Zone businesses may already suffer from a false sense of security because they earn positive economic profits based solely on a favorable industry structure, not because they are advantaged players. To add to that false sense of security by using additional discretionary debt to further increase their ROEs would not ordinarily be wise. However, there is a dilemma here because Yellow Zone companies with low debt levels may be attractive takeover targets, especially for private equity firms. The mere existence of this threat should be a strong incentive for Yellow Zone companies to rethink their strategies and address their disadvantaged business models rather than relying on financial engineering to boost their returns or protect them from takeover.

Finally, there are the Green Zone companies. These are the companies for which the question of trading the risk of higher debt levels for higher returns is most relevant. On the one hand, even without the use of debt their ROEs are typically well above the cost of equity so, unlike Red Zone companies, they do not need to use any debt to be economically profitable. Further, these companies are mostly able to finance their Gold strategies without recourse to other than normal operating debt and an occasional bridge financing, so permanent debt financing is not usually needed to maximize EP growth. On the other hand, as was shown in Exhibit 7.2, even a modest amount of discretionary debt can, for a reliably profitable company, increase EP and equity value a significant amount while still maintaining the safety of more than adequate interest coverage. Although it would be hard to fault the CEO of a Green Zone company for choosing not to use any discretionary debt, a good case can be made for using at least some discretionary long-term debt, perhaps maintaining the equivalent of a minimum AA or A+ credit rating, to strike a good balance between risk and reward. The freed-up equity would flow back to the shareholders in the form of higher dividends or share repurchases over time.

Once a company has set its general capital structure policy, thereby establishing its target interest coverage and the approximate mix of debt and equity financing it seeks to maintain, it still has decisions to make regarding the management of its equity. With respect to EP growth, if Gold strategy choices require investment of more new equity than can be immediately funded through retained earnings, then the company should certainly go to the capital markets and issue new shares to fund value-creating growth. In the more usual case where mature companies earn enough to fund their Gold strategies internally, any "excess" equity can be managed in one of three ways: increasing cash, paying dividends, or repurchasing shares.

As noted earlier, holding cash beyond what is needed for operating requirements is not a profitable investment for shareholders, so building a cash hoard is usually not the best use of excess equity. The remaining choices, whether to return cash to shareholders through dividends or share repurchases, do not impact Gold strategies or future EP growth one way or the other. The excess equity should certainly be returned rather than held in the company for no value creating purpose, but by which means it is returned is not an important risk management or strategic consideration. There may, however, be financial considerations impacting the choice. If management feels investors are undervaluing the company's Gold strategies, then repurchasing shares may result in improved returns for the shareholders who retain rather than sell their shares. Conversely, if management feels the market is overvaluing the company, paying out more in dividends would be the better choice.

ETHICAL CHOICES

Maximizing economic profits over time demands that companies conduct themselves in a highly ethical manner. This is not only a moral imperative but an economic one. A strategy that relies on deceiving customers, endangering employees, mistreating suppliers, flaunting the law, or misleading investors cannot be a Gold strategy because, as a result of the company's or business unit's own bad behavior, its economic profits are much more likely to implode at some point. Regrettably, in recent years there have been far too many examples of ethical failures that have severely damaged or even destroyed major U.S. corporations, among them Fannie Mae and Freddy Mac, Worldcom, Enron, Tyco, Arthur Anderson, Adelphia Communications, and Bank of America. Making the right strategic management choices should never cross the line, as the CEOs and other executives of these companies did, into decisions that contain the seeds of their own destruction.

The broad sweep of ethical issues a CEO may have to address is not in the scope of this book. However, certain information and process issues will be highlighted briefly because they exist at every company and go to the heart of management integrity: They are the quality and transparency of economic profit information, the quality and rigor of the creative construction process, and the accuracy and positioning of externally communicated information. Deficiencies in any of these areas can be symptoms or causes of deeper ethical challenges that could limit or threaten economic profit growth.

The Ethics of Economic Profit Information

The need for the CEO and other executives to have excellent and detailed economic profit information in order to make the right strategic management choices, including risk management choices, is seemingly self-evident. Yet few companies capture, report, or analyze this kind of information well. It remains one of the most shocking and inexcusable deficiencies of modern business practices that in a world with GPS, digital maps, and radar, CEOs are often navigating with the informational equivalents of a sextant and the sun—exposing the company to enormous and unnecessary risks of missing EP growth opportunities, of investing in EP consuming strategies, or of suffering outright EP implosions.

How can this be?

One answer might be that it is hard. For reasons noted earlier, capturing, maintaining, reporting, and analyzing good economic profit information at a granular level is a huge task, it is challenging to do well, and no one group within the company has the clear responsibility to produce it. Further, the institution imperative often causes people to hoard information, so a CEO trying to make strategic decisions may never see the true economics of a business unit—even if the data actually reside somewhere in the organization. But the fact that producing and reporting detailed economic profit information can be difficult is an insufficient excuse for not having it. No one would accept such an excuse for a lack of product or employee safety information, for example, so a failure to produce information so critical to wealth creation—the company's very reason for existence—should never be tolerated by the CEO.

Tolerance of poor information indicates that management is not, in a sense, being entirely honest with itself. If economic profit information is unavailable, it means the CEO does not really insist on having it. Whether the excuse is that the data are too hard to get, or that sharing it violates some tribal sense of ownership, or that executives simply don't know what to ask for (i.e., they are still in the operating income growth and earnings per share mind-sets), making decisions without solid economic profit information reflects a lapse of duty not only to investors but ultimately to all stakeholders who benefit from the process of wealth creation.

Failure to capture, report, and use good economic profit information, including external information on competitors and markets, is not unethical in the sense of being a deliberate bad act, but perhaps in the sense of not really doing what is in the best interest of the company. It is an error of omission, not commission, and any CEO determined to do so can fix it.

The Ethics of the Creative Construction Process

Protecting against declining or imploding economic profit requires complete honesty among executives, especially when big strategic management issues are being reviewed or decided. Otherwise, the best information, the best insights, and the best options may never surface in the creative construction process. To achieve this level of candor, at least two norms must be in place: There can be no avoiding action on "bad" news, and tribal agendas must be checked at the door.

No Avoiding Action on Bad News

Bad news comes in many forms, from product safety problems, to the loss of a major customer, to a competitor's roll out of a clearly superior offer. Responding to these acute threats to economic profit is often nondiscretionary: Management knows it must do something to address them, usually quickly. The fact that the news is often public and may have adverse consequences for the company's reputation adds to the sense of urgency.

There is a different kind of bad news, usually of a more chronic nature, that many executives find harder to deal with objectively and expeditiously; that is the bad news of underperforming people and underperforming capital. Chronic poor performance, which can be more threatening by orders of magnitude to the resiliency of long-term economic profits than its acute cousins, is considered more of a "family" matter and, like many family matters, can be swept under the rug for months, years, or even decades. Its adverse impact is insidious and quietly cumulative, and taking direct action is to a degree discretionary, more a matter of executive will than of obvious urgency.

Dealing with chronic bad performance news poses some complicated ethical issues for management. Inevitably, it requires making painful decisions, which may include shrinking or eliminating participation in some product lines, markets, customer segments, and activities, or even changing leadership or reducing headcount. No one enjoys making these decisions, which have real consequences for customers, suppliers, and employees, as well as local communities. Thus, the capacity for denial of the scale and chronic nature of these problems is almost limitless. Many executives, understandably, try to avoid making the hard choices and hope the problems will go away. But, of course, they won't.

This means the CEO and the rest of the management team have to be prepared to deal objectively and often with this kind of "bad" news, ideally while the problems are still small and manageable. This is the essential purpose of the compliance dimension of the creative construction process. The CEO will set the tone for the candor and speed with which decisions are made about underperforming people and capital. If the CEO is inclined not to want to hear bad news, then these problems will be buried by other executives and emerge only when they become too large to be ignored. By then, the consequences of delay, such as a massive restructuring, the loss of an investment grade bond rating, or even the change of CEOs, will likely be very unpleasant and very public.

The ethical issues that can accompany the resolution of chronic performance problems do no got away or become smaller with time. They must be dealt with no matter when decisions are made. It is far better for employees, suppliers, customers, and shareholders if decisive action is taken on this kind of bad news quietly, professionally, and every day rather than periodically in the massive, infamous upheavals that will otherwise surely occur.

Checking Tribal Agendas at the Door

Business unit heads are corporate executives. They have an affirmative responsibility to help the CEO ensure that all of the company's resources are employed to maximize the growth of economic profit. But they are also the leaders of their own business unit "tribes." The tribes expect their chiefs to protect them from tiresome interference from the center while simultaneously fighting for ample corporate resources to be earmarked for the unit so that it will be able to grow regardless of its performance. Reconciling these conflicting objectives can present the head of a business unit with some serious dilemmas.

Apart from the normal tensions between units and the center, two related factors exacerbate the conflicting allegiances a business unit head might feel. One is the damaging presumption that the business units are in competition with one another for resources, and the second is a failure to enforce the Gold strategy standard.

As long as business units believe they are competing with one another for a limited amount of capital, with the CEO acting as the dispenser of that capital, tribal tensions will be high, among the units themselves and between the units and the center. Because most companies, consciously or not, do treat capital as a scarce resource for which the units must compete, it is not surprising that business unit heads sometimes sit in strategy and budget meetings eying each other like hyenas circling a fresh kill. No one wants to be left at the edges of the meal looking for scraps.

Exhorting the business unit heads to be good corporate team players will not resolve this conflict. The only permanent solution is for the CEO to treat every business unit as a largely independent strategic entity and to fund it separately from the other units. When this degree of independence is established each business unit can feel confident that its objectives, strategies, and resources are not being impacted by choices being made about other, unrelated, units in the portfolio. Circumstances at other business units are no longer relevant and pose no threat to being properly funded. This also frees business unit heads to be more effective contributors to the creative construction process—as they come to believe it is not an adversarial process, they can be more forthcoming with information and more open to direction from the CEO.

A second problem tribal agendas sometimes pose is their antagonism to the Gold strategy standard. As noted previously, pursuing Gold strategies often requires painful decisions, possibly with important adverse consequences for some members of the business unit tribe. Faced with these competing objectives, maximizing value or protecting the tribe from unpleasant changes and upheaval, business unit leaders frequently try to find a middle way that ultimately accomplishes neither objective. The best antidote to this problem is to have very high quality and transparency of information so that the tough decisions cannot be buried or avoided for long. A business unit leader should not expect to be able to go into a creative construction review meeting and have any material performance issues escape the notice of the CEO, so attempting to soften or hide these issues would be a waste of time and a career-limiting act. It would also be unethical.

The Ethics of External Communications

The way in which a company communicates with the outside world tells a great deal about its character and the leadership qualities of the CEO. For instance, when the CEO's annual letter to the shareholders is full of platitudes, excuses, and grandiose strategies and betrays a poor understanding of the capital markets, then the signal to both outsiders and the company's own employees is that the CEO may be inept, in denial, or worse, attempting to deceive investors and others about the company's real issues. From a risk management standpoint, the board of directors should consider this kind of communication failure a trigger to review whether the company has the right CEO.

In Western economies, and increasingly elsewhere, regulators, account-ants, and equity analysts require or request massive amounts of information about public companies, and then they dutifully publish that information in regulatory documents, financial reports, and analysts' reports. Indeed, with laws such as Sarbanes-Oxley in the United States, the CEO and CFO can be held legally liable for reports containing accounting errors (a standard we can only dream could be applied to the work of lawyers, journalists, and politicians). This puts CEOs, CFOs, and boards under enormous pressure to actually care about all of this information, much of which is of absolutely no use in running a company well. Of course companies cannot disregard even wasteful and misguided laws and regulations that govern their external reporting, but the output should not be taken too seriously. Much of what is reported is the result of years of bright but misdirected minds looking for ever more convoluted ways to present the financial condition of a public company so that absolutely no one can understand it.

Inevitably CEOs are sucked into this maelstrom of obligatory but largely useless external information sharing. Nevertheless, there are some important choices regarding a company's external reporting practices that can affect the resilience of future economic profits.

General Rule

With respect to reporting any material news that is bad, or potentially bad, the ethically and pragmatically correct choices are the same: Report the news quickly and accurately. The classic case of this course of action was Johnson & Johnson's response in 1982 to the appearance of cyanide-laced capsules in some bottles of its best-selling product, Tylenol. Once the company became aware of the product tampering, CEO James Burke immediately went public with the news and recalled every single package of Tylenol to protect consum-ers from harm, costing the company $100 million. Despite this huge cost and the initial damage to the brand, sales of Tylenol and the company's share price had nearly recovered within a few months' time.[8]

Neither reputations nor economic profits will ultimately benefit from any other course of action. Even the appearance of a CEO suppressing negative information is a sign that other executives are probably engaged in doing the same, behavior that is contrary to the interests of all external stakeholders.

Guidance

A fact little appreciated by CEOs is that there is no evidence of systematic error in pricing the common stocks of individual companies. This does not mean companies are always correctly valued. It means that the stock market's valuation errors do not seem to be biased, up or down. At any point in time a company is as likely to be overvalued as undervalued, reflecting the endless oscillations caused by investors guesstimating a company's value based on whatever information is in the market at that time.[9]

One implication of this fact is that CEOs should not try to influence stock price by providing guidance. Announcing a guidance number may cause a short-term tick in the stock price, but over time the company's market capitalization will be influenced primarily by the levels of performance the company has proven it can deliver rather than by management's predictions for the next 12 months of earnings. If that were not so, then companies with great public relations and celebrity CEOs would see their shares systematically overvalued relative to peers. But over time, there is no evidence of this.

Even if the CEO is not trying to influence the stock price but merely trying to be a good sport and supply analysts with his or her best estimate of earnings guidance, there can be no benefit to economic profit growth or shareholder value from doing so, and it should be avoided. Once offered, meeting the guidance number can become an obsession in its own right ("We can't afford to disappoint the Street!"), possibly leading the company to resort to creative accounting gimmicks or, worse, playing havoc with business unit strategies to engineer the desired short-term accounting results. The best information a CEO can provide to investors is the long-term average economic profit growth rate he or she believes the company's Gold strategies will produce, the biggest opportunities and risks the company faces in achieving that performance, and the general tenets of how the company's strategic management choices are made. The rest is delivery.

Financial Reporting Practices

Despite, or perhaps because of, the staggering number and complexity of accounting and regulatory rules imposed on public companies, company management retains considerable flexibility as to what accounting policies or methodologies to follow. Regrettably, it is not rare that CEOs and CFOs opt to use this flexibility primarily to boost reported earnings (which in the United States, at least, can be presented two or three different ways in the same reports, thereby providing something for everyone). This practice is not always motivated by the purest of intentions, particularly if executive bonuses are tied largely to the preferred reported earnings number (see Fannie Mae and Freddie Mac, among many shameful examples). Boards that routinely resort to this "flexibility" to trigger executive bonuses are doing their shareholders no favors.

In addition to the possible conflict-of-interest problem, when choosing accounting policies and methodologies there is the problem of addiction. Once the rules have been used to report the highest possible earnings in one year, they must usually be stretched further to generate the desired rate of reported earnings growth in subsequent years. This earnings inflation can be pushed only so far until no amount of legitimate accounting wizardry can sustain the illusion. After a time, the true economics of the company will become evident to investors and the stock price will undergo a major correction. Frequently, investors are not even fooled at the outset by inflated earnings reports and stubbornly refuse to buy what the CEO is selling, leading to the often heard lament that "the market doesn't understand" the company and awards it too low a price.

Over time, following conservative accounting practices will likely yield the same or higher reported economic profit growth than supposedly more aggressive practices, but with fewer gyrations and restatements. And conservative accounting sends investors a more positive message about management's own confidence and ethics than a very aggressive approach. Attempting to gild the lily can make a CEO look like a weak or superficial leader rather than a knowledgeable and disciplined strategic manager. This goes to the issue of trust. If investors (or employees) come to believe a CEO is willing to massage the numbers to look good or to meet bonus targets, the resulting distrust is likely to be reflected in increased uncertainty about the company's future prospects, meaning it will have a higher cost of capital and, ultimately, a lower share price. Such an outcome is antithetical to the responsibility of a CEO.

 ## CHAPTER SUMMARY

For a CEO, the primary objective of risk management is to prevent the implosion of the company's economic profits. The same financial thresholds and targets used to make strategic decisions should act as trip wires to stimulate remedial action long before a business unit or the company is in real danger of losing its ability to grow economic profits over time.

The strongest line of defense against EP deterioration is the composition of the company's portfolio of businesses. The greater the concentration of Green Zone business units, the more resilient EP will be. Conversely, a portfolio containing business units in the Yellow and Red Zones is much more vulnerable to EP deterioration. This is why the CEO should not be swayed by arguments that portfolio diversification lowers risk—usually it does the opposite.

Balance sheet management can have a material impact on both the size and sustainability of EP. For some companies, holding high levels of cash can be a competitive advantage, but under most circumstances excess cash generates negative EP and poses a constant temptation to make poor investments, especially acquisitions. Adding discretionary debt—over and above the company's operating, bridge financing, and industry structure needs—can increase EP and be value creating. However, using debt in this way may only be suitable for companies in the Green Zone because for them it poses very little risk in exchange for a significant increase in equity value (at least in the United States).

Among the ethical choices that can impact EP growth are the quality of internal management information, the effectiveness of the creative construction process, and the honesty of communications with all stakeholders. A failure to maintain integrity in any of these areas is a danger signal for the resilience of future economic profits. The CEO and top management team have a duty to be informed, objective, and honest about the state of their businesses and about their choices for making the businesses better. This is an essential foundation for achieving the broader ethical standards that all companies should be striving for.

CHAPTER EIGHT

Making It Work

T HE IDEAS PRESENTED IN this book offer a general blueprint for how CEOs might improve their companies' strategic management capabilities. Many of these ideas have been applied to different degrees by a wide range of companies. The majority of these companies were able to significantly improve their economic profit growth rates and total shareholder returns, outpacing their peers by wide margins. This chapter looks at some of the lessons learned from these implementation efforts, including the conditions that seem to be conducive to success, the initial priorities for improving the quality of strategic management, and the outcomes a CEO might reasonably expect to achieve.

 ## CONDITIONS CONDUCIVE TO SUCCESS

Two conditions that have an especially large impact on efforts to improve the quality of strategic management are CEO commitment and cultural alignment.

CEO Commitment

Strategic management is the essence of the CEO's job, so any material changes to the company's strategic management practices have to be led by, or "owned" by, the CEO. Other executives can certainly propose changes or lead change initiatives, but no one else in the organization shares the ultimate responsibility for the quality of strategic management or the overall financial performance of the company. Three manifestations of a CEO's level of commitment are his or her clarity of purpose, decisiveness, and investment of time.

Clarity of Purpose

The CEO must be comfortable that economic profit growth (or equity value growth) trumps all other financial and strategic objectives. This is not to say that it trumps product or employee safety, complying with regulations, or obeying the law. It means that, subject to the requirements of good citizenship, choices will be made in favor of those options with the highest expected economic profit growth over the planning horizon. The goal is not to balance competing objectives such as earnings growth, return on equity, revenue growth, cash flow, or market share. These are not proxies, equivalents, or substitutes for economic profit growth, nor are they equally valid alternative decision criteria.

Are there great CEOs who do not subscribe to economic profit growth or who stress other financial objectives? Absolutely. But there are no great CEOs whose companies fail to produce superior economic profit growth during their tenure, whether or not they assert that objective. A competently managed company or business unit that is operating in profitable product markets with a competitive advantage will, under most scenarios, produce reasonable economic profit growth whether or not it set out explicitly to do so. The CEO may, as an example, be pushing earnings or sales growth, with good EP growth resulting as an unconscious by-product. But even in these happy circumstances, the company is unlikely to be *maximizing* economic profit growth or equity value because that is not really what it is trying to do.

As an example, even before 1981 when Roberto Goizueta became CEO and adopted EP growth objectives, it would not have required a very sharp pencil to determine that increasing the sales of bottled and canned Coke would create a lot more value for the Coca-Cola Company's shareholders. So had Goizueta decided to focus just on growing the volume sales of Coke and the company's other carbonated soft drink brands, he would still have produced pretty good results. But the economic profit lens brought two things into focus that helped the company perform at an even higher level. First, lacking the proper metrics, management had seriously underappreciated just *how much* additional value was generated every time someone bought a Coke anywhere in the world; adding that economic profit per bottle insight brought phenomenal new energy and investment into driving volume growth on a global scale. Second, apart from bottled and canned carbonated soft drinks, the company had less insight on how other parts of its business created or consumed value, including fountain soft drinks, orange juice, bottled water, wine, and the bottler system itself. Once the discipline of understanding market economics, competitive position, and economic profit had been applied to all parts of the company, major strategic changes were made—including restructuring of the bottler network and the fountain network, repositioning of the orange juice business, and sale of much of the wine business.

So favorably positioned companies may perform well, though probably not their best, even if EP growth is not the CEO's dominant objective. Of course, companies or business units that are not participating in good product markets or that are competitively disadvantaged are not so lucky. They are unlikely to improve their low or negative EP status by single-mindedly pursuing earnings or revenue growth targets and may well suffer the opposite fate.

Decisiveness

Some aspects of improving strategic management may be met with outright resistance. Setting demanding EP growth objectives, creating a high-quality management information system, shifting from a culture in which top-down funding and control systems define strategy to one in which bottom-up strategies determine funding and control targets—all of these and many other organizational changes will require a determined CEO to implement successfully. In addition, there will usually be significant changes to business unit strategies and accelerated capital restructuring, some of which will be welcomed and some of which will be fiercely resisted by the affected units. The CEO has to be prepared to be absolutely resolute in overcoming all the inertia and inevitable pushback that he or she will encounter.

Being decisive does not mean change will be instantaneous. In large companies some of the changes a CEO will want to make may take years to imbed completely in the organization, so a degree of patience is in order. People need to learn and internalize the new metrics and rules, older management systems need to be upgraded or replaced, and some trial and error needs to occur to discover what works best within a particular corporate culture. But the progress of change should be steady, and from the very beginning, with whatever tools are in place, the CEO should be seen as approving only those strategies that are expected to maximize the growth rate of economic profit over time.

Investment of Time

Modern CEOs are challenged with utterly unreasonable demands on their time: attending to the normal press of business; fighting fires; making site visits; attending internal and external board meetings, employee events, customer meetings, security analyst meetings, trade or industry events, civic events, meetings with bankers, auditors, lawyers, and regulators; and participating in lobbying efforts—all of which may require travel to many countries and across many time zones and can easily consume 80 or more hours a week even before the CEO has time for thoughtful consideration of the big strategic management issues. This presents the CEO with a stark choice of either cutting back considerably on the standard CEO agenda, especially outside activities, or of letting strategic management slide in the expectation, unlikely to be fulfilled, that other executives will take care of it.

As a rough rule of thumb, assuring that all resources of the company are invested in strategies that maximize economic profit growth will require the CEO to devote at least one half of his or her time exclusively to that effort. No other responsibility of a CEO merits this level of time commitment. An economically profitable, well-run company will not suffer in any way if the CEO never attends a security analysts' meeting, does not join outside boards, or is a no-show at Davos. Something has to give for the CEO to devote the requisite time to lead the company to its highest possible level of performance. This does not mean a CEO has to become a hermit, never leaving the company cave. Meetings with employees, key customers and suppliers are often essential, as are some civic commitments. But any demands on the CEO's time that do not advance the strategic management agenda should be held to an absolute minimum.

Alignment with Company Culture

One aspect of culture that infuses all companies is the institutional imperative. The institutional imperative is the natural enemy of excellent strategic management, resisting efforts to improve clarity, decisiveness, performance standards, and the proper allocation of resources. No CEO can avoid having to deal with this creature, especially in large and complicated companies; it will test his or her will on a daily basis. The institutional imperative cannot be eliminated, but its worst effects can be mitigated through good strategic management practices.

In addition to the ubiquitous institutional imperative, companies have their own cultural characteristics, two of which can have a significant impact on whether and how improvements to strategic management practices might be achieved. The first characteristic is the core convictions that infuse a company's business model, and the second is the general mind-set or commercial comfort zone of its executives.

Core Convictions

Any effort to change strategic management practices needs to align with the core convictions of the business. Otherwise, the odds of failure are very high. For companies that are doing well with their current business model, this alignment is not difficult to achieve. In the Coca-Cola Company example cited earlier, aligning the CEO's drive for increased "share of stomach" with increasing economic profit growth was a natural fit, as the two ideas were mutually reinforcing. And because the changes being made in the strategic management process not only validated but further energized efforts to execute on the core business model, the credibility of the new approach was more easily acknowledged in other parts of the company where existing business models were not always as successful and had to be challenged.

In companies or business units where the current business model is broken or in dispute but convictions have not yet adjusted to the new realities, aligning new strategic management practices with managements' core beliefs can be difficult. As an example, at one large money-center bank during the late1990s, a prevailing conviction of the CEO and most of the top management was that retail banking was an unattractive business and that investment banking was a great business (this, in itself, is a false distinction). Even when careful analysis showed that the retail-oriented business units consistently produced equal or greater absolute economic profits than the investment banking business units, the CEO and a majority of the senior management simply would not accept the strategic implications of those findings. Their misplaced convictions could not be altered by mere facts. This was a real blow to the leaders of the retail businesses, who already felt like second-class citizens, and the prospect of making EP growth the basis for decision making at that bank was set back for years.

Executive Mind-Set

Some CEOs and executive suites have a strong management mind-set that can significantly influence the quality or nature of strategic management practices:

Examples include sales, marketing, engineering, financial, operational, and transactional mind-sets. Executives with engineering and financial mind-sets tend to be more comfortable with systematic approaches to strategic management, executives with sales and transactional mind-sets less so. This has nothing to do with their respective intelligence, energy, or desire for their companies to perform well. As much as anything, it has to do with differing time horizons.

An executive at ExxonMobil, with an engineering and possibly also a financial perspective on the world, tends to think in terms of enormous, and enormously complicated, strategic investments that play out over many years. He or she has the luxury of taking much more time to evaluate strategic options than a deal-oriented investment banker who must respond almost instantaneously to changes in customer demands and capital market conditions. Indeed, the words "long-term strategy" and "investment banking" almost don't go together because so much of the business is opportunistic and the response times are so short.

Clearly, businesses with such different mind-sets and time horizons need to adopt different strategic management practices: The principles and the nature of the five big choices remain the same, but the processes and practices have to be adapted to the prevailing executive mind-set. As one simple example of such an adaptation, sales and marketing executives may respond much more positively to a metric like EP per unit or per dollar of sales than to a metric like EP per share, which is too far removed from their everyday goals to give them much guidance. As another example, companies with long-lived assets need long planning horizons and rigorous restructuring criteria because of the inherent difficulty of changing their participation choices and business models. But companies that are mostly transactional are accustomed to making frequent changes in their participation and positioning choices because profitability feedback from their customers is rapid and their asset commitments are comparatively light or self-liquidating. For these fast-paced companies, a planning horizon of even five years might be too long.

There are other examples of strong executive mind-sets that can have a significant impact on the quality of strategic management. One is competitive intensity, the difference, say, between a regulated public utility (often open to new process but not necessarily driven by competition or regulation to perform at its highest level) and a mass-market merchandiser (faces fierce competition daily and driven to improve performance with or without new process). Another example is an executive culture that dwells in the past (we were such a great company) and may be in some denial about the future (we need to make a lot of fundamental changes if we ever expect to recover our greatness). And, of course, there are *real* cultural differences between companies headquartered in different countries and led by executives of different nationalities: The path to improving strategic management in a big U.S.–based company will definitely be different from the best path for a company headquartered in Brazil, India, or China.

Core convictions and strong mind-sets cannot be ignored in determining how to improve strategic management. To the extent a CEO is able to leverage, adapt to, or work around these cultural realities, the odds of overcoming the institutional imperative and improving the company's economic profit growth will rise dramatically.

 ## PRIORITIES FOR CHANGE

The impetus for improving strategic management will vary by CEO and by company, as will the underlying conditions and the starting point for change. Therefore, the path to improvement will also be different for every company. The desire for change might begin with a CEO's concern about the company's capital management practices, or with the quality of strategic options coming from the business units, or with the company's lagging shareholder returns. When addressing these concerns, questions may then arise about the appropriateness of the company's performance objectives, about the quality of its product and customer information, or about its compensation or portfolio management practices. Because the big strategic management choices are so interconnected, the CEO's concerns about underperformance in one or two areas are frequently linked to issues in other areas that may not be immediately apparent. The path to improving strategic management is, to some degree, a path of discovery.

Although each CEO and company will follow its own unique path, there are a number of fairly common strategic management issues that need to be addressed by most companies at some point. What follows are six general suggestions for addressing those issues. The suggestions are based on the actual experiences of several dozen companies that have made serious efforts to improve their strategic management capabilities.

1. Focus on the Five Choices

Obvious as it may seem, it is essential for the CEO and top management team to agree on precisely what it is they are being paid to do, and getting the five big choices right is a good place to start. Although the CEO has to take ultimate responsibility for the quality of strategic management for the entire company, it is the responsibility of every executive to play a constructive and effective role in that effort. In this sense, the five choices form an evergreen agenda the entire management team can share, with each individual focusing on the subchoices within his or her sphere of accountability. Business unit heads may have primary responsibility for making the right participation and positioning choices, but they are also accountable to follow the choices the corporate center makes regarding matters such as performance objectives, information transparency, and risk management. The five choices (and subchoices) constitute not only an agenda at a point in time but a modus operandi for the management team members to set their collective priorities and assist each other in continually growing the economic profit of the company.

2. Upgrade Performance Objectives

The foundation of exceptional strategic management is choosing and properly employing the right performance objectives. Consequently, some important changes need to be made early in the effort to upgrade the strategic management process.

- *Agreeing on a "governing" objective.* Many companies measure economic profit in some form and use it in various ways for decision making, but few give economic profit growth primacy over all other financial or strategic objectives. If EP is used at all, it is one of several powerful competing objectives. It is a big step to choose maximizing EP growth as a single governing objective, but it brings enormous benefits, not the least of which are clarity of purpose and a focus on the right strategic and organizational drivers of the company's long-term performance.
- *Adopting the minimum acceptable performance objective.* The one element of setting objectives that should come from the top down is the requirement that every business unit, and every part of every business unit, must earn at least its cost of capital. Some may argue about whether management has a duty to maximize shareholder value, but there can be no argument that the CEO should tolerate activities that destroy shareholder value. If a company does not already have and enforce this rule, adopting it should be one of the first improvements made.
- *Shifting from top-down to bottom-up target setting.* Letting go of top-down target setting is a big step, but if the change is made properly, CEOs need not fear the consequences. Aligning the business unit EP and revenue

targets with their Gold strategies will actually result in choosing more demanding objectives and establishing more legitimate accountability for achieving those objectives than will a generic top-down performance mandate. The speed of this change is dependent on progress in other areas, particularly improved information, but it should start as early as possible to foster better strategy formulation.

3. Improve Information Quality

This aspect of the improvement effort is normally the most complicated, time consuming, and sometimes also the most contentious. Thus, it must be executed with considerable care but without losing momentum. Early priorities for change should include the following:

- *Agree that the CEO and center "own" the information.* Business units are entitled to have their own opinions, but not their own facts. The business unit heads and the CEO should all be operating with the same high-quality information covering product, market, and customer profitability, competitive position, and forecast assumptions. The business unit needs this information to formulate its Gold strategies, and the CEO needs this same information to approve strategies and funding, to set performance targets, and to assure compliance.
- *Peel the onion.* Usually the first step in upgrading information is to create pro forma income statements and balance sheets for each business unit, allowing for the measurement of EP. There will be cost and asset allocation rules to be set, debt and equity imputation methods to be established, and cost of equity to be estimated. Once there is reasonably good EP measurement at the business unit level, it is possible to move on to product (or product group) profitability, followed by the geographic market and then customer (or customer segment) profitability measurement. Sometimes the most difficult challenge is capturing good external information on competitors' EP and EP drivers, but with time and experience this too can be added to the complete database.
- *Keep it simple.* There are always trade-offs between the precision and the utility of management information. Some companies that have floundered on EP measurement have done so because the effort became an exercise in financial exegesis, with endless debates about methodologies for cost of capital estimation, cost and asset allocations, and even revenue allocations between business units. Some of these issues are indeed difficult, often the

more so because they are perceived by some executives to have political implications (e.g., increased transparency is viewed as diminishing their control). Nevertheless, it is better, at least in the beginning, to err on the side of making simple but reasonable estimates that may be somewhat "incorrect" rather than to lose the enormous benefits of good estimates by insisting on false accuracy or by trying to make everyone happy with the allocation rules.

4. Embrace Creative Construction

The primary activity of the creative construction process is the series of dialogues throughout the year between the CEO and business unit and function heads. These dialogues are focused entirely on finding or renewing and executing Gold strategies. These are not budget review meetings (for which there would no longer be any need), nor are they formal strategic planning presentations to the CEO (for which there would be very little need). They are an ongoing exploration of ways to improve a business unit's economic profit performance between the two individuals ultimately accountable for that performance.

Transitioning from a budget/planning culture to a Gold strategy execution culture starts with a few key steps:

- *Make Gold strategies management's real focus.* The idea of a Gold strategy has intuitive appeal because it is a relative concept, implying that it is the best of all the strategic options a business might pursue. When linked to the objective of maximizing economic profit growth, the Gold strategy becomes a concrete expression of how a business will put its human and capital resources to their highest and best use over the planning horizon—or until an even higher EP growth option emerges to become the new Gold strategy. Formulating and executing Gold strategies should occupy more of management's time than any other endeavor.
- *Make business unit strategy, funding, and target approval all one decision.* Once the necessary business unit information reporting system is in place, it becomes possible for the CEO to make funding and target choices simultaneously with the approval of, or a change in, a Gold strategy. These decisions should be made for each business unit independently of decisions made for other units. If this is accomplished, the consolidated funding requirements and performance targets of the business units will be the right ones for the company overall. This is a huge change for most companies and needs to be undertaken with considerable care. Yet it

cannot be put off for too long because the creative construction process cannot be effective as long as the legacy short-term planning or budgeting processes remain in place as the *de facto* determinants of financial targets and funding decisions.

- *Ensure that compliance and growth are the perpetual agenda items.* A Gold strategy is not a static plan but a work in progress, constantly reforming at the margins to remove economic weakness and build on economic strength. Thus, the continuous dialogue between the CEO and business units is always about issues of compliance (economic weakness) and growth (economic strength). Some executives would not normally consider compliance discussions to be strategic, but properly understood such discussions are essential to formulating and executing great strategies. A business unit must justify the investment of all of its capital all of the time. It has no ongoing entitlement to the capital it already has and should never assume it cannot be taken away. Regular compliance discussions allow for relatively small strategy corrections and small capital restructurings to take place more or less continuously. Conversely, businesses should have the full backing of the CEO to invest in economically profitable growth, whether that is to be found in new products, new markets, or new customer segments. Profitable growth opportunities occur throughout the year, not just at annual planning time, so decisions about growth need to be made continuously and, usually, in comparatively small increments over time. This change in the management of strategies should be made as soon as the information set allows.

5. Identify Value Creators

A goal of any CEO or board is for the company to build and sustain an executive team of proven EP growth producers. In the early stages of improving strategic management, there may or may not be enough insight into the potential of each executive in the company. Some executives may have a terrific track record of increasing revenues, others at managing costs, but it does not necessarily follow that these are the individuals who will be the best at formulating and executing Gold strategies. It may take some time to determine who has the required capabilities. As the CEO begins to identify these individuals, making the most of their abilities will be a high priority.

- *Give high-potential EP growth producers the best opportunities.* The biggest opportunities to increase EP growth and equity value are often found in the "tails" of the ME/CP Profitability Matrix, either in the best-positioned (e.g., High Octane) or the worst-positioned (e.g., Ream Maker) business units. Appointing the right leader in either one of these situations can have a dramatic impact on performance, and because such leaders are usually in short supply, the company will benefit by focusing their energies where they will do the most good. These will not necessarily be the most senior executives or even the most experienced executives; they will be the executives whom the CEO would choose to run the business unit if he or she were the principal owner.

- *Redirect the energies of value consumers.* Inevitably there will be executives who do not have the requisite talent and leadership abilities to take a business up to the Gold strategy standard. Some may even have a proclivity for making value-consuming decisions. These executives may or may not have other important contributions to make to the company, but they should not be business unit leaders. Making such appointments sends the wrong signal to the organization, weakening considerably the effort to improve strategic management.

6. Make Bold Choices

Even in the early stages, focusing on the five choices, upgrading objectives, improving information, and making the other changes outlined previously will unleash a flood of opportunities to accelerate economic profit growth. In the companies that have employed these strategic management practices most successfully, the CEOs took almost immediate action on selected high-profile opportunities to show the organization that they were fully committed to a better way of doing things and that significant performance improvement was possible even over a relatively short period of time. This decisiveness and getting early "points on the board" are critical factors in getting the full organization engaged.

The early high-profile opportunities will be different in every company, but there are some situations that arise frequently. One is orphan businesses. An orphan is a business unit, or perhaps part of a business unit, that earns good returns, that has probably been part of the company for a long time, that is generally midsized or small relative to other units, and that no one pays much attention to. It just goes along each year, gets its dollop of capital, produces its positive EP, and creates few if any headaches for the CEO. These orphan businesses are usually competitively advantaged in profitable product markets, though total product-market EP may be slow growing or even declining. But because they have had so little visibility (perhaps happily so in their view), they have not been encouraged to find their Gold strategies. Once they are "discovered," however, it is usually possible to reenergize these units and quickly put them on an accelerated EP growth track, sometimes more than doubling their equity value in just one or two years.

Inescapably, some of the early high-profile opportunities will come from exiting or restructuring business units. No corporation of any size is free of this obligation. The CEO's willingness to take the necessary action on these business units, or parts of business units, will be essential for building the credibility of the new approach to capital management. If the organization senses a lack of decisiveness in these difficult matters, the forces of the institutional imperative will ultimately win the day.

In addition to the six changes outlined here, other aspects of strategic management including business unit boundaries, compensation plans, and communications policies will likely also have to be reevaluated. Normally, these changes would come later in time because they are difficult to address until new agendas, objectives, information, strategy formulation, and funding practices are at least partly in place.

 ## THE PRIZE

What are the concrete benefits of good strategic management, of making the right targeting, participation, positioning, organizational, and risk management choices? Among the benefits a CEO should reasonably expect to see are large improvements in transparency and the quality of decision making and communication ("soft" benefits), and significant improvements in the company's financial performance and resource strength versus the competition ("hard" benefits).

Soft Benefits

At a personal level, the CEO will be able to set clearer priorities for where he or she and other members of the management team should be investing the majority of their time and effort. Given the often unreasonable demands on a CEO's time, even very able leaders can be frustrated by how little time is left for them to focus on the choices that really shape strategy and drive performance. By reviewing constantly where the company stands with respect to the five big choices, by insisting on the Gold strategy standard, by meeting often with the business unit heads on the critical questions of compliance and growth, and by elevating the quality of information available to all decision makers, the CEO can achieve much better alignment between time spent and benefits to the company. There will always be a short list of high-impact EP growth and compliance issues to be addressed, and it will be clear to everyone what those issues are and the sense of urgency the CEO feels in getting them resolved.

The CEO should also find it easier to communicate with the board and with outside investors. As a high-level agenda, the five choices can be very effective in board meetings, allowing the CEO to highlight the top issues, initiatives, and expected outcomes in each area. The board should also be apprised periodically of the major aspects and performance potential of the business unit Gold strategies. This is a relatively efficient way of giving directors the big picture, along with the opportunity to ask questions about, or offer advice on, the choices to which the CEO is clearly giving priority. Much less detail would be provided to the investment community than to the board, but the CEO will still be in a position to communicate effectively what he or she sees as the big issues, how they are being addressed, and what long-term financial performance the company is targeting and believes it can sustain.

Similar benefits will accrue to business unit heads and their teams. Their strategic and financial priorities will be clarified; they will be liberated from the tyranny of top-down targets, cross-subsidies, and capital budgeting (while at the same time being held to much higher standards of capital efficiency); and they will manage strategy formulation as a continuous improvement process and not as an annual regurgitation of a strategic plan. Ideally, their relationship with the CEO will be a partnership for maximizing economic profit growth. Their ability to explain to their own teams why the business is pursuing certain participation or positioning choices and not others will also be enhanced, helping less experienced managers learn the foundations of good strategic management as they move up in the organization.

Hard Benefits

Will building strategic management capabilities based on the principles and practices in this book result in higher EP growth and superior TSR performance? Experience strongly suggests the answer is yes.

The performance history of 10 very successful CEOs and their companies are summarized in Exhibit 8.1. These CEOs have different personalities, backgrounds, and leadership styles, but two traits they all have in common are (1) a commitment to extremely high financial performance standards, and (2) a deep

EXHIBIT 8.1 Selected Exemplars

Company	CEO and Tenure
Bank of America	David Coulter (1996–1998)[a]
Bank of Hawaii	Michael O'Neill (2000–2004)
Bank of Montreal	Matthew Barrett (1990–1998)
The Coca-Cola Company	Roberto Goizueta (1981–1997)
Dow Chemical Company	William Stavropoulos (1995–2000, 2002–2004)
Ford Motor Company	Alan Mulally (2006–)
Gillette	Jim Kilts (2001–2005)[b]
Lloyds TSB	Sir Brian Pitman (1983–1997)
Nordstrom	Blake Nordstrom (2000–)
Roche	Dr. Franz Humer (2001–2008)

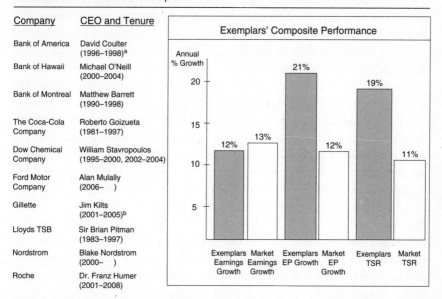

Exemplars' Composite Performance

Sources: Datastream, company documents.

Notes:

Performance measures and comparisons cover periods of CEO tenure.

Relative measures are comparisons with Datastream "market" composite.

[a]Merged with Nations Bank in 1998.

[b]Acquired by Procter & Gamble in 2005.

understanding of how their strategic and organizational decisions affect value creation in their companies. They serve as excellent examples of what is possible when capable leaders consciously pursue, in their own distinctive ways, the thoughtful application of the principles and practices discussed throughout the book.

The phenomenal performance of this group of companies needs little elaboration. It is interesting to note that the economic profit growth rates of the group far outstripped their earnings growth rates, a pattern similar to the one observed in the S&P sample presented earlier (see Appendix I). Also similar to the results from the larger sample, the exemplar group achieved very high total shareholder returns relative to the general market. These results were not random. The CEOs explicitly set out to change key elements of the companies' strategic management processes and practices as a prerequisite to achieving exceptional financial performance, and they were obviously successful in doing so.

Along with exceptionally high economic profit growth and shareholder returns come other hard benefits to management and shareholders. Most importantly, exemplar companies typically have much stronger balance sheets and cash flows than their competitors, giving them better access to the capital markets, lower borrowing costs, and greater resiliency during periods of adversity in their industries or in the general economy. Along with this financial strength comes the capacity to invest more in research, product development, information technology, and marketing than competitors, giving an exemplar the potential to continually increase its positioning advantages. A third significant benefit is the ability to attract and retain top talent relative to competitors, not only because an exemplar company can better afford it but because the best executives are more likely to want to be part of the best team.

An important qualifier regarding the exemplars' performance results is that they are CEO-specific. Some companies, like Lloyds TSB or Bank of America, can experience tremendous performance improvement during one CEO's tenure but they are not necessarily able to sustain that improvement—and may even see it reversed—during a successor's tenure. A good strategic management process can help a good CEO enormously, but process is not destiny. If a successor CEO is determined to grow the company's earnings, revenues, market share, or scale and scope at almost any cost, then economic profit growth will become irrelevant. The organization will recognize the change and respond to the new CEO's priorities immediately, no matter how deeply embedded good strategic management practices may have been under his or her predecessor.

The 10 exemplars shown here are only a subset of a larger group of CEOs and companies who have made similar changes, also with very good results. At the same time it is fair to point out that some companies attempting to adopt these ideas have not achieved their aspirations in terms of economic profit growth or TSR performance. The specific reasons vary, but one common factor in nearly all cases has been that the CEO's core convictions were ultimately in conflict with making the kinds of choices proposed here. The façade of the strategic management process may have changed, but behaviors did not.

CHAPTER SUMMARY

Making the strategic management process work—getting the five big choices right—should certainly be at the top of a CEO's agenda. The CEO's own clarity of purpose, decisiveness, and time commitment will largely determine whether the process can be continuously improved and sustained at a high level.

Improving strategic management usually involves conquering important technical challenges to elevate the quality of decision making. But what may be even more important is adapting these technical changes to a company's cultural realities, including the institutional imperative, embedded commercial and financial convictions, and established management mind-sets. Any effort to improve strategic management must resolve both the technical and cultural issues equally well if it is to succeed.

The journey to improved strategic management may be a long and winding road, but steady, important progress can be made every quarter and every year, with major performance improvements occurring all along the way. As the exemplars and others have demonstrated, a determined, decisive, and able CEO pursuing these improvements can have a transformative impact on the economic profit growth and shareholder value of his or her company.

Economic Profit Growth, Earnings Growth, and Total Shareholder Returns

HE ANALYSIS THAT PRODUCED the results shown in Exhibits 1.1 and 2.11 was designed to answer two related questions:

1. What relationship, if any, does there seem to be between a company's economic profit growth rate and its total shareholder returns (TSRs) over time?
2. What relationship, if any, does there seem to be between a company's earnings growth rate and its total shareholder returns over time?

THE DATA

Determining the relationships between financial metrics, like economic profit and earnings, and stock market metrics, like market capitalization and TSR, is complicated by several factors, among them: (1) there are many variations to choose from when measuring economic profit or earnings; (2) the financial metrics capture a company's past performance, whereas the stock market metrics are determined by investors' expectations of a company's future performance; and (3) the apparent strength or weakness of relationships can vary a great deal depending on the particular group of companies in a sample or the specific time frame over which an analysis is done.

To conduct this analysis, the following data choices were made:

- Company earnings, book equity, share price, and dividend data were taken from Datastream, with no adjustments.
- The group of companies tested consists of companies included in the Standard & Poor's 500 as of the end of 2009, reduced by the number of companies that (1) were not in the index during the entire measurement period or (2) for which usable data were not available during the measurement period.
- The total time period examined was from 1988 to 2007. For some of the analysis, single-year data were used. For most of the analysis, 10 overlapping 10-year spans, from 1988–1997 through 1998–2007, were used. All growth rates and shareholder returns were measured using only data from the first and last years of the 10-year periods.
- Economic profit was calculated using annual earnings and beginning period book equity.
- The cost of equity capital estimate applied to each company in every year was 10 percent, a simplifying assumption made because finding robust estimates of cost of equity for each company going back in time was not feasible. This assumption is not believed to have affected the measured growth rates of economic profit (EP) in a material or systematic way.
- Total shareholder return for each company was calculated as the 10-year compound annual rate of return from share price appreciation (or depreciation) and reinvested dividends.
- Calculations were done both on a per-share and on a total-company basis.

 THE ANALYSIS

In looking for relationships between financial metrics and shareholder returns, a natural starting point would be to test for a statistically significant "fit," or correlation, between each company's historical EP growth or earnings growth and its historical TSRs across the entire sample of companies. This regression analysis was done for 1-year and 10-year periods. The correlations between 1-year TSRs and same year EP growth or earnings growth were generally close to zero, meaning that neither EP nor earnings growth seems to explain much about changes in share price over these short periods. The data do show a positive but fairly weak correlation between 10-year TSRs and 10-year EP or earnings growth ($0.2 < R^2 < 0.5$ in most cases), meaning less than half of longer-term shareholder returns can be "explained" by either variable.

One reason for these modest correlations is that share prices, which are the main component of TSRs, are based on investors' *expectations* of future dividends and share price appreciation. If Company A is *expected* to produce better future performance than Company B, then its current share price will already reflect that expectation. If both companies go on to perform as expected over a given time period, then, even though Company A will have had the better reported financial performance, both may have the same risk-adjusted returns over that period. Thus, we would expect to see a company achieve above-average TSRs only if it delivers a positive surprise to investors in the form of better than expected financial performance. This characteristic of TSR behavior is the primary reason it should not be relied on too heavily when evaluating company or management performance, especially over shorter time periods.

To try to gain more insight than we found in the regression analysis, a different approach was taken. Of particular interest was the *relative* influence of economic profit growth versus earnings growth on total shareholder returns. To address this question, companies in the sample were divided into three groups:

- EP-Dominant Group: Companies that had a compound annual EP growth that exceeded their compound annual earnings growth rate by a specified differential (ranging from 1 to 11 percentage points)
- Earnings-Dominant Group: Companies that had a compound annual earnings growth rate that exceeded their compound annual EP growth rate by the same specified differential
- Middle Group: Companies with EP and earnings growth differentials that fell in between the other two groups

The representative case used in Exhibits 1.1 and 2.11 specified a 5 percentage point differential for the 10-year period from 1998 to 2007, the results of which are shown in Exhibits AI.1 (per-share basis) and AI.2 (total-company basis).

EXHIBIT AI.1 TSR versus Per-Share EP Growth and Earnings Growth (5 percent differential)

Group	10-Year CAGR Earnings per Share	10-Year CAGR Book Equity per Share	10-Year CAGR EP per Share	10-Year TSR
EP Dominant (51 Companies)	15.0%	7.6%	30.3%	13.6%
Middle (165 Companies)	10.8%	10.7%	10.7%	9.8%
Earnings Dominant (51 Companies)	8.9%	14.9%	−5.3%	7.0%

Notes:
CAGR: compound annual growth rate.
EP-Dominant Group: All companies with compound annual EP-per-share growth greater than earnings-per-share growth by 5 percentage points or more.
Earnings-Dominant Group: All companies with compound annual earnings-per share-growth greater than EP-per-share growth by 5 percentage points or more.
Middle Group: All companies with earnings-per-share and EP-per-share CAGR differentials of less than 5 percentage points.

EXHIBIT AI.2 TSR versus Total Company EP Growth and Earnings Growth (5 percent differential)

Group	10-Year CAGR Earnings	10-Year CAGR Book Equity	10-Year CAGR Economic Profit	10-Year Change in Shares Outstanding	10-Year TSR
EP Dominant (50 Companies)	16.5%	9.3%	32.4%	+7.6%	13.6%
Middle (165 Companies)	11.5%	11.7%	11.5%	−2.0%	9.9%
Earnings Dominant (52 Companies)	12.1%	19.8%	−2.4%	+43.7%	6.8%

 ## DISCUSSION OF THE RESULTS

Looking first at the per-share analysis displayed in Exhibit AI.1, the middle group of 165 companies were those whose EP per-share growth rate from 1998 to 2007 was within plus or minus 5 percentage points of their earnings per-share growth rate. As it turns out, their group average EP and earnings per-share growth rates were nearly identical (10.7 percent and 10.8 percent, respectively), as was their book equity per-share growth rate (10.7 percent). Their average total return to shareholders was 9.8 percent, which was close to their average cost of equity capital over this period.

Comparing this middle group first to the 51 companies in the EP-dominant group, the differences are pronounced. The EP-dominant group experienced an average EP per-share growth rate of 30.3 percent versus an average earnings per-share growth rate of 15.0 percent, while book equity per share grew at only 7.6 percent. For this group, the average TSR was 13.6 percent, meaning share prices in this group were compounding about 40 percent per year faster on average than those in the middle group—a significant difference.

What might explain the TSR differences between these two groups? It does not appear to be random: the same analysis over multiple 10-year time periods, and using differentials ranging from plus or minus one percentage point to plus or minus eleven percentage points, yielded very similar results in virtually all cases. Nor is it solely because the EP-dominant group experienced higher absolute EP growth and earnings growth than the middle group: as noted earlier, the analysis of these variables individually showed a fairly weak correlation to TSRs (for this 10-year period, the correlation coefficients for EP growth and earnings growth versus TSR for the total sample were 0.35 and 0.34, respectively).

One explanation might be that investors' expectations of a company's future earnings per-share growth rate and their estimates of the company's future EP per-share growth rate may tend to be similar (because investors appear to focus so heavily on earnings forecasts, the similarity with expected EP growth rates might well be implicit rather than explicit). If this hypothesis is correct, then when EP growth turns out to be higher than earnings growth, investors' expectations have been surpassed—the company has delivered a positive EP growth surprise. But this surprise would translate into a higher than expected TSR only if EP growth itself was a bigger driver of share price than earnings growth (otherwise the surprise wouldn't particularly matter to investors). In the case of the EP-dominant group, achieving an average EP per-share growth rate two times higher than its earnings growth rate does appear to have been a positive surprise to investors, causing them to adjust their valuation expectations upward as reflected in the relatively high TSR performance versus the middle group.

If this reasoning holds, then we would predict the opposite outcomes between the middle group and the earnings-dominant group. And that is exactly what we found. The 51 companies in the earnings-dominant group experienced an average EP growth rate that was 14.2 percentage points below their average earnings growth rate. This negative differential was driven by the combination of a somewhat lower earnings per-share growth rate (8.9 percent vs. 10.8 percent) with a much higher book equity per-share growth rate (14.9 percent vs. 10.7 percent) compared to the middle group. If these relative results were largely unexpected by investors (i.e., if this relatively poor EP growth performance was a negative surprise), then the earnings-dominant group would be predicted to have had a lower TSR than the middle group, which it did: 7 percent vs. 9.8 percent.

Although this analysis alone cannot entirely prove that economic profit growth is the primary driver of share price growth, it strongly suggests that it is at least an extremely important factor. For CEOs, the main message in this analysis should be clear: maximizing economic profit growth does not absolutely guarantee the company will enjoy high TSRs during any particular time period, but pursing that objective successfully offers the best odds that the company will deliver positive surprises and higher TSRs over the longer term.

A final word on earnings growth: Given that earnings growth is itself a large component of economic profit growth, the effects of the two are necessarily interconnected in ways that can be difficult to separate empirically. However, Exhibit AI.2, which looks at total company rather than per-share financial data, does contain an intriguing result that CEOs should take to heart. Notice that the average earnings growth of the earnings-dominant group is actually slightly *higher* than it is for the middle group of companies (12.1 percent vs. 11.5 percent). This means that, on a total company basis, the group with the higher earnings growth rate actually generated a much lower TSR (6.8 percent vs. 9.9 percent). And this is not a complete anomaly—it is a result that was repeated in about 60 percent of the scenarios that were analyzed.

Because this result was not observed in the per-share data, one implication seems to be that at least some of the companies in the earnings-dominant group were issuing (net) new shares at a faster rate than the companies in other groups, and the data show they were. One reason for issuing a lot of new shares is to make large acquisitions, and within the earnings-dominant group were several companies that did so in a big way, including AT&T, Verizon Communications, Bank of America, JPMorgan Chase, Pfizer, and Procter & Gamble. In the eyes of their investors, most of the investments funded by these newly issued shares appear to have been detrimental to EP growth and to TSRs. So caveat emptor: Those big "strategic" acquisitions that are EP dilutive for more than a year or two seem to have low odds of creating shareholder value or fueling above average TSRs.

APPENDIX TWO

Economic Profit and Equity Value

M OST READERS WILL HAVE some familiarity with the concept of valuation and present value models. This appendix provides a brief review of the models and related factors needed to understand the key points and examples found in the book.

 VALUATION MODELS

Dividend Discount Model

All examples of equity value (EV) used in the book are based on the well-known dividend discount model:

$$EV = \sum \frac{D_t}{(1 + COE)^t}$$

where

Dividends **(D)** = Equity cash flow of the company or business unit
Cost of equity **(COE)** = Minimum rate of return required by shareholders

The dividend discount model is commonly used by companies to evaluate potential acquisitions. When estimating the investment returns (or net present values) of major project proposals, including research and development projects, new factories, and other large capital equipment purchases, most companies use a related discounted cash flow model based not just on equity capital but on total capital investment.

The equity and total capital valuation models are equivalent, and either can be used. Examples in the book use equity models because putting business units on an equity basis enables them to determine directly the impact their strategic decisions are likely to have on shareholder value.

Economic Profit Discount Models

With a little algebra, the dividend discount model can be transformed into an economic profit discount model:

$$EV = \sum \frac{EP_t}{(1 + COE)^t} + BE_0 \text{ or } \sum \frac{BE_{t-1}(ROE_t - COE)}{(1 + COE)^t} + BE_0$$

where

Book equity (BE) = actual or imputed book (common) equity.
Return on equity (ROE) = current period earnings divided by beginning book equity

This multiperiod version is the model most suitable to use when forecasting and estimating values for business unit strategies. Typically, there will be an explicit planning horizon forecast of economic profits for each strategy, followed by an estimate of "terminal" value, all discounted back to the present using the cost of equity capital. With a little more algebra, the "steady state," or "constant growth," version of the economic profit discount model can be derived:

$$EV = \frac{EP_1}{COE - G} + BE_0$$

where

Growth (G) = estimated or assumed constant growth rate of economic profits into the far future

This is the version of the model used most often in the book for expository purposes only. It would not normally be the best model to use when evaluating strategic options because too much detail about individual strategies and their performance in comparison to other strategies would be lost.

MAXIMIZING ECONOMIC PROFIT GROWTH VERSUS MAXIMIZING EQUITY VALUE

In Chapter 2 the point is made that choosing a business unit strategy that maximizes EP growth over time will in almost all cases also maximize its equity value. This assertion requires an explanation.

The key point is that strategy formulation and execution are continuous and dynamic events. Business units are (or should be) constantly searching for options that will increase economic profit: introducing new products and discontinuing old ones, adding new services, reducing production costs, adding new customer segments or exiting old ones, entering new geographic markets, revitalizing business models, and so on. Thus, a strategy is continuously evolving, meaning that the prospects for future EP growth are also changing constantly, as is implied equity value. This means that a business unit with, say, a five-year EP forecast horizon will be making an almost continuous series of decisions, always searching for options that will maximize economic profit growth over a moving five-year time horizon. As the business unit moves through time, these continuous decisions are intended to keep it at the highest EP growth rate available to it at any point. If a business unit is able to stay on this continuously updated highest forecast EP growth track, it will also be achieving the highest equity value growth of which it is capable.

How should a business unit select its EP forecast horizon? The minimum forecast horizon would be the time frame over which the EP benefits from investments made today (broadly defined to include brand building, research, and new product development, as well as fixed and working capital and human capital investments) are likely to be largely captured. This may be 20 years or more for a mining company and 3 to 5 years for an investment bank. For multibusiness companies, this means that different business units may have different EP forecast horizons and that those with shorter horizons are likely to make strategic adjustments more often than those with longer horizons.

One concern about making strategic decisions based on multiyear EP forecasts, versus full equity value calculations, is that an EP-based decision might be biased toward the short term. Specifically, the concern is that managers may shy away from making long-payback investments that would lower EP growth over the next several years. Although this cannot be eliminated as a possibility, it is easy to overstate the problem:

- If large, long-payback investments are the norm for a business, then it should be using a longer-term EP forecast horizon consistent with the economic life of those investments. In some cases, such as acquisitions or the development of oil fields or new pharmaceuticals, a full valuation of the options may well provide the best answers.

- For many businesses, however, forecasting expected financial performance beyond three to five years is an exercise in fantasy, so adding more forecast years and a terminal value (the estimation of which comes with its own set of complications) in order to do a complete equity valuation may look impressive but adds little or nothing to the quality of strategic decisions. For these businesses, equity value will be maximized over time by continuously improving and executing against their highest EP growth options.

- Some managers instinctively think an investment that lowers return on investment (ROI) or ROE will also reduce EP, but this is not necessarily the case. EP is a function both of returns and of the size of the investment base. As a simple example, a strategy requiring equity of $1 billion that earns a 25 percent ROE and grows at 5 percent (forever) with a 10 percent cost of equity would have a first-year EP of $150 million and an equity value of $4 billion, but an alternative strategy for the same business requiring $2 billion of equity that earns only a 20 percent ROE and grows at 5 percent (forever) would have a first-year EP of $200 million and an equity value of $6 billion. Thus, the lower ROE strategy is also the higher EP and higher equity value strategy. This result is not always intuitive, especially if the business unit or company has a strong focus on sustaining high ROIs or ROEs.

VALUATION ISSUES

The basic concept of valuation is better understood than the actual practice of valuation. A full discussion of valuation practices is not being undertaken here, but a few practical considerations for evaluating business unit strategies are discussed next.

Focus on the numerator. There has been far more research and writing about estimating the cost of capital (the denominator) to use in valuation models than about the estimated future cash flow or economic profit streams (the numerator). The finance literature is overflowing with ideas and papers about the cost of capital but offers few practical ideas for estimating future economic profits (the strategy literature generally does not pay much attention to either factor). But the numerator is by far the more important concern of investors and managers because it normally has a much bigger impact on equity value and, therefore, on decision making.

Stay grounded in reality. Make sure forecasts are well grounded in the market economics and competitive position of the business. For example, business unit planning forecasts often show enormous ROE and EP improvement, particularly in the later years of the forecast period. This may be justified if the unit clearly has a superior business model in an economically attractive market, or if it is undergoing a major restructuring to eliminate negative EP activities. But in other circumstances, such fanciful forecasting is not justified and is not a sound basis for decision making. The actual product-market economics and competitive position of the business unit will impose a range of possibilities for future ROE, EP, and EP growth, and forecasts should normally fall within that range.

Focus on the critical differences between strategic options. The participation and positioning choices a business unit could make must be explicitly linked to the differences in sales growth, margins, and asset efficiency that underpin future EP growth estimates for each option. The objective of evaluating options is not to determine the exact absolute result for each option but to get the right *relative* result. The important thing to estimate with confidence is the likely difference between EP growth from Strategy Option A and Strategy Option B over the forecast period. It is management's understanding of these differences and the reasons for them, not the absolute estimates, that should guide the best choices.

Keep cost of equity capital estimates simple. For expository purposes, a 10 percent cost of equity is assumed throughout the book. Over longer time periods, the nominal average cost of equity capital for larger public companies in the United States is typically in a range of 8 percent to 12 percent, although with smaller companies or across business units there may be a larger range. There are many sources of data to help develop good cost of equity estimates for most businesses.[1] A key point to keep in mind is that the choice of the best strategy available to a business unit will rarely turn on the exact precision with which the cost of equity is estimated.

Don't complicate the management accounting. The seemingly simple identity of EP = BE(ROE − COE), when applied to a company's external financial reports, can be disrupted by modern accounting conventions, particularly those that require changes on the balance sheet that do not flow through to the income statement. However, these conventions apply to historical events and should not disturb the forecasts used to determine the highest EP growth or equity value strategies at the business unit level. The projected income statements and balance sheets of the business units should be constructed to minimize accounting complications so that measures of EP in future periods are not distorted.

APPENDIX THREE

Economic Profit and Equity Value: Illustration

Diversa Corp Illustration ($000's)

Business Unit	Earnings	Book Equity (Imputed)	Return on Equity (ROE)	Capital Charge	Economic Profit (EP)	EP Growth	Equity Value (EV)
High Octane	$ 1,600	$ 10,000	16%	$ 1,000	$ 600	4%	$ 20,000
Shop Smart	2,400	20,000	12%	2,000	400	4%	26,667
Big Dog	1,200	10,000	12%	1,000	200	4%	13,333
Wahoo	600	7,500	8%	750	−150	4%	5,000
PopulAir	1,200	15,000	8%	1,500	−300	4%	10,000
Ream Maker	500	12,500	4%	1,250	−750	4%	0
Diversa Corp	$ 7,500	$ 75,000	10%	$ 7,500	$ 0	4%	$ 75,000

Notes:
Cost of equity = 10% all units
Capital charge = Book equity × .10 (cost of equity)
EP = Earnings − Capital charge
$$EV = \frac{EP}{(COE - G)} + \text{Book equity}$$

Reconsidering the Corporate Center

*T*HE FOLLOWING IS AN *excerpt from a Marakon Commentary titled "Off-Center," which I wrote in 2002. It offers an alternative model for organizing the corporate center around the principle of maximizing economic profits and equity value rather than strictly around the functional silos that dominate the structure of many corporate centers today. Some of the terminology differs slightly from that in the book, but the meaning and connections should be clear to the reader.*

At most large companies today, the activities and structure of the corporate center are based on a traditional functional support model that is no longer appropriate for maximizing the value of the company. In the modern corporation, thought should be given to organizing the center not around support functions, but around clearly defined value-creating activities. The resulting structure would look very different from the traditional model, but would give the CEO added leverage for achieving superior performance over time.

 ## THE NEED FOR CHANGE

The primary role of the modern corporate center should be to assure that company resources are invested to maximize profitable growth and long-term intrinsic value. But corporate centers were not originally created for this purpose. They were created primarily to assure control (targets and plans), compliance (policies and standards) and cost efficiencies (scale economies) in largely single-business national market companies, which then grew into the multi-business global market companies of today. These traditional centers were generally comprised of functional silos organized around finance, human resources, marketing, IT, legal, etc., mostly reporting directly to the CEO.

While companies themselves have changed enormously over the last 30 years, most corporate centers today are still a legacy of this traditional structure, presenting management with significant problems, including:

- ◼ *Unclear roles and responsibilities for creating value*—The functional silos do not share commonly based performance objectives, measures or decision processes for managing their activities. For example, the finance, strategic planning and IT units often have completely different and competing views on what key information executives require, with the result that businesses units are presented with multiple and often conflicting performance objectives, performance indicators and decision criteria. As another example, HR departments often design and implement incentive compensation plans that are not aligned either with capital market requirements or with the capital management practices of the company, and this can have unintended, but costly, consequences for future financial and strategic performance.

- ◼ *Hard to measure contributions to value creation*—These units are actually very hard to benchmark in terms of quality or cost of outputs. While measuring these factors properly within and across companies would present challenges in the best of circumstances, the fact that there is so little clarity of mission and so few common measures of success across these silos makes the task of benchmarking almost impossible. Thus, no one seems to know what is the "right" amount to be spending on (or the right amount of output to be receiving from) the finance function, or the HR function, or the IT function.

- ◼ *Added complexity of decision making*—Because of their relatively narrow functional focus, it is often difficult for these functional units to contribute meaningfully to broader strategic and organizational issues. On issues that do require multi-functional inputs (i.e., almost every important issue), these silos can be difficult to align and coordinate, with one result being too much upward delegation of process decisions to the CEO.

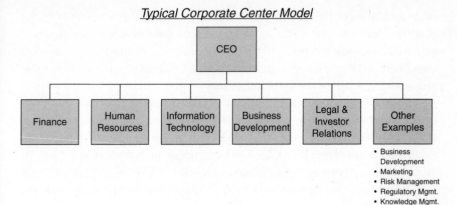

Typical Corporate Center Model

Most companies actually do recognize the need for change and have attempted, with varying success, to modify or adapt the traditional corporate center structure to contemporary needs. For example, in many companies, some form of a business development function has been added to the center, and IT has been elevated from a narrow technical function to a broader information management role. Some companies have also created corporate-based centers of excellence, such as marketing and knowledge management, to leverage competitive advantages spanning multiple business units. And in almost all companies, the role of the CFO has been expanded from reporting, treasury, audit and tax to include a more "strategic" scope of responsibilities.

In our view, these modifications, while directionally helpful, cannot overcome the inherent shortcomings of the traditional corporate center: it is imperfectly aligned with the objectives, the complexity and the scale of the modern corporation. Consequently, we believe top management should consider redefining the activities and changing the structure of the center to become a powerful enabler of, and not an obstacle to, superior performance.

 ## CREATING A NEW MODEL OF THE CENTER

The corporate center has a complex role. It serves as both a wealth creator (formulating and executing corporate strategy) and as a wealth creation catalyst (enforcing standards, allocating resources and building capabilities). These tasks, in turn, can be subdivided into a number of specific activities such as target setting, strategy formulation and executive development. As a first step, management needs to specify what activities are essential to maximizing value and, of these, which ones should be the responsibility of the center rather than the business units. The next question is how best to organize these activities to ensure a consistently high standard of performance around each one. These activity "clusters" can then become the basis of a new structure and process for managing the corporate center.

There can be many ways to think about clusters of activities that drive value, and the best answer will vary by company. One way that can be helpful is to consider the idea of corporate "value creation centers," units that have an explicit objective of creating value for the company and the resources to do so. These units comprise activities related to specific drivers of profitable growth and value, and can be managed by multi-functional teams to achieve the company's objectives.

As a starting point for designing a new model, value-creating activities could be clustered into six types of units, each accountable to the CEO: an enterprise strategy unit, a strategic management unit, an executive develop-ment unit, specialized centers of competitive excellence, a finance unit and a corporate services unit.

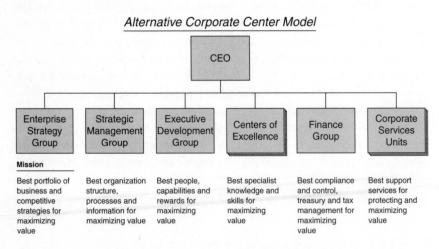

Alternative Corporate Center Model

Enterprise Strategy Group	Strategic Management Group	Executive Development Group	Centers of Excellence	Finance Group	Corporate Services Units
Mission					
Best portfolio of business and competitive strategies for maximizing value	Best organization structure, processes and information for maximizing value	Best people, capabilities and rewards for maximizing value	Best specialist knowledge and skills for maximizing value	Best compliance and control, treasury and tax management for maximizing value	Best support services for protecting and maximizing value

1. Enterprise Strategy Group: The mission of this unit would be to help the CEO and top management create a distinctive and profitable growth strategy for the overall enterprise, including:
   - determining the highest value-at-stake issues that should comprise the top management agenda (linking management activity to capital market requirements)

- determining the highest-value corporate strategy, including:
  - the highest-value corporate participation or portfolio strategies (which new products, markets or businesses to enter and which to exit—as well as the best means of entry and exit)
  - the highest-value corporate competitive strategies (how to leverage corporate assets or competencies to increase value across the portfolio)
  - the highest-value corporate financial strategies (what credit rating to manage to and how best to distribute cash to shareholders)

  Note that this is not a strategic planning unit focused mainly on process, but a strategy formulation unit focused primarily on helping resolve high value-at-stake enterprise issues. Nor is it a business development unit out looking for deals, although at some companies this activity could be a part of its responsibilities. And finally, it is not a unit with responsibility for business unit strategies which the units themselves must formulate to maximize their value to the corporation.

2. Strategic Management Group: The mission of this unit would be to help the CEO and top management build an enduring enterprise-wide advantage in creating value, including:

- establishing exemplary financial performance standards for the corporation and lines of business (linking strategic performance to capital market requirements)
- establishing and maintaining best practices for key strategic management processes, including strategy formulation, resource allocation and performance management
- establishing and maintaining best practices for strategic management information, including standards, metrics, methodologies and reports
- establishing and maintaining best practices for management of organization structure, including business unit boundaries, management roles and responsibilities, and intra-company transaction rules (transfer pricing, etc.)

  The operating role of this unit would be to help ensure the best possible alignment between the corporation's standards, processes, information and structure and the goal of maximizing value. This is a continuous process of improving decision-making standards and practices at all levels, driving always to increasing profitable growth and value faster than the competition.

  It should be noted that while setting financial performance standards and determining financial strategies are normally thought of as purely "finance" issues, they are actually critical elements of enterprise and line of business strategies. Financial performance standards in the form of economic profit growth goals and relative shareholder return targets should be at the very foundation of superior strategy formulation and approval.

Finally, as described here, the Strategic Management Unit really has no analog at most companies today. It includes activities that are sometimes found in strategic planning, some that are found in finance, some that are found in IT, some that are found in HR and some usually not found in any part of the corporate center.

3. Executive Development Group: The mission of this unit would be to help establish a competitive advantage in the quality and capabilities of the senior management team. These are the executives who have the most impact on enterprise and line of business strategy formulation, execution and delivery—and therefore the most impact on the profitability, growth and value of the company over time. As such they form a distinctive resource that should legitimately be managed by the CEO, with the support of a dedicated executive development group.

Ideally, every member of the senior management team would be a superior value creator. To achieve that goal, companies must be very proactive in identifying, developing, promoting and rewarding individuals who clearly meet that test. To further these objectives, the role of this unit would include setting standards, policies and practices for key activities, including:

▪ Placement and promotion of senior executives
▪ Capabilities development, including continuous education and knowledge sharing
▪ Recruitment of high-caliber senior executives from outside the firm
▪ Compensation aligned with value creation performance

4. Specialized Centers of Competitive Excellence: Where specialized capabilities are essential to sustaining and growing the value of multiple business units within the company, the CEO may establish specialized units focusing on those capabilities. These units would have accountability for setting enterprise-wide standards, policies and practices and helping to ensure that the required capabilities are established at the appropriate levels of the company. Depending on the industry and company itself, examples might include: a marketing management center of excellence (e.g., for consumer products companies); a regulatory management center of excellence (e.g., for pharmaceutical companies); or a risk management center of excellence (e.g., for financial institutions).

5. Finance Group: The mission of this unit is to provide excellence in the classical functions of financial reporting and control, legal and regulatory compliance, treasury and tax management. Post-Enron, there is certainly a heightened awareness of the absolute necessity for performing these functions to the highest standard to protect not only shareholders, but employees, creditors and all other stakeholders in the company's financial well-being.

6. Support Services Groups: The mission is to support the corporation and business units with excellent capabilities in activities where enterprise-wide standardization (e.g., compliance) and efficiency (e.g., scale economies) justify centralization. Examples include human resources, legal, IT, investor relations and facilities management. Along with finance, these activities are each important and need to be well managed, but they should not determine the core organization structure of the corporate center as they often do today.

CONCLUSION

Organizational structure and process do not solve all problems, but they are critical determinants of the potential of any organization to perform at the highest level. We believe the new direction for the corporate center we are proposing here could support and stimulate far higher value creation than the legacy models with which most companies are trying to cope.

CEO Pay Practices: An Alternative

*T*HE FOLLOWING IS AN *article I wrote for* Directors and Boards *magazine in 2003, originally titled "Rethinking Today's CEO Pay Practices."* It offers an alternative framework for setting CEOs', and by implication, all of top management's pay.*

Some caveats should be noted. Since this was written there have been changes in the accounting for and use of stock options, making them somewhat less important than they were in 2003. Also, if I were writing the article today I would give less weight to total shareholder return (TSR) and more weight to economic profit growth in the calculation of a CEO's variable pay. I would also note that the example of a 15 percent economic profit target is probably too high for most companies, but the basic point that the actual target must be based on the expected EP performance of the company's best strategies remains valid.

Few elements of corporate governance have received more negative publicity or calls for reform in recent years than executive compensation, especially CEO compensation. Among the leading schools of thought on the subject are social engineers (pay is too high in relation to that of ordinary employees), financial engineers (pay is not linked effectively to economic performance), and legal

---

*This article originally appeared in the Spring 2003 edition of *Directors and Boards* (www.directorsandboards.com). Reprinted with permission.

engineers (the process of setting CEO pay is not sufficiently objective or independent). We have limited comment on the social engineering perspective, but there is much to consider in the financial and legal engineering positions.

In practical terms, most suggested reforms have focused on stock option programs, with the general view being that whatever good intentions boards have had in granting stock options, the actual results have ranged from compensation levels that seem arbitrary at best to iniquitous at worst. There has been less commentary about reforming the overall structure of executive compensation packages, including base salary and short- and long-term cash compensation as well as stock options and other awards. We believe effective reform will require this more comprehensive perspective.

TYPICAL PACKAGE

Briefly, the typical CEO pay package in a large U.S. public company today looks something like this:

1. Annual base salary: usually around $1 million paid in cash.

- Short-term incentive bonus: usually ranges from 50% to 200% of annual base salary, paid in cash, for achieving annual or "short-term" objectives—most commonly, an earnings or EPS target is the major driver of this component.
- Long-term incentive bonus: size, forms, and timing of payments vary widely, with stock option grants usually being a significant component—often as high as 60% to 70% of total compensation prior to the recent bear market.
- The details may vary widely, but the overall compensation structure is remarkably similar across companies, with relatively low "fixed" and high "variable" pay for CEOs. While this may seem sensible in theory, in practice the results have often been disappointing. Most notably, many companies with unexceptional performance have nevertheless paid their CEOs tens or even hundreds of millions of dollars in bonuses over the past several years, primarily through the use of ordinary stock options. Shareholders are rightly outraged, and boards have sometimes been clumsy and unconvincing in explaining why they allow this to happen.

AN ALTERNATIVE APPROACH

What is being proposed here is to turn this conventional structure around: Pay much higher annual base salaries but have much more selective payment of bonuses, with only truly exceptional company performance driving exceptional CEO pay. Two important observations underpin this proposal: *Current practices are not well aligned with CEO labor market requirements; they are also poorly aligned with capital market requirements.*

With respect to the CEO labor markets, the annual base salary levels for CEOs appear too low in relation to minimum labor market requirements. The strongest evidence of this is seen in how boards almost always grant CEO bonuses regardless of company performance, either by moving the goalposts on the short-term program or by repricing or reissuing stock options. For example, *BusinessWeek's* "Executive Compensation Scoreboard" shows that in 2001, when many companies performed below expectations, the median annual cash bonus was still $1.5 million, which is at the higher end of the range for many companies.

Whatever the mechanism, the message seems to be that even CEOs with mediocre performance records have a minimum market value that is higher than the $1 million or so annual base salary they receive. (CEO base salaries are commonly set at $1 million or less because of an ill-conceived tax regulation—IRS Code 162(m)—providing that any cash compensation over $1 million is nondeductible unless the excess is related to "performance"; some larger companies have wisely begun to set base salaries above $1 million while absorbing the tax.) If this is so, it argues for setting higher annual base pay to better reflect labor-market realities. More important, higher annual base salaries would enable boards to avoid even the appearance of abrogating previous CEO pay agreements or of not enforcing the company's performance standards, both of which are corrosive to the boards' legitimate authority.

The capital market requirements are that the compensation of top management, and the CEO in particular, should be well aligned with measurable wealth creation over time. For this to happen, boards will need to be completely clear about two things:

- First, any executive compensation above annual base salary should not be thought of as "incentive" compensation. Bonuses should be designed as a reward for performance actually achieved and not as an inducement to achieve something in the future. Competent individuals at this level should not need inducements to perform well in the first place, and incompetent individuals cannot perform well regardless of the inducements; in addition, inducements are slippery to define, measure and enforce.
- Second, performance objectives themselves must be closely linked to the growth of the company's intrinsic value over time (intrinsic value being

defined as present value of the company's expected future equity cash flows, discounted at the cost of equity capital). Two of the best measures for this are growth of economic profits (an internal measure defined as net income minus a charge for capital) and total shareholder returns relative to peers (an external measure). To achieve capital market alignment, compensation above base annual salary would be paid only when the company has objectively achieved superior economic profit growth and/or superior total shareholder returns.

ILLUSTRATIVE COMPENSATION PLAN

Following the guidelines suggested above, boards would be able to establish compensation plans that are simpler and better aligned with the capital and labor markets, and that should be perceived generally as more equitable. To illustrate how it might work, the board of a Fortune 100 company might design a CEO compensation plan as follows:

1. Set the CEO's annual base salary at, say, $4 million. This is an estimate of the de facto "minimum wage" for the CEO of an average-performing Fortune 100 company today. As noted above, the median pay for large-company CEOs in 2001 was about $2.5 million (base plus short-term bonus, even in a year when many companies did not meet their performance objectives). In addition, some portion of so-called long-term incentives seems actually to be hardwired in practice, so we are estimating another $1.5 million of annual salary to reflect this. The annual base salary would be paid in cash or, possibly, a combination of cash and straight stock.

2. Set two concrete minimum performance objectives for earning rewards above base salary:
   - Achieving annual top-quartile TSR relative to peers.
   - Achieving an annual economic profit (EP) growth target of, say, 15%, a level that is generally consistent with top value-creating companies over time (but the actual EP growth target should be based on the performance expected from delivering on the company's strategy in any given year).

3. Set an annual bonus of 50% of base salary for achieving each performance objective. Achieving both earns a reward of 100% of base salary (total pay of $8 million), achieving either one but not both earns a reward of 50% of

base salary (total pay of $6 million), achieving neither earns no bonus in that year (total pay of $4 million). The annual bonus could be paid in cash or some combination of cash and straight stock.

4. Provide two additional rewards for achieving consistently superior performance over time:

   ▪ In any one year, multiply annual bonus by the number of consecutive years each performance objective has been achieved. For example, if both the EP growth and relative TSR objectives are achieved two years in a row, then in the second year the CEO's bonus would be $8 million (2 × $4 million) and total compensation would be $12 million. In addition to its simplicity, this approach has the benefit of eliminating the need for separate short- and long-term bonus plans that are often based on vague or even false distinctions between one-year and multiyear performance standards. Here, the emphasis is rewarding consistently superior performance with powerful multipliers, always using the same metrics and standards.

   ▪ In years when the company achieves above-average TSR (i.e., first or second quartile relative to peers), add a grant of $1 million worth of performance stock options. Performance stock options are designed so that the company must exceed a performance hurdle for the options to be in the money: the hurdle can be set either so that the company's TSR must exceed the peer group average or so that the company's TSR must exceed its cost of equity capital over time.

Ordinary stock options do not create proper alignment with investors' interests or returns and should not be a significant part of top management compensation at large public companies. However, boards do have a desire to include stock options in CEO pay, and CEOs clearly like to have them as part of their package. The use of stock options as proposed here has three objectives: (a) to recognize achievement of second-quartile TSR, but in a way that must be sustained to be of value to the CEO; (b) to grant the options as a reward for performance actually achieved and not as an incentive or inducement to perform; and (c) to index the reward so that the options are in the money only when the company actually outperforms its peers. Of course, a more straightforward alternative to performance options would be simply to grant $1 million worth of actual stock in each year when the company achieves above-average TSR relative to peers. The upside potential for the CEO would be lower, but so would the downside potential. See exhibit for examples of the plan in action.

The Plan in Action

One-Year Payout Matrix With 15% Economic Profit (EP) Growth Target

	Relative Total Shareholder Return (TSR)			
	1st Quartile	**2nd Quartile**	**3rd Quartile**	**4th Quartile**
EP growth ≥ 15%	100% cash/ $1m options (17% CEOs)	50% cash/ $1m options (13% CEOs)	50% cash/ no options (3% CEOs)	50% cash/ no options (1% CEOs)
EP growth <15%	50% cash/ $1m options (8% CEOs)	no cash/ $1m options (12% CEOs)	no cash/ no options (22% CEOs)	no cash/ no options (24% CEOs)

Note on multiyear performance rewards: Annual dollar amount cash rewards would be multiplied by number of consecutive years performance objectives have been achieved.
Note on percentage of CEOs: Estimate of typical distribution that might be expected in any given year.

Multiyear Higher-Performing Company

	Performance	Cash Bonus	Performance Options
Year 1	1st Quartile TSR, EP growth ≥ 15%	$4 million	$1 million
Year 2	2nd Quartile TSR, EP growth ≥ 15%	$4 million	$1 million
Year 3	1st Quartile TSR, EP growth ≥ 15%	$8 million	$1 million
		$16 million	$3 million (issue value)
	Base Pay (3 years)	$12 million	
	Total Compensation	$28 million cash +	$6 million + (est. market value)

Explanation of Cash Bonus: *Year 1:* Both TSR and EP performance targets achieved ($2 million + $2 million =$4 million); *Year 2:* TSR target missed, but EP target achieved for second consecutive year ($2 million 2 = $4 million); *Year 3:* TSR target achieved and EP target achieved for third consecutive year ($2 million + [$2 million x 3] = $8 million).

Multiyear Lower-Performing Company

	Performance	Cash Bonus	Performance Options
Year 1	3rd Quartile TSR, EP growth <15%	0	0
Year 2	2nd Quartile TSR, EP growth <15%	0	$1 million
Year 3	3rd Quartile TSR, EP growth <15%	0	0
		0	$1 million (issue value)
	Base Pay (3 years)	$12 million	
	Total Compensation	$12 million	<$1 million (est. market value)

Observations

• Over a three-year period, the CEO of the higher-performing company has earned more than two and one-half times what the CEO of the lower-performing company has earned, reflecting his or her greater success at growing the value of the company. For companies of this size, the three-year difference in value creation could easily exceed $15 billion in market capitalization.

• The CEO of the lower-performing company has still been well compensated, but because the annual base salary fully reflects labor market realities, the board has not had to resort to any *ex post facto* revisions of the bonus plan or performance targets, or to reissuing or repricing stock options.

ALERTING THE BOARD EARLY AND OFTEN

The CEO compensation framework proposed here is an attempt to address both the capital market and the labor market problems of existing plans. A critical condition for success is that boards and CEOs must be prepared to accept the outcome: relative pay for relative performance within their peer group. If boards continue to insist, illogically, that "their" CEO's pay must be above average for their industry or other peer group, then no plan will produce results that are equitable with respect to other employees, shareholders, or even to the best CEOs.

By setting base salary to the de facto "minimum wage" level for average-performing CEOs, boards will eliminate the need, or even the temptation, to revise bonuses when performance objectives are not met. And by setting performance objectives that are properly aligned with value creation, together with a clear focus on rewards rather than incentives, this framework assures that only the best-performing CEOs will be compensated at very high levels. Finally, by eliminating any need for separate short-term and long-term plans and by shifting to performance options (or straight shares), boards will have a much more straightforward and investor-friendly way of paying for consistent delivery of superior value creation.

No executive compensation plan will produce perfect results under all circumstances. For instance, it could be argued that what is proposed here might result in overpaying some truly underperforming CEOs. That is possible, but the amount of "overpayment" would be very modest compared to what can happen (and has happened) under current plans. The compensation guidelines proposed here are designed to alert the board early and often to the company's real performance issues, which must be addressed by superior strategies and leadership standards, and not by continuously revising the CEO's pay plan.

Notes

CHAPTER TWO

1. As an example, G. Bennett Stewart, *The Quest for Value* (New York: Harper-Collins, 1991).
2. Some readers might wonder about the need to recognize "synergies" between two or more business units, meaning their strategies and financial performance are closely interrelated. Where synergies truly exist, their economic benefits can usually be captured either through arm's-length transactions or effective transfer pricing between units, which still allows them to plan and execute their strategies independently. If "synergies" are forced onto the units (i.e., they probably are not really synergies), or if the linkages between units truly are too extensive for them to operate as independent economic entities, then business unit boundaries probably need to be redrawn to encompass the full extent of the interdependencies.
3. The estimated changes in equity values assume, for purposes of example only, that the three companies were all valued at $10 per share at the beginning of the base year and then revalued in year 5 assuming in each case that EP would grow at 5 percent in perpetuity. (See Appendix II for the valuation methodology.)
4. Airbus: EADS annual reports.

CHAPTER THREE

1. Spencer Stuart, *Route to the Top*, 14th annual ed. (2008), 6.
2. This estimate is based on direct observations by the author while acting as an advisor to approximately 30 large public companies over the period 1978–2009. However, it is also possible to infer directly from public data that a substantial amount of capital is underperforming at many companies. For example, for a company with a cost of equity of 10 percent that normally earns an ROE of 15 percent, it is likely that about one-fifth of its equity capital is actually generating ROEs of 30 percent or more (twice the company average).

If this is the case, then a typical distribution of returns on the remaining capital would suggest that roughly one-third is generating an average less than its 10 percent cost of equity and therefore negative EP. If the lowest-performing one-third of capital were redeployed or if strategies were changed to bring returns up just to the minimum 10 percent, then the company's average ROE would increase to approximately 20 percent and (assuming 5 percent long-term EP growth) its equity value would increase by more than 50 percent.

3. This presumes there are no material expenses, assets, or liabilities held in a separate "corporate" account, which normally there should not be. The company has no reason to engage in corporate activities that are not EP and value accretive, and therefore allocable, to the business units.

4. The 2001 to 2007 time period for analyzing GE's results was chosen to coincide with the first year of Jeff Immelt's tenure as CEO and to end before the 2008–2009 implosion of the U.S. capital markets. These later events were arguably beyond the control of any CEO. Had they been included in this analysis, the underlying message regarding GE's poor EP performance would actually have been stronger, but that would have been an unfair distortion. The 2001–2007 period tells the story well enough.

5. "GE has six strong businesses [segments] . . . we expect these businesses to achieve 10%+ earnings growth most years, with long-term returns [ROCE] of 20%," GE 2006 Annual Report, 5.

6. Datastream.

 CHAPTER FOUR

1. Retail Banking: The profitability of many U.S. banks has been severely tested from 2007 to 2010. However, most of the underlying factors that normally allow retail banking to be economically profitable, particularly the interest rate spread between the cost of deposits and the returns on securities and loans, do not appear to have changed fundamentally. Regulators may require banks to carry more capital, and other regulatory changes may adversely impact specific operations such as credit cards, but well-managed banks should still generate ROEs above their cost of equity over time.

2. Apple: See, for example, Joe Wilcox, "Apple has 91% of market for $1000+ PC's, says NDP," Betanews.com, July 22, 2009.

3. Aluminum Industry: Among the world's largest aluminum producers, only Alcoa has managed to eke out positive cumulative economic profits of $3.52 per share for the decade ending 2007. ALCAN has earned a positive economic profit in only two of the ten years ending 2007. Other large players, including Norsk Hydro, Calco, and RUSAL have had volatile and generally poor overall earnings records. Datastream and public sources.

4. Exploration and Production: Based on results of approximately 100 North American exploration and production companies from 1998–2007. Datastream.
5. Refining: Based on an analysis of refining margins and capital investment levels of major U.S. refiners and profitability information in annual reports.
6. Mutual Funds: ICI, 2009 Investment Company Fact Book, Table 1.
7. Mutual Funds: See, for example, Philip Coggan, "The Triple Whammy Packs a Wallop," *FT Business*, April 23, 2007.
8. Mutual Funds: Because the vast majority of mutual funds are run by private companies or as units within larger public companies, data on industry profitability are not extensive. Data available on public mutual fund companies (Value Line) indicate they enjoy good to exceptional EP performance in rising equity markets when their operating leverage works in their favor, and mixed EP performance in declining equity markets when their operating leverage works to their disadvantage. But the top-performing companies still earn high economic profits even in down markets.
9. Money Transmission: Estimated 2007 global product-market economic profit of $4.0 billion based on proprietary analysis by a major market participant. For further confirmation of how strong and profitable the incumbents in this product market are, see David Enrich, "A Citi Unit Grows—With Fed's Help," *The Wall Street Journal*, January 11, 2010, 1.
10. U.S. Education Services Companies: The seven companies followed by Value Line are Apollo Group, Corinthian Colleges, ITT Educational Services, Learning Tree International, Renaissance Learning, Inc., SkillSoft PLC, and Strayer Education.
11. U.S. Entertainment Industry: The companies included here are CBS Corp, the Walt Disney Company, DreamWorks Animation SKG, News Corp, Sinclair Broadcast Corp, Time Warner, and Viacom. Company data are from Datastream, except NBC/Universal, which is based on analysis of GE financial statements and other public data.
12. U.S. Paper Industry: Four major U.S. companies—Weyerhaeuser, International Paper, Louisiana Pacific, and Wausau Paper—collectively earned a negative EP of $7.7 billion during the years 1998 to 2007. Datastream.
13. Nucor: Average annual EP per share growth of 24.6 percent and TSR of 19.7 percent over 1998–2007 period. Datastream.
14. Intel: Datastream.
15. The Coca-Cola Company: EP per share grew from $0.11 in 1984 to $1.42 in 1997, a compound annual growth rate of 22 percent. Datastream.
16. U.S. Airlines: Analysis includes American Airlines, Continental Airlines, Delta Airlines, Jet Blue, Northwest Airlines, and Southwest Airlines. Datastream.
17. Executives often argue that more patience is needed with emerging market investments and that even years of economic losses can sometimes be offset when the local market takes off, at which point the early movers will then be in

a position to do well. In effect, the company is buying an option to participate profitably at a later date. This argument has the virtue that it cannot be proven wrong, and there are examples of patient capital being well rewarded in time. Executives should keep in mind, however, that economically unprofitable markets do not normally turn themselves around, and even when they do it can take far longer than expected. As a result, these Scenario III investments either should be very small placeholders or should be based on entering with an enormous near-term competitive advantage in the local market.

18. Nokia: Datastream.
19. 3M: Datastream.
20. IBM: 2008 Annual Report. Chairman's Letter
21. IBM: Louis V. Gerstner, Jr., *Who Says Elephants Can't Dance?* (New York: Harper Business, 2002).
22. ExxonMobil: In 2008, ExxonMobil has announced its plans to divest its approximately 2,000 company-owned service stations in the United States. The company will continue to have "branded distributors" for more than 10,000 sites in the United States and is keeping its retailing operations outside the United States as well [March 5, 2009, analyst meeting].
23. JPMorgan Chase: Datastream.
24. Emerson and Danaher: Contrary to the experience of many active acquirers who fail to create value through acquisitions, these two companies have sustained excellent EP results while making acquisitions a core part of their growth strategies. In the decade 1998–2007, Emerson earned a total EP of $7.8 billion with average annual EP growth of 8.5 percent, and Danaher earned a total EP of $3.1 billion while growing its EP at over 22 percent per year.

 CHAPTER FIVE

1. For a company or business unit that achieves a dominant EP share position, there may come a time when further increasing its share of product-market EP is not feasible owing to legal or regulatory constraints or to the improved abilities of other competitors to withstand further incursions into their own EP shares. The dominant EP player may still have a net competitive advantage but will find it more difficult to exploit its position fully because of exogenous constraints on its overall growth.
2. Mark W. Johnson, Clayton M. Christensen, and Henning Kagermann, "Reinventing Your Business Model," *Harvard Business Review* (December 2008), and Michael E. Porter, "What Is Strategy?" *Harvard Business Review* (November–December 1996).
3. ExxonMobil: 2007 performance vs. Royal Dutch Shell, BP, Chevron, Total S.A., and ConocoPhilips. Datastream.

4. Intel: Fortune, November 23, 2009, 123.
5. Warren Buffett: Letter to Shareholders, Berkshire Hathaway 1992 Annual Report.
6. Disney: Datastream.
7. General Electric: Datastream.
8. Intel, Pfizer: Datastream. During the 1998–2007 period, EP declined for both companies. Whereas Intel's earnings in 2007 were almost unchanged from 10 years earlier, Pfizer's earnings were nearly four times higher in 2007 than they were in 1997 (base year). This serves as a particularly striking example of how earnings and EP can move in opposite directions.
9. Coca-Cola: During Roberto Goizueta's tenure as CEO, the company's annual EP per share growth averaged 19.6 percent and annual TSRs averaged over 30 percent. Datastream.
10. Roche: "Can Roche Leave Genentech Alone?" *BusinessWeek*, December 7, 2009, 48.
11. Danaher: For a good description of Danaher's approach to integrating acquisitions, see Bharat Anand, David Collis, and Sophie Hood, Danaher Corporation, Harvard Business School Case (9-708-445), revised July 23, 2008.
12. C. K. Prahalad and Gary Hammel, "The Core Competence of the Corporation," *Harvard Business Review*, May–June 1990.
13. Nucor: Ken Iverson, *Plain Talk* (New York: John Wiley & Sons, 1998), 27.
14. Disney: The profitability of motion pictures is difficult to pin down. A frequently mentioned estimate is that 60 percent of movies do not even earn an accounting profit. There is reasonably good evidence to suggest R-rated movies are significantly less profitable than G-rated and PG-rated movies. See Arthur De Vany and W. David Walls, "Does Hollywood Make Too Many R-Rated Movies? Risk, Stochastic Dominance, and the Illusion of Expectation," *Journal of Business* 75, no. 3 (2002), 425–452. From available evidence, there is little likelihood that R-rated category could, on average, be generating an economic profit.
15. Disney: Touchstone profitability data are found in Michael G. Rukstad and David Collis, "The Walt Disney Company: The Entertainment King," Harvard Business School Case 9-701-035, revised January 5, 2009.
16. Danaher: Datastream.
17. Danaher: For a more detailed description of Danaher, see Anand, Collis, and Hood, Danaher Corporation, Harvard Business School Case.
18. Danaher: Danaher Corporation 10K filings.

CHAPTER SIX

1. For expository purposes, the business unit examples used throughout the book have avoided complex boundary drawing issues. This should not be taken as

suggesting that boundary drawing in real companies is always easy or straightforward, which of course it is not. Indeed, not only will the choice of participation and positioning strategies be affected by the way boundaries are defined, but different strategic options might presuppose changing boundaries as well. A key principle in drawing boundaries, between and within business units, is to allow for the clearest possible insight into the sources of and accountabilities for EP growth. Other important factors, such as span of control needs and executive process design, should follow this principle whenever possible.

2. In late 2009, GE announced its intention to divest most or all of its interest in NBC/Universal through a complex transaction with the Comcast Corporation.

3. 3M: Datastream.

CHAPTER SEVEN

1. Nassim Nicholas Taleb, *The Black Swan* (New York: Random House, 2007). As many others have noted, this is a superb book on risk, providing a much-needed sense of perspective and humility on our ability to forecast or properly plan for truly bad outcomes.

2. Business unit risk-reward characteristics. The observation that higher returns can be consistent with lower risk is true for the typical customer facing business units within a nonfinancial company. However, it does not apply to some financial services activities, particularly those involving a significant amount of trading. The trading of financial instruments, or even nonfinancial assets like commodities, incurs risks that rise with returns (especially if those higher returns are enhanced with high leverage), just as conventional theory suggests. Part of the distinction is that conventional customer facing businesses can choose to participate in product markets with positive economic profit, and, if they can gain and hold competitive advantage, they will earn a growing share of that EP, further protecting the resilience of their own future EP prospects. In a trading unit, the expected net present value of all market participants' trading activities is zero—there is no positive EP to be had from market economics alone. Even with a short-term competitive advantage in trading (e.g., from having better information than other participants), a disproportionate share of zero is still zero. Over the longer term, during which it is assumed markets are reasonably efficient and no player can hold a lasting competitive advantage, the economic benefit to outside shareholders from purely financial trading activities has to be assumed to be zero at best. If traders are imposing large costs in the form of transaction fees or their own compensation, then risk-adjusted returns to shareholders will be negative.

3. Corporate portfolio diversification and stock prices: Philip G. Berger and Eli Ofek, "Diversification's Effect on Firm Value," *Journal of Finance and Economics* 37 (1995), 39–65.
4. Conglomerate discount: Berger and Ofek, "Diversification's Effect on Firm Value," 39–65.
5. Microsoft and Intel acquisitions: Both companies have a history of making between 10 and 20 acquisitions per year, generally for prices totaling well over $1 billion. Thompson SDC, company publications.
6. Capital in financial services companies: In companies where both assets and liabilities are composed largely of financial obligations, the definition of "capital" itself can become very complicated. In banking, for instance, there are different definitions for regulatory capital, economic capital, and book capital. Ultimately, banks, like every other business, should earn positive and growing economic profits, but the management of risk and balance sheets in these institutions is fundamentally different and more difficult than it is for non–financial services companies and is not being directly addressed here.
7. Nucor: From 1990 through 2007, Nucor's average debt-to-equity ratio was well under half that of its peer group. Datastream.
8. Johnson & Johnson, Tylenol: Judith Rebak, "Tylenol Made a Hero of Johnson & Johnson: The Recall That Started Them All," *New York Times* online, March 23, 2002.
9. The presumption that the stock market is an unbiased estimator of company value is consistent with the "efficient market hypothesis," the proposition that stock prices reflect all information that is known by investors at a point in time. Whether market efficiency operates perfectly in practice is a subject of debate, but for managerial purposes it is best to assume that it does.

APPENDIX II

1. One estimation technique is to use a simplified capital asset pricing model:

$$COE = RFR + B(MRP)$$

where

COE = Cost of equity capital

RFR = Risk free rate: Use nominal long term government bond rate

B = Company "beta": estimates can be found in various sources, including the Value Line Investment Survey

MRP = Market risk premium, the difference between the average expected return embedded in stock prices and the risk free rate. MRP in the United States is usually between 4 percent and 6 percent.

Index